PRINCIPLES OF THE DOCTRINE SERIES

BOOK I: *This Is The God Of Israel*

ENDORSEMENTS

FOUNDATION IS THE KEY to any structure. Jesus Himself states that if a building is built on a foundation of sand, it will crumble when the storms of life come upon it. Just like the building built on a foundation of sand crumbles, so do many Christians in their walk with Christ. As soon as adversity hits, it seems to be, as if by nature, to buckle and backslide in some way, shape, or form. I believe this is due to a lack of knowledge and revelation of who God truly is. Ask your average Christian who God is, at His basic core, and a myriad of responses will be given. Without knowing who God is, how can we accurately represent Him in this natural world? This book is an answer to so many questions regarding the nature of God. In my life, since reading this book, my entire Bible is viewed differently. It is almost a shame to say that I have been viewing God through rose colored glasses. Now, as I read the Bible, and as I experience life, scales are no longer over my eyes, and I see God clearly, hear Him easier, and I know Him more. In a way, it is as Jesus stated, that eternal life is to know the Father and to know the Son in whom He sent. With a book like this, every Christian can tap into eternal life on a level that has been hidden from Christians by the enemy for well over 1500 years. It would be no understatement to say that this book will revolutionize the state of Christianity moving forward for generations to come. I recommend every Christian read this as a prerequisite to any study. With the Principles of the Doctrine available for a new member or a new Christian, years, perhaps even decades of struggles will be nullified, and joy unspeakable will flow throughout the body. May God be praised as you read.

—Pastor Jamal Smith

ENDORSEMENTS Cont.

THE FOLLOWING is a quick retelling of my own story that connects me to the heart of Stan Albuquerque, and this life changing book, "This is the God of Israel."

Growing up, my parents made my older sister and I attend Hebrew school twice a week. Our Rabbi was a tremendously respected, learned man whom I later discovered the students at Hebrew Union College studied his many writings while preparing for the Rabbinate. I was thoroughly indoctrinated into my Jewish culture, albeit in a reformed setting. I never entertained or even remotely thought about what other people did in terms of their "religion." As I reflect on this, I may have had a sense of, "Ha.. I'm Jewish and therefore I have some kind of 'leg up' on you." However, I never outright said that to anyone, and it was never discussed. I just might have thought that in my subconscious to be completely transparent.

I am describing all this to you so you'd have a sense of the evolution I experienced growing up and always having a profound sense of God's presence as it had nothing to do with my "religion." I was always somehow "rocked" by hearing His word. It could have been in synagogue listening to words from the Tanach recited; or watching a movie where even a Christian Minister or Priest was reciting scripture, it always pierced me.

While in college I met a lovely Italian, Catholic lady and fell madly in love. After finishing school we got married, much to the 'disgruntled-ness' of her parents, who would not allow me a "Christ Killer" into their house.

After finishing college I met some business colleagues who were, lo and behold, studying from a book I had never yet opened; the Brit Ha'Dasha (New Covenant). Scripture speaks of the Ruach Adonai (Spirit of the Lord) or the Ruach Ha'Kodesh (Holy Spirit). All I know is that when I read this New Covenant, this Ruach breathed into me somehow. As it says in Jeremiah 31:31, "…He will write His word on our heart…." It was as if the Lord himself was speaking in my ears, and He was! The struggle I was now undergoing was, "Oh My God, how do I explain what I'm experiencing to my family and friends!?" What I was experiencing in my spirit was that I knew, that I knew, that I knew. There was no denying that this sense of spirituality which had always been upon me, this 'kinship' with the word of God, was exploding within me. Yet, I still kept these things to myself.

ENDORSEMENTS Cont.

One of my colleagues said that he had a friend who was a Messianic Rabbi in Brooklyn, NY and that I should look him up. It just so happened that my wife and I were soon headed in that general direction to visit family, so we decide to go off the track and visit Dr Howard Morgan in Brooklyn. We were not there more than 20 minutes when he sensed in his spirit that all he needed to do was blow on us like blowing out birthday candles. We were ready to open our hearts, surrender to, and accept the Jewish Messiah, Yeshua (Jesus) into our hearts to be our Lord and Savior. My next thought was… Lord, give my intellect permission to believe. Yeshua was sitting on my right shoulder whispering , "you know you are doing the right thing." I did know and we both did just that.

Again, what would family and friends think? There is such a huge cultural divide, and Dr Morgan made it quite clear that I was NOT converting to Christianity, nor was I going to stop being Jewish!!! I was, in fact, doing the most Jewish thing I could ever do, and that was to surrender to the Jewish Messiah, the one whom my Jewish brethren are still waiting for. I was Home free!!! We prayed to receive him as our Lord and Savior right then and there and life has never been the same since. That was 1981. After much prayer and incredible amount of studying, I was ordained as a Messianic Rabbi in 2006.

This is where Stan Albuquerque came into the picture, and nothing happens by accident. When I met Stan, we actually lived in the same Condo building. We spent many a late-night walking on the dock behind the building in deep discussions over the D'var Adonai (Word of the Lord). His passion for the word and desire to have a clear understanding of what he was reading compelled me to read more deeply between the lines. By studying the entire word of God, we grew a deeper understanding of the One true God we serve. As we gain that deeper understanding, we can more effectively engage the non-believer, the Jew and Gentile alike, thereby being the ambassadors and disciples he commissioned us to be. This book has created in me, and I pray in you, a sincere and masterfully researched look at what we may think we understand about the Trinity. This book by Stan has given me a deeper knowledge of the Godhead. He doesn't only share his thoughts, but he also backs up his comments by what ought to

ENDORSEMENTS Cont.

be the only way we must all do so…by the Scripture itself. You will be transformed in your understanding, and even more so as you share this new understanding with others. This is the main reason, among others, that you should read this book.

To quote Stan, "I intend to demonstrate that certain traditions have played a significant role in formulating our collective theology, perhaps more than we are willing to admit at first." He goes on to say, "The focus of this book will be addressing the doctrine of the Trinity in light of the scripture; how our approach to it can directly impact what we believe of biblical doctrine and the expression of our faith." It is with much enthusiasm that I encourage you to read "This is the God of Israel!" and ask the Ruach Adonai to minister to you. He wants you to enjoy what it is like to have an eternal walk with Him. "He who has the ears to hear, let him hear" (Luke 8:8).

—Rabbi Peter Gaines
   Associate Rabbi
   Beth Yeshua Messianic Synagogue
   Coral Springs, FL

ENDORSEMENTS Cont.

FROM CHILDHOOD, I have always believed in God. During troubled times, I sought the Father through prayers of desperation. But I never fully committed, as I never knew how. This is a constant theme for a lot of individuals. The basic steps I knew were: Believe in Christ, and pray every day. That's it.

I grew up in church, played the bongos during worship, and was always mesmerized by the atmosphere of prayer and speaking in tongues until, one day, probably around seven or eight years old, the preacher laid his hand on my forehead and began to pray, and then … he shoved me backward. On the floor, I thought to myself, *I don't feel God, I don't feel what everyone seems to be feeling.* In some way, I believed it could happen because I would see my Grandmother experience those moments of speaking in tongues and "falling in the spirit."

I felt bad, so I didn't get up. I stayed there with my eyes closed. And ever since that day as a young kid, I did not believe in people. I did not believe it when people fell while praying. Oddly enough, I continued to believe in God, but my trust for people was stripped away.

I say all this to explain that I never had pastoral care, never had a teacher to show me how to learn about God or to read scripture, let alone understand it. I guess you can say I was a product of tradition. Believe, go to church, pray, repeat. Finally, in 2018, through the grace of God using my wife to declare and say to me, "I'm giving my life to Jesus Christ," I turned to God fully.

Intrigued by apologetics, it confirmed for me that there is truth to God's Word, and you *can* defend it. Wow, I'm all in. It was still difficult to understand scripture, as it was so foreign to me. I wanted to understand The Trinity so I could explain it to my family and help them to understand why God is important and why Jesus is the way. At least to me, the combination of knowing the Gospel and The Trinity is and was very important, especially to teach it to my kids.

It wasn't until the pandemic (on a zoom fellowship call) that I was exposed to Stan's study on The Godhead. This revelation changed EVERYTHING. It was so revealing that I became emotional during the study. It was like a new dimension had opened, and I was experiencing the scripture

ENDORSEMENTS Cont.

and the history.

With the Godhead study, I began to yearn to read the Bible. The words became 3D to me. I could see the people and history. This experience was nothing but clarity on the nature of God and The Godhead. If you want to understand God (which is still a mystery), then the first step is this book. It truly-truly strengthened my faith in God and in the Scriptures. Often people who oppose Jesus as Lord will say, "Show me in the Bible where Jesus said, *I am God!*" Christian Apologists usually address this by quoting John 8:58: *"Jesus said unto them, Verily, verily, I say unto you, Before Abraham was, I am."* But in this study/book you will see WHY. It is so basic but so profound that no apologist I follow has ever explained WHY Jesus didn't just plainly say, "YES, I AM GOD."

After reading this book, if you think this book is amazing, wait until you experience the next one. May this book bless you with the revealing of The Godhead as you probably never heard it before, using Scripture!

—Richard Carmelo Soto

HAVING BEEN RAISED in the Roman Catholic tradition, I knew only shame and guilt. Rediscovering my faith in the new traditions of the "come as you are" non-denominational churches posed even more challenges for me. I was eventually baptized. I had prayers answered, and I even experienced the healing power of God. Yet, still, my faith felt flimsy rather than steadfast.

Principles of the Doctrine laid the groundwork for what I see to be the future of the church in putting a biblical culture over modern traditions. It builds on a foundation by answering two essential questions: *Who am I?* and *To whom do I belong?*

Knowing that repentance is an essential part of forgiveness was pivotal in rediscovering my own redemption. Understanding the constant and consistent Presence of God is to know that the promise that God IS what he ALWAYS has been and ever will BE.

I know the feeling of being lost. The traditions, both old and new, had given me the feeling of being found. It wasn't until I read Stan's insights that I really felt saved and experienced the freedom of a new beginning.

—**Ricardo Castro**

ENDORSEMENTS Cont.

AS THE EDITOR AND PUBLISHER of Stan Albuquerque's first presentation in the **"Principles of the Doctrine Series, Book I: This is the God of Israel,"** I have had the honor and extreme blessing of being immersed into its message.

Through this book, I have been re-introduced to the Heavenly Father. Even though I have known Him, I never really understood Him on this deep, personal level. I have come to know Him, not just from the perspective of the Trinity, but as my Father God Who loves me beyond my imagination, Who moves mountains on my behalf, Who makes ways for me where there are no ways, Who is with me constantly and directs my path! He knows my thoughts, my needs, even my wants. He knows every aspect of my being and the purpose for which I was created.

I learned that our Father's greatest desire is that we, His children, might be a reflection, substance if you will, of His invisible Holy Presence in the physical world. He sees me, and He sees you every second of every day. We must learn to reflect the true light of His Holiness, His Love, His Forgiveness, and His Purpose for creating man.

If you want a more intimate relationship with our Father God, and to learn what His purpose and direction is for you and your life, this book is a wonderful place to begin. I can honestly say that it has changed my life for the greater. It truly makes the Word of God come to life in your life.

★★★★★

—**Nancy E Williams**, President
The Laurus Company, Inc.

PRINCIPLES OF THE DOCTRINE SERIES

Book I

THIS IS THE GOD OF ISRAEL

Stan T. Albuquerque

LAURUS BOOKS

PRINCIPLES OF THE DOCTRINE SERIES
BOOK I: *This Is The God Of Israel*

By Stan T. Albuquerque

Copyright © 2023 by Stan T. Albuquerque

All rights reserved. This book is protected under the copyright laws of the United States of America. This book may not be copied or reprinted for commercial gain or profit, or reproduced, stored in a retrieval system, or transmitted in any form or by any means—electronic, mechanical, photocopy, recording, scanning, or any other means, without written permission of the copyright owner. The use of short quotations or occasional page copying for personal or group study is permitted and encouraged. Permission will be granted on request.

Paperback: ISBN: 978-1-957528-04-5

Mobi-ePub: ISBN: 978-1-957528-05-2

Published by LAURUS BOOKS

Cover Design: Brenda Lance

Scripture quotations, unless otherwise noted, are taken from The Holy Bible, King James Version, available in the Public Domain.

Scripture quotations marked (NASB®) are from the New American Standard Bible®, Copyright © 1960, 1971, 1977 by The Lockman Foundation. Used by permission. All rights reserved. www.lockman.org

Scripture quotations marked (AMP) or (AMPC) are from the Amplified® Bible (AMPC), Copyright © 1954, 1958, 1962, 1964, 1965, 1987 by The Lockman Foundation. Used by permission. www.lockman.org

Scripture quotations marked (ESV) are from The ESV® Bible (The Holy Bible, English Standard Version®), copyright © 2001 by Crossway, a publishing ministry of Good News Publishers. Used by permission. All rights reserved.

Scripture quotations marked (GNT) are from the Good News Translation in Today's English Version-Second Edition, Copyright © 1992 by American Bible Society. Used by Permission.

Scripture quotations marked (NIV) are taken from The Holy Bible, New International Version® NIV®, Copyright © 1973 1978 1984 2011 by Biblica, Inc. TM. Used by permission. All rights reserved worldwide.

Scripture quotations marked (MSG) are taken from THE MESSAGE. Copyright © 1993, 1994, 1995, 1996, 2000, 2001, 2002. Used by permission of NavPress Publishing Group.

LAURUS BOOKS
AN IMPRINT OF THE LAURUS COMPANY, INC.
www.TheLaurusCompany.com

This book may be purchased in paperback from TheLaurusCompany.com, Amazon sites around the world, and most other online retailers. Also available in formats for electronic readers from their respective stores. Available to booksellers at Spring Arbor.

ACKNOWLEDGMENTS

TO THE LORD GOD, OUR HEAVENLY FATHER AND CREATOR, Whose thoughts and ways are loftier than all things created. I worship You with my whole heart, and I honor You with my entire life, giving praise to Your holy and precious Name. To Christ Jesus, the Son of God, the Word of God made flesh, and Whom I completely adore. I bless You forever as my Lord and King. You reign forevermore, and Your rule is to the ends of the earth. To the Holy Spirit of God, my Teacher, my Liberator, and my Comforter. May Your work in us all be thorough and complete. May Your Presence always be welcome, and may You never be quenched in me. I offer continual praise, and everlasting glory to You, my God and Father of lights, King over all kings, and Holy One. I worship You, for You alone are worthy.

TO MY BELOVED WIFE, MAYUME, my partner in life, and my best friend. I dare to out-love you each and every day, to cherish and honor the vows I made to you since the day you made me the most blessed man on earth. I thank God Who, in His infinite Wisdom, saw fit to bring you into my life. I look forward to many more years of loving you the way Christ teaches a man to love His Wife—with passion and devotion, with strength and gentleness, with unfailing love and gratitude. I bless and cherish you and the life we have built together. I look forward to many more years and opportunities to love you more.

TO MY CHILDREN: BEN, CECILIA, LAURA, and CLARA. You are the arrows in my quiver and the legacy of my life. I bless all of you with everything I am and everything I have to give. May you walk worthy of the Lord our God all of your days. May His everlasting life be evident within you for all the world to see. May your lives be a testament to His faithfulness to our family, the Church, and to all the nations of the earth. May you lead your generation into the Kingdom of God with jubilant praise on your lips and great joy in your hearts. Be strong in the Lord, be holy in all you do, in all you speak, and in all you think. May the favor of God be upon you, in you, and work through each of you.

TO MY EXTENDED FAMILY: My father Jurandir for your strong work ethic, leadership, and generous spirit. Your diligence, discipline, and demeanor are without question singularly inspiring. I love you, Dad ... so very much. You really are the best. **To my sister Jennifer,** the smartest and hardest working girl in the world! No one matches your devotion to our family! I cherish your fighting spirit and your desire to excel in all things. You are a warrior! **To my precious brother Phillip**, I love you more than you can know. Of all the people in my life, you have not only been my brother in blood but also my closest friend and confidant. **To my in-laws Carlos and Cecilia Goncalves**, your love and devotion to God, commitment and care for our families, and formidable generosity is unparalleled. Thank you for giving me my beloved.

TO ALL OF MY FRIENDS who have made invaluable contributions to my walk with God: **Rabbi Peter Gaines and wife Susan** for your friendship and insight into our shared Hebraic ancestry. May you both prosper enormously in ministry and life. **Pastor Jamal Smith and wife Tawanda** for your brotherhood and deep friendship. Thank you for your investment into my own life and that of my family. Jamal, thank you for the early morning phone calls and encouragement, and most of all, for your friendship. To **Douglas Grinnell**, my close friend and brother in Christ, who is an inspiration to me, and whom I emphatically trust. You are gracious and kind. Thank you for your devotion to our friendship, despite the geographical distance between us. I will forever be in your debt. I look forward to many years of ministry together. To **Dimitre**, you are one of the greatest men of God I have ever known. Your sensitivity to the things of God and your servant heart demonstrate a greatness that has yet to be revealed to the world. Thank you for being an example of the believers.

I have so many other precious individuals I want to acknowledge, but I have little room to write all I want to say. So, I would like to at least mention in no particular order **Duane Finnie, Randall and Shirley Wright, Obadiah and Nydia Schimp, Bryce and Melanie Little, John and Jacquelyn Lambert**, and so many others I cannot mention here, who have followed along with me in this journey of life, and who made it so worthwhile throughout my trials. Thank you all for being my close friends and family in Christ.

Finally, I would like to mention once more, **The Most High** for His grace and mercy in my life. **Lord Jesus**, I thought it proper to acknowledge You here once again because You ARE the Alpha and the Omega, The Beginning and The End, The First and The Last. You encompass everything, and You are above all things. By You all things consist, and all things were made by You and for You. I give You double honor because You are more than worthy to receive everything good that any of us can ever give or hope to offer. I bless You, my God. A thousand times over, I bless You. I do not have the sufficient vocabulary to describe the magnitude of Your greatness. I offer You myself and all of my household in Your service, to honor Your Presence in all places, at all times. I love You, Lord, and I will forever lift my voice to give You the glory that You are due.

—Stan Albuquerque

TABLE OF CONTENTS

ACKNOWLEDGMENTS. 13

TABLE OF CONTENTS. 17

PREFACE 19

A NOTE FROM THE AUTHOR 22

INTRODUCTION 25

CHAPTER 1 – *My Personal Story*. 33

CHAPTER 2 – *Paradigm Shift*. 41

CHAPTER 3 – *A Different Perspective* 49

CHAPTER 4 – *The Trinity and Church Doctrine* 57

CHAPTER 5 – *Persons and Pronouns*. 65

CHAPTER 6 – *The Essence of God* 71

CHAPTER 7 – *The Mystery Revealed* 79

CHAPTER 8 – *The Stubbornness of Dogma*. 87

CHAPTER 9 – *The Father* 93

CHAPTER 10 – *The Father Revealed* 103

CHAPTER 11 – *The Word and The Son* 111

CHAPTER 12 – *The Name and Presence* 123

CHAPTER 13 – *The Name*. 129

CHAPTER 14 – *The Divine Profile* 135

CHAPTER 15 – *The Holy Spirit of God* 143

TABLE OF CONTENTS Cont.

CHAPTER 16 – *Spirit Nature* 149

CHAPTER 17 – *Function of the Spirit* 157

CHAPTER 18 – *Living and Led by the Spirit (Part 1)* 163

CHAPTER 19 – *Led by the Spirit (Part 2)* 169

CHAPTER 20 – *Walking and Being Filled* 175

CHAPTER 21 – *The Spirit in Context* 183

CHAPTER 22 – *The Divine Conflict* 191

CHAPTER 23 – *Faith and the Believer* 199

CHAPTER 24 – *Faith and the Divine Profile* 205

CHAPTER 25 – *The Plan of God* 211

CHAPTER 26 – *The Plan for Holiness* 219

CHAPTER 27 – *Government and Divine Profile* 225

CHAPTER 28 – *Faith and the Kingdom* 231

CHAPTER 29 – *The New Creation* 239

CHAPTER 30 – *The Word of Reconciliation* 245

CHAPTER 31 – *The Ministry of Reconciliation (Part 1)* 251

CHAPTER 32 – *The Ministry of Reconciliation (Part 2)* 259

CHAPTER 33 – *The Administration of Forgiveness* 267

ABOUT THE AUTHOR 277

BIBLIOGRAPHY 279

PREFACE
By Philip Albuquerque

In 1997, when I was 14 years old, my brother Stan came home from deployment with the United States Navy to visit for a month. It was during this trip that he introduced me to my Lord Jesus. He preached the Gospel to me, and I was captivated. Partially, it was because I had always looked up to my brother, and I saw how much he loved God. I wanted to be like him, so I thought, "I should love God, too."

I remember the day I got saved. I told my brother that I wanted to accept Jesus (internally, I wanted him to be proud of me, and that was the driving force AT FIRST), but I was a bit startled when he asked me the simple question, "Why? Why do you want to become born again?" I wasn't sure how to answer that exactly, so I said, "I just do." He replied with, "Okay, that's good enough for me." We prayed, and before I could finish my prayer, tears overwhelmed me. I realized something had changed inside. I still wasn't sure what it was, but I knew I was different. From there on, I would go on to live my life for Christ.

About a year after I got saved, I went to visit my brother in Japan where he was stationed. It was there that he introduced me to apologetics. That trip catapulted me into the world of evangelism. At 15 years old, I started preaching the gospel and reading every book I could find on all sorts of Christian topics and doctrines. I hungered for God's Word and revelation about Himself to mankind. Through the years, my life did not always exemplify Christian conduct, but I always believed the truth of God's Word.

Fast forward to 2020. I was always aware of my brother's keen insights, but when it came to the doctrine of the Godhead, I felt I had a very good grasp on the concept and on how to give arguments to support my position. I never shied away from dialogue with JW's, Mormons, Oneness, etc. I was very confident in defending my position when speaking with anyone.

However, one day, I was having a conversation with Stan about the nature of God, and he said to me, "I have a really cool study on the Godhead, if you're interested in hearing it." I told him we could do it sometime, but that I was very well equipped on the subject matter. (My overconfidence would soon be shattered. lol) He replied with, "I promise it's like nothing you have ever heard before." Well, needless to say, he piqued my interest with that one statement. From there, he proceeded to share with me some of what you will read in this book. From the onset of our discussion, I was hooked.

In all the books I have read on this topic, I have NEVER read something like this that is so transformative and prevailing. Stan approaches the nature of God from a perspective that is, in my opinion, never addressed in the modern-day Church. He brings into light, key aspects of God's nature that are often overlooked when reading the Bible. I believe the reason it is often overlooked is because of our Christian traditions. Let me be clear, I do believe traditions can be good, but what happens when our sacred traditions conflict with something we clearly see in scripture?

More often than not, we tend to interpret those passages to fit our tradition. It's just a normal thing we do as Christians. We have a difficult time letting go of traditions we have held on to for so long. However, if our pursuit is truth, we have to be willing to at least scrutinize our traditions to see if they stand the test of time. This is exactly what I did, but I did it with the information you will read in this book. Let me explain ...

After Stan walked me through this study (over a period of 2 hours a day for 3 days), I decided to go into apologetics mode, scrutinize his study, and try to counter his arguments. I needed to see if what he was saying was able to stand up to the toughest arguments I could find in scripture. To make a long story short, every verse I could think of, every passage of scripture I would read to try and counter what he addresses in this book only reaffirmed what he showed me.

It came to a point where I had to let go of some precious traditions of mine, but in doing so, there was a freedom and joy that I experienced that is very hard to put into words. I saw God more clearly (no pun intended) than I ever had in my entire Christian life. I remember calling Stan one day, and while we were talking about the Godhead, I broke down in tears at the beauty and awe of what I was learning and the freedom I was experiencing. I begged him to put this into a book format because I believed it would REVOLUTIONIZE the body of Christ and bring the same freedom and joy I was experiencing to many others. He understood how serious I was and told me he would begin writing it immediately.

Here we are today with this book in your hands. With that, I want to present a challenge to the reader. Read the book in its entirety and, once you are finished, put this book under your own scrutiny. Test if what you read isn't truly based in what the Bible says. Also, test your traditions and compare them with what you read here. I believe the outcome will not be what you expect it to be. I also believe that no matter what you conclude, you will walk away from this with a deeper understanding and revelation of God that you have never had before.

A NOTE
From The Author

Before I submitted this manuscript for publishing, I had the opportunity to share its contents with a number of people who provided some keen insight into the general feel and direction of this book. My own Pastor sat down with me, and for three hours, he went over his critique of the manuscript. He warned me that too many "shock factor" moments within one volume can be hurtful to the veracity of a book. He wisely recommended that I revise some of the more radical sounding statements I had written. I decided to heed his counsel and make some necessary adjustments. I feel responsible to provide as much information as I can to eliminate the potential confusion that may arise from some of my statements, as much as possible.

So, after careful consideration, I decided I would augment additional content in order to provide the much needed context for those "heavier" sections of my rhetoric. I am well aware that by writing this book, I am placing all my reputation on the line. I recognize that by publishing this work, I run the risk of being subjected to unfair scrutiny and may very well be criticized by well-known and respected leaders and Bible teachers, some of whom I have a profound respect. It is with great humility toward all those who hold authority in the Church that I truly hope they will not rush to judgement without first applying some careful analysis of what they read. Please take some time to mull all this over before issuing an opinion. I believe you will come away more blessed and excited about this topic than ever before.

That being said, I would like to address you, the reader, as my fellow companions traveling with me on this precarious road. I will inevitably challenge the status quo that most of us in the evangelical Christian community often take for granted. It is my intent to push the envelope for a bit so that perhaps you too can see exactly what it is that I see when reading the Bible. I said it here first … so that no one is surprised. However, if you do follow along with me on this path, you may be confronted by some uncomfortable realities, and that is perfectly okay. In fact, if you don't have any reservations at some point as you read along, I would sincerely question your own commitment to truth. I say that because no one should flippantly make a decision to leave behind any deeply held convictions without first conducting some serious self-reflection and reasoning.

None of us can afford to be wrong about something so profound, so true, and so paramount to the meaning of our very own existence as human beings as this topic. It is my heart's desire that as we probe through this book, you will walk away with a far greater sense of awe, love, adoration, and worship toward the Lord, the God of Israel, the Maker of heaven and earth.

Blessings,

Stan A.

INTRODUCTION

Before I get into the specifics, I would like to share with you a quick story about an epiphany I had a few years back that opened my eyes to the deep truths I explore in this book.

In the Spring of 2006, I was listening to an MP3 seminar on biblical divine healing. In it, the speaker brought up a familiar passage from the book of Isaiah. He explained that oftentimes what we believe can be the very opposite of what the Bible actually has to say. As he delved deeper into Isaiah 61:1, my attention was drawn to a minute detail that blew me away. In my mind, the broader implications were staggering. The first part of the verse says, *"The Spirit of the Lord GOD is upon me, because the LORD has anointed me to bring good news to the poor ..."* (ESV).

The speaker made the observation that the verse emphatically states that the Spirit will come on the believer *after* having been anointed. That is to say, the anointing is what happens *first*, and then what follows afterward is the Spirit coming *upon* you. There is much more to this than meets the eye, so allow me to elaborate.

In certain church circles, when a preacher gives a fiery message, those in the pews might say things like, "Wow, the pastor was on fire!" "The

Spirit was all over the pastor today!" "Man, he was anointed!" It might seem rather insignificant, but I can assure you it is not. Its implication heavily impacts our approach to theology. In fact, it plays an important role in the premise for this book.

Different churches have developed a peculiar theology over the years, teaching the idea of different kinds of anointings, such as a healing anointing, a teaching anointing, or even a pastoral or preaching anointing. On the surface, it all seems harmless and gives the impression of being biblical. But, in reality, this is not the case. In fact, you might be surprised to learn there is no such verse anywhere in scripture that says anything remotely close to such a thing as a "teaching" or "healing" anointing. These are literally fabricated terms developed solely by "in-house" tradition. Biblically speaking, there is only one anointing in the New Testament. That is the anointing of Jesus Christ. There is NO other anointing. It simply does not exist. This sort of "anointing" language is usually derived from our vernacular, the unique vocabulary of our religious community used to describe our spiritual experiences.

What we see and hear in a church service all contributes to this experience and informs how and what we believe as we describe our experience. We refer to this type of communication as "Christianeez," otherwise known as the lingo of the Christian church. It is basically the familiar language of a Church body. We mention these terms so often amongst ourselves that we consequently end up accepting them without questioning whether or not they are accurate. We just assume it is in the Bible by default. However, if we were to dig just a little bit deeper, we would discover it is nowhere to be found in scripture. Our Christian lingo is so intermingled with our traditions that we don't realize just how much those traditions formulate our beliefs, at times even more so than the Bible itself.

My own epiphany was in recognizing that I had been using that same kind of traditional Christian lingo whenever I read the passages in Isaiah. I would read the verse, and then interpret it according to the "christianeez" I was familiar with. It occurred to me that if I did it in Isaiah, then I must have done it elsewhere in the Bible, too. Initially, when I re-read the passage, it became increasingly apparent that my eyes were merely glossing over the specifics of the text. In my mind, I thought I already knew the verse. Even though I had memorized the passage in question, it became suddenly obvious to me that what I believed about that verse was the exact opposite of the way it was written.

In other words, even though I would read, "the Spirit of the Lord God is upon me *because* the Lord has anointed me … ," what I actually believed about it was, "the Spirit anointed me because He came upon me." This realization hit me squarely between the eyes. This was the exact opposite of what the verse says. After some digging and self-reflection, I had to conclude that much of what I had come to know over the years was a mixture of church tradition with scriptural truth. The problem was that even though it sounded biblical on the surface, it was still only tradition. It was not pure biblical truth, not really.

This set me on the path to further investigation. The more I searched, the more I uncovered. You will be surprised to learn that other reputable ministries around the country have conducted their own research and concluded that what Americans believe suffers from a mingling of biblical truth with foreign concepts. In fact, in 2020, the results of a survey sponsored by Ligonier Ministries in 2014, 2016, and 2018 showed that of the 3,000 Americans surveyed, the majority claimed a traditional belief in the Trinity. Over fifty percent of the same group also held views that contradict Trinitarian doctrine, such as the outright denial of the deity of Christ, and included the belief that the Holy Spirit is only a mere impersonal force.[1]

This is only one of many such surveys and is evidence that much of what we believe is simultaneously mixed with ideas and concepts that contradict the basic fundamentals of traditional Christian doctrine. That means people are holding to conflicting ideas about what they believe and turn a blind eye to the lies they embrace. Traditions that we hold up to par with scripture are difficult to undo in the minds of people.

Generally speaking, traditions are good, as long as they don't replace

---

[1] Earls, Aaron. "Americans Hold Complex, Conflicting Religious Beliefs, According to Latest State of Theology Study." *Lifeway Research*. Ligonier Ministries, August 12, 2021. Last modified August 12, 2021. Accessed October 12, 2022. https://research.lifeway.com/2020/09/08/americans-hold-complex-conflicting-religious-beliefs-according-to-latest-state-of-theology-study/

the plain reading of the text. I am all for any tradition that reinforces scripture and supports truth. However, we ought to take issue with blind adherence to any tradition. As the people and children of God, we ought to know *exactly* what we believe and why. See if you can follow my logic. Jesus said, *"And ye shall know the truth, and the truth shall make you free"* (John 8:32). The apostle Paul wrote, *"So then faith cometh by hearing, and hearing by the word of God"* (Romans 10:17). Logic would therefore dictate: If faith comes by hearing the Word of God, then if what we are hearing is more tradition than truth, our faith becomes compromised.

If we consider why so many modern believers do not experience the freedom Jesus promised, it is no wonder why this is the case. Could it be that our experiences, or even our lack thereof, may be tainted simply because we hold so dearly to our traditions at the expense of truth? In a world so riddled with lies and deception, it is definitely worth our time to re-evaluate what it is we really believe. I don't see the point in believing in lies, regardless of how many warm fuzzies the lies may give.

What Is The Point?

The main purpose for addressing the nature of God in the first half of this book is to lay the groundwork for what is the second half, which involves the role we play in revealing our God to the world in a manner that is cohesive with His nature. I believe that revisiting those passages in scripture that speak of God's nature will have a revolutionary effect in the life of the believer. What we believe about God really does have a direct effect on how we behave and perceive the world around us. Filtered ideas can skew our understanding and have a direct impact on our witness.

I intend to demonstrate in this book that certain traditions have played a significant role in formulating our collective theology, perhaps even more so than we may be willing to admit at first. These traditions have bled into almost every discipline of Christian thought and practical everyday life. The focus of this book will be in addressing the doctrine of the Trinity in light of scripture; how our approach to it can directly impact what we believe of biblical doctrine and expression of our faith.

My hope is that this book will help bring the reader's own beliefs into closer alignment with the more precise language of scripture. This will, in turn, be useful when you come across opposing arguments often designed to confuse those who don't apply the necessary elbow grease to really learn about their own Bible. Some of the most challenging questions I have been asked were related to the traditional approach of the doctrine covering God's nature (the Godhead). I say *challenging* because I have been called out in the past for *certain details* surrounding the Trinitarian approach, which, as we shall see, should not be overlooked or ignored.

When explaining the doctrine of the Godhead, we ought not fall spectacularly short of its grandeur, as many of us do with complex and sometimes contradictory arguments. However, as we press further into this book, these rough edges can be smoothed out. While the traditional answers may fail to provide a clear picture of what we truly believe as Christians, we are still tasked with persuading unbelievers to make the conscious choice of believing in the New Covenant based on our imperfect explanations. I figure we can fix it by addressing this very issue with the most foundational part of our theology ... what we believe about God.

Our definitions and arguments need not be so complicated that we resort to unbiblical language in order to explain the claims of scripture. Yet, we should ask ourselves, "What if I'm wrong? What if the assumptions I bring to my own arguments are the very things that make my job of persuading others more difficult?" This book will take steps in that direction to clarify some of our claims about God's nature and how that knowledge both influences and motivates us.

Moving Forward

We must examine the biblical text to better understand God's own nature, but without the lens of our traditions. We will take an in-depth look at the undergirding theme about Who and What the True God is really like. We will also identify those assumptions that have brought so much confusion to the body of Christ. We will highlight certain passages that don't exactly fit within the paradigm of what we've been taught about

God in the most fundamentalist Christian circles.

So let me be blunt here: I fully intend to impress into your mind the consistent themes of God's nature that the *Bible* emphasizes over and over again, not what we *think* it says. It may lead us to question some of our formal education on the matter, and especially what some of our favorite Bible teachers may have taught us. It will require you to actually open up your own Bible and read it for yourself. Even when scripture passages are provided in this book, it shouldn't relieve any of us of the responsibility to research it within our own Bibles. The most valuable resource in our possession for truth is the Holy Scripture itself.

We will take a quick tour of some of the historical views on God by the ancient Hebrews who gave us the Tanakh (Old Testament), and how it influenced New Testament theology. We must also look more closely at the words of Christ referring to God (as they were recorded), while keeping in the forefront of our minds that Jesus instructed the people of His day by using the Tanakh (from here on referred to as the Old Testament)[2] as the foundation for His teachings. Every now and then, I may refer to some extra-biblical sources from established scholarship, academia, or articles in order to make a valuable point. But the Bible will be the primary and most crucial source material for this book.

Jesus' commentaries on God were built on the platform of Old Testament concepts. The New Testament narrative is perfectly in line with that platform. Fortunately for us, we have the privilege of hindsight. We can look back through past history armed with the wealth of both Testaments. You will see how God weaves His thread consistently between the Testaments and communicates the same themes that were universally understood among ancient Hebrews. This is especially important in areas where

---

[2] The term "Old Testament" was first used in the second century by Melito of Sardis (the first known Christian Pilgrim). He was mentioned by Eusebius. Some have even postulated that Constantine may have referred to the old testament so as to make people believe that it had no longer any value.

[3] Eusebius of Caesarea, "The Church History of Eusebius," in *Eusebius: Church History, Life of Constantine the Great,* and *Oration in Praise of Constantine,* ed. Philip Schaff and Henry Wace, trans. Arthur Cushman McGiffert, vol. 1, A Select Library of the Nicene and Post-Nicene Fathers of the Christian Church, Second Series (New York: Christian Literature Company, 1890), 206.

our Western Christian theology strays from the pattern of God's design.

I should mention here that I am not a scholar by profession, nor am I a student spending all of my time in university libraries doing endless research for term papers. I am simply a person who wants to bring attention to certain motifs in the biblical account that, in my estimation, are simply ignored at large by the Church. This knack of seeing things outside the box has done me well in the past, and I am of the opinion that the Church is placing too much emphasis on the wrong part of the story, as you will see.

We will also correlate our understanding of God's nature with the Church's attitudes and best practices. Directly linking a clearer understanding of God's nature to our application of His Word provides practical reasoning behind our claims as Bible-believing Christians. Furthermore, by clarifying what we know about God, we are compelled to set aside our long-held presuppositions, thus enabling us to re-evaluate our beliefs to be aligned with truth instead of lies. I am not just talking about giving mental assent to what the Bible says about God's nature. What I am proposing is the potential overhaul of certain precious doctrines held dear. You may have to make some hard decisions by the time you finish reading this book.

How should we as Christian believers peer into this mystery and yet walk away with greater clarity? What is God's intended purpose for us in light of the Revelation of Jesus Christ in the New Testament? Finally, how does His nature make its way into defining our faith? I sincerely doubt your traditions will come away unscathed. But, if the goal of your pursuit is truth, then your traditions can be relegated to their proper place in the hierarchy of things, secondary to the Scriptures. We will explore all of this and more in this book.

King Solomon once said, *"Wisdom is the principal thing; therefore, get wisdom: and with all you're getting get understanding."* Our main objective here is for greater and deeper understanding of the God we serve, not just knowledge and wisdom. So, come with me as we journey together into the mystery of His reality, and to behold our ultimate destiny in Him.

CHAPTER 1

My Personal Story

It was January of 1994 when I became a Christian and experienced what it means to be truly "born again" as a believer. Since then, I have acquired a voracious appetite for studying God's Word, specifically in areas of theology and apologetics. In the course of my walk of faith in Jesus, there were times when I had to put off and also take on different perspectives. This was a direct result of being compelled to look at my own interpretation of certain biblical passages. Over time, my own worldview was shaped and challenged the more I learned. I have many friends in active ministry around the world with whom I have had scores of discussions and even debates, all of which have heavily informed my perspectives over the years. Among some of these relationships, I have also met with people from all walks of life, varying in both culture and even religious beliefs.

Throughout this process, I wrestled with certain aspects of my own belief system on a number of occasions in lieu of these encounters. I defined and redefined certain particulars of my own beliefs as I came to realize that much of what I was taught was in dire need of a reformation of sorts. Shortly after becoming a Christian, I made it a point to share the good news of Jesus the Messiah with nearly everyone in my sphere of influence. I did not really have a church background growing up, so when I became a believer, I was so on fire that I hit the ground running.

In my zeal, I wasn't always polished, but I did the best I could to share my newfound Christian faith. As I engaged with people about the Gospel, I was increasingly confronted with questions for which I did not have an immediate answer. This compelled me to do deeper research for just about everything I claimed to believe. The need to find the correct answers forced me to acknowledge and address what seemed like apparent discrepancies in my understanding of the biblical text.

If someone asked me a question and I had no answer, I would say, "I don't know the answer to that, but I *will* get back to you." Regardless of how long it took, I would do my due diligence to get back to them with the correct answers. It sometimes took a full day. At other times, it took a week or more. But I always returned with what I considered a compelling and persuasive response. There were times when they had forgotten about the questions they had asked and were surprised when I suddenly showed up two weeks later with my response in hand.

In my mind, the Bible always has all the answers to just about any question you can ever have. I figured if I did not know the answer to a question, it simply meant that *I* did not know it. I would therefore research until I found what I was searching for. I felt uncomfortable with flippant answers to profound questions. The idea of pending judgment for leading others astray lingered in my mind.

With the passage of time, more frequently than not, it seemed the majority of the questions hurled my way were basically the same kind of questions posed from different angles. My answers would usually revolve more or less around the same thing from my previous discussions. However, every now and then, I would have questions posed to me that made me think hard, producing inquiries of my own in the back of my mind and propelling me into further research to discover deeper, more profound answers. I figured that if the question popped up in my mind, then I was certain someone else would bring it up at some point down the road. Have you ever asked yourself a question about your faith that got you stumped? If you were asked to break down what you believed, could you do it without hesitating or scrambling for some reference book?

Well, it's accurate to say that tackling certain fundamentals of Christian doctrine could be a daunting task for many of us, especially if there is not a thorough grasp of the material. I am sad to say that many professing Christians are biblically illiterate and never take the time to really study the Bible. Not everyone who believes is necessarily a Bible scholar or theologian.

Even though I don't consider myself a theologian or even a scholar, I can honestly say I do study the Word of God to *"be ready always to give an answer"* to every question about my faith (study 1 Peter 3:15). When attempting to break down what we claim to believe to someone, many times our hearers may still be left asking questions, and at times without clear answers. My goal is to give you the benefit of my experience in answering certain questions raised to me over the years.

Understanding and knowing God through the person of Jesus Christ has enriched my life in more ways than I can describe. My personal experiences, relationships, and biblical studies have resulted in what some might consider a rather peculiar, yet faithful, view of the nature of God and the powerful role that knowledge plays out in our lives. I am, of course, referring specifically to the Godhead and the implications of its theology.

This affects not only how we relate to Him as God, but it affects also our disposition toward other people, and even toward our adversaries. It is my belief that as we tackle the questions raised in this book, your own life will be changed in the process. We will explore exactly what it is that we believe about God and use scripture to scrutinize those beliefs. You may be surprised to discover that what you think you know may not be so.

My Personal Story

As the son of Brazilian immigrants, I grew up in Brooklyn, New York, and Rio de Janeiro, Brazil. My parents immigrated from Brazil a year before I was born. I was raised as a non-religious Roman Catholic by parents who chose not to pursue the priesthood and convent to start a family. Nevertheless, even though I grew up in a non-religious home, I still retained a healthy curiosity about the Bible. Don't get me wrong. I was no saint. In fact, my parents' friends would refer to me as the devil from Brooklyn because of my infamous exploits.

Still, contrary to what most Catholics do, I would occasionally pick up my parent's huge family Bible from the shelf and peruse through its contents. I recall as a kid watching movies like *The Ten Commandments*, then immediately searching for the specific passage in Exodus where Moses received the tablets with the Ten Commandments. *"Honor thy father and thy mother ..."* was an important commandment I came across, and would occasionally be reminded of the verse when my mom would scold me for being disrespectful.

Eventually, I would come across other more conflicting passages where Jesus would say things like, *"And call none your father upon earth; for one is your father, who is in heaven"* (Matthew 23:9 DRA). As a kid, I thought I understood what the Bible said about honoring your father and mother. However, coming across Jesus' words made me rethink what He must have meant. He could not have meant "father" in the natural sense because the Bible had tons of examples where that was normal. Therefore, Jesus must have meant it in a spiritual sense. But that created even more problems for me as a Catholic. If Jesus meant it in a spiritual sense, then why did we refer to our Catholic priests as "Father"? It was a direct violation of the commandment.

Another passage that drew my attention and made things even more complicated for me was, *"Thou shalt not make to thyself a graven thing, nor the likeness of any thing that is in heaven above, or in the earth beneath ..."* (Exodus 20:4 DRA). To make things worse, not only does the passage say NOT to make images, but it also says NOT to bow down to them either. This confounded me because, as a Catholic, I was supposed to do all these things; yet, everyone was okay with doing exactly what God said not to do. So I did what any good Catholic would do ... I went to the priest.

There was a local Catholic church a few miles from my home. One day, I decided to pay a visit to the local priest and ask him questions specifically about these two passages. His response would impress me for years to come. He said, "Well, that's our tradition. It's just how we've practiced for centuries. You know you shouldn't really bother reading your Bible anyway. That's why I'm here."

Well, that did not sit well with me, and it certainly did not satisfy my curiosity. So I began searching for answers. This set the stage for me to search for the truth.

As I began asking more questions, I discovered by my parents' admission that our family originally came from Jewish stock. They were refugees who immigrated from Europe to northern Brazil. In fact, to this day, there is still a large Jewish population where my parents were from. I wasn't sure what I could do with that information, but I took it in stride and tucked that information away. Later, when I became a Christian, I relished in the thought of sharing in some heritage to the Jewish people, especially now that I believed in Jesus, the Jewish Messiah.

My initial experience in the church where I got saved was "interesting," to say the least. Even though they introduced me to my Lord and Savior, they had some peculiar beliefs. I wondered, *They couldn't all be wrong ... could they?* Well, there were some considerable drawbacks. I eventually came to recognize that the doctrine and methods of that ministry were highly suspect, and to a large degree manipulative. The church was known for their King-James-Only-ism, which is the view that the KJV Bible is the only version considered to be inspired in the English language. Other Bible versions were rejected as uninspired and even demonic. According to their doctrine, water baptism (that is, full submersion) was viewed as essential to salvation. This meant that if your mode of baptism differed from theirs, you were not considered saved, no matter how much you "believed" and "loved" Jesus as your Lord and Savior. It made no difference to them.

That ministry also held to the "oneness" doctrine, which meant they were adamantly opposed to the Trinity, citing it as unbiblical and even pagan. They believe that Jesus IS the Father, and the Son, and the Holy Ghost in bodily form. Having myself come from a Catholic background, I was wary of having anything to do with pagan practices, so I somewhat agreed with their position on the issue. However, I would later learn this church was labeled a cult by certain awareness groups. I also came to discover their brand of religion wasn't the norm of the Christian experience. They feigned themselves to be a traditional Christian church. Man, oh, man, I still had so much to learn, and so much to see before I would come to my senses.

There was a considerable amount of control being imposed over that fellowship. This was especially true when it came to those doctrinal points that enforced obedience to the leadership, a clear marker of a cult, by the way. On a number of occasions, I was caught up in the crossfire of a Pastor yelling at someone or a group for "… not doing what you were told!" Of course, we were being made to feel guilty over what I perceived as a non-issue. One example that comes to mind was their idea that preaching the gospel on the streets was only meant to invite people to the church. Witnessing on the streets was not really telling them about Jesus. It was getting them into the building for a Bible study. If you did not follow their instructions, you could expect to be called into the Pastor's office to receive a "loving rebuke." I had my fair share of such rebukes at the behest of a red-faced Pastor. He would aggressively defend the ministry's doctrine and was inflexible and dogmatic. Mind you, it was not like that in the beginning. It was more of a progression of sorts with me. Eventually, it made my experience in that church increasingly intolerable and unbearable.

On many occasions, when I tried witnessing, I found myself having to twist a passage or two in the Bible to make it mean what the ministry wanted me to teach, while ignoring the plain reading of the text as the basis for my arguments. In spite of everything I experienced, this is what grated on me the most. Since I had come to faith through that ministry, I did not want to be unappreciative, and I did not want to simply leave over what might be a misunderstanding on my part. I did not have anywhere else to go since they were all I knew since becoming a Christian. I felt a deep sense of obligation to stay with them. Even though I had my reservations, I did not want to be seen as divisive or rebellious. However, that all came to a head sometime after I was stationed overseas in Japan while serving in the Navy. This was where the tide began to turn for me.

Prior to arriving overseas in 1994, it was made abundantly clear to me that I was required to call the church's leadership back in the United States on a regular basis since they disapproved of me attending any other church. They considered other organizations to be deceived and apostate. However, shortly after arriving in Japan, I began reaching out to others who claimed to be Christian believers so as not to venture in my newfound faith alone in a foreign country. Despite the rules they gave, I attended the church services in the local chapel, and participated in Bible studies held on the ship without informing my home church stateside. I figured what the leadership did not know would not hurt them.

I was 19 years old, alone in a foreign country, serving in the military. For the first time, I was on my own in the world. Furthermore, calling back to the U.S. multiple times a week was pretty expensive. I really felt like I needed the support of a local fellowship. Eventually, I did find a handful of evangelical Christians on the ship who believed differently than me, but who genuinely loved God. Among my new friends was a young man named Samuel. He was a preacher's kid of a Church of God in Christ ministry back in his home town. The longer I remained overseas, the easier it became to disregard the influence of my home church. I did eventually break away and leave that ministry. I offer the following account of the events that led to my departure from them.

I noted how effectively my friend Sam was being used of God in his witness of the gospel. He was always patient, kind, loving, and wise. He was always sharing his faith in Jesus with others, both with his words and his actions. On a number of occasions, I saw God use him in supernatural ways. God answered his prayers. He had divinely ordained encounters, and he even experienced some of the more mystical things like visions and dreams revealing things about other people and situations of which he had no way of knowing. His life and testimony both touched and challenged me, compelling me to ask more questions. I observed his walk closely, and I can say that I saw authentic Christianity being lived out before my eyes. Don't get me wrong; he was not perfect or anything like that, but I had no doubt that he was certainly the genuine article.

One particular day, I called the General Pastor of that ministry I was affiliated with, and proceeded to tell him everything about my friend. The pastor seemed more and more apprehensive over the phone as he intently listened to me basically admitting to being in fellowship with someone he considered an "unbeliever." I informed the pastor that I had personally witnessed Jesus use Him to lead others away from sin, and to turn to God by calling Jesus *Lord*. I also conveyed to the pastor how he believed in the same method of baptism, with one exception. He did not see baptism as *essential* for salvation.

This was a major touch point of the church I was saved in. They believed that if a person was baptized they had to believe it essential for their salvation, and the person doing the baptizing had to say the words "In the name of Jesus Christ" for it to even be valid. After I said what I wanted to say, the pastor retorted with, "Well, then, Stan … he's clearly not a brother."

I will be frank with you. I had some serious problems with that statement. I had difficulty reconciling what I knew about my friend with what the Pastor was telling me. How could someone whom I had personally witnessed being used mightily of God not be a brother in Christ? It went against everything I had observed and come to learn about Sam. After I hung up the phone, I wandered around the next two weeks contemplating what I should do.

On the one hand, the Pastor quoted scripture to support his view that to fellowship with anyone who disagreed with the Bible was wrong because the Bible says, *"Be ye not unequally yoked with unbelievers…"* (2 Corinthians 6:14). On the other hand, my friend was living out what I saw as an exemplary biblical lifestyle according to what was written in scripture, *"… be thou an example of the believers …"* (1 Timothy 4:12). So … who do I trust?

CHAPTER 2
Paradigm Shift

For two weeks, I agonized over the decision of whether to remain with that ministry, which would require that I end my friendship with Sam. Thankfully, I had finally reached a breaking point. To live in that conundrum for any prolonged period of time would be impossible. I felt like I was at the point of being driven mad with confusion. I vividly recall walking down the street in Sasebo, Japan, while reading my Bible, and came across the following passage:

> *"For what if some did not believe? Shall their unbelief make the faith of God without effect? God forbid: yea, let God be true, but every man a liar; as it is written, That thou mightest be justified in thy sayings, and mightest overcome when thou art judged."* (Romans 3:3-4)

From this verse, I concluded that my problem was with my perception of the truth, not the truth itself. I decided the best thing to do was to consider everyone to be a liar and only God to be true. My friend, my pastor, and yes, even myself were all liars as far as I was concerned. I figured that by seeing things from that vantage point, all I could do is look up knowing

God would never lie to me. Only God was true in that moment, and if I was to be justified in my decision and overcome this confusion in my life, then I had to trust God to show me what to believe. I could not trust in my own understanding.

That was when I came up with a plan. I surmised that since God knows everything in advance. He was well aware of what I was about to ask Him long before I ever understood the question. So by relying on His sovereignty alone, I closed my Bible and prayed, saying, "Lord, I can no longer continue losing sleep over this. Either the pastor is wrong or my friend is wrong, and I do not know what to believe or decide. I am taking the position that we are all wrong, except for You. Therefore, I am trusting You to show me whether or not my friend is a brother. If indeed he is my brother in Christ, then I ask that You send him here exactly to where I am, to pull up in his car, and ask me to go with him to the mountain to pray. If that happens in the next five minutes, then I will know without a doubt that he is indeed my brother, and I will ignore what the pastor said and leave that church for teaching me lies."

In that very moment I stopped walking, crossed my arms, and just stood right there on the sidewalk. Mind you, I was in a random place at a random time with no way of determining what would happen next. Pretty bold, I know. It was an ultimatum for sure, but it was not directed at God. To be clear, I don't typically make such decisions as common practice, but it was an ultimatum to my own self for a decision in the moment. I also knew the chances of it happening were slim to none. That is how I rationalized that if the answer came in those moments, it would be God answering my prayer specifically according to my request.

About a minute or two later, I saw a car turn a corner onto the road coming toward me about two blocks away. As it approached, I recognized it to be my friend's vehicle. Without even motioning to him, he pulled right up next to me on the sidewalk, rolled down his passenger side window, and called to me, "Hey, Stan. So glad to run into you, man! Hey, you want to go up to the mountain with me to pray?" With great relief and gathering tears of joy, I responded, "Yes, brother, I do." From that day forward, I cut off all communication with that church and never looked back.

You might be wondering how I could have stayed so long in that situation, where error was so rampant. You might ask why I did not notice what the Bible said about the proper behavior of leadership? Shouldn't I have had discernment about the wrong beliefs they held? These are all legitimate questions. In my defense, I did not grow up in a biblically-based home. When I got saved in that church, that was all I knew. My conversion experience was real, and I experienced a genuine relationship with God. Though what they taught was certainly wrong on a number of points, I don't hold grudges against them. I realized the majority of them were going along with what they had been taught, just as I was for a time.

But what about the rest of the Christian Church? Well, I opened myself up to learning from others, and even accepting teachings in line with the more traditional orthodoxy of the Christian faith, including Trinitarian doctrine. I re-evaluated my pre-conceived views of the Trinity to align myself more with my brothers and sisters in Christ abroad. I studied a number of authors such as Norman Geisler, Josh McDowell, and R.C. Sproul, to name a few. I read books on apologetics, heard various Bible teachings from pastors and theologians, and also participated in a number of Bible studies that specifically touched on the Godhead, most likely because the topic was such a major part of my initial exposure after getting saved. I figured I needed to catch up.

I frequently engaged in minor debates, and even led a number of people to Christ without incident. It was such a blessing to share Jesus with everyone and not have the shadow or pressure from that church over me. Every now and then, I even found myself passionately defending the Christian faith using the Trinitarian approach to the consternation of some of my Jewish shipmates. Of course, that would have been forbidden in that other ministry. Still, I didn't care … I was free from the oppression of a cult-like atmosphere, and I surrounded myself with like-minded believers who genuinely loved and served God.

I witnessed to others about Christ every time I had the opportunity. During these encounters, I became increasingly uncomfortable with how I was teaching about the Godhead. My discomfort was not the doctrine of the Trinity itself but the methodology in explaining the Trinity that kept getting in the way of my peace with it. Then one day, while conferring with a Jewish co-worker about the Trinity, he said to me, "I don't get it, man. How can you stand there and say you are preaching the Bible alone, and yet you keep referring to the 'Trinity' when that word is not even in your Bible?" I shrugged off the question, even though it had merit, and stored it in the back recesses of my mind. I knew I would have to revisit this question, and I would eventually need to know the answer.

It wasn't long until I revisited the topic and began asking questions of my own. "Why do we use the 'Trinity' to describe God if the New Testament itself makes no point at all in defending the concept?" Or, "Why wasn't a defense of the Trinity the biggest point of contention in the disciple's interaction with the Jewish leadership at the time?" More importantly, "Why didn't Jesus do it? Since He is the Son of God, why wasn't the defense of the Trinity at the core of His message? Wasn't He here to show us what God is like? Isn't He God?" Finally, "Why doesn't the Bible emphatically use this term?"

The more I asked these questions, it became clearer to me that I was deviating in my logic from both the traditional Christian view of the Trinity, as well as from the Oneness doctrine of the church I had left a few years earlier. I simply could not agree with either side, at least not fully. I kept my views to myself, not willing to discuss something I wasn't sure of. I would mull it over in my head all the time. I still had to acknowledge in later discussions that even though the traditional terminology was not in the Bible, there is still indeed a biblical justification for the "triunity" of God. Yet, I could not in good conscience bring myself to conclusively use the traditional model as the lens for understanding Christian doctrine, at least not in the way it was taught to me.

It appeared I was approaching a similar crossroad with my understanding of God's very nature as it was in the scenario with Sam. Understand, I had not done away with the concept of the Trinity altogether, since I do see a trinity of sorts in the Bible. However, I have simply shifted my vantage point, having come to reconcile these ideas that only appear conflicted. A triune revelation of God is not unique to the New Testament. So why is it that we assume it is merely a Christian tradition? That is exactly what this book is about. So, before we go any farther, let's agree to approach this subject, and each other for that matter, with respect and humility that we may not have given this in the past. Before you label me a heretic, hear me out first. Allow me to make my case.

I want to make it clear that I do not reject the triunity (or trinity) of God as Father, Son, and Holy Spirit as revealed in the New Testament. I recognize this doctrine to be principally scriptural and appropriate. Nor am I against using the term *Trinity*. However, I am purposefully steering away from using Trinitarian language when referring to God's nature precisely because of all the baggage associated with the term. Therefore, my reasons for refraining from using Trinitarian language toward God are mainly due to the absence of such language in the New Testament.

Furthermore, I do not believe that using the term is necessarily wrong. It is not evil in itself, nor is it inherently good. However, I do think it is insufficient. It can be misleading from a certain point of view for reasons we will explore further, i.e., the baggage. Therefore, to prevent ostracizing or alienating any segment of the Christian community, I prefer to replace the terms "Trinity" or "Trinitarian" with more precise terms such as "tradition" or "traditional" respectively, since it more accurately reflects the point I am making. I am also not against all tradition. Even Rabbi Paul (aka Rav Shaule) encouraged the Thessalonians to hold on to the traditions they were taught (2 Thessalonians 2:15). What I do oppose are those traditions that either contradict or attempt to replace biblical language with the jargon that brings confusion. Instead of using the words *Trinity* or *Trinitarian*, think more along the lines of *tradition* or *traditional* instead. With that said, let us dive in.

⟵⟶

Jesus' own descriptions of the Father are particularly revealing. Jesus always chose His words carefully and was consistent with His semantics. When the Lord appeared on the scene, He did not simply begin teaching a Trinitarian understanding of God that was foreign to the Jews. It simply was not in His purview. Jesus was thoroughly Jewish in every way. This view is not limited to a "Christian" sentiment. Popular Orthodox Jewish Rabbi Shmuley Boteach, affectionately called *America's Rabbi*, argues that, "Jews should claim him (Jesus) as one of our own. Through Jewish sensibilities, we can see in the Christian Bible one of our rabbis, Jesus, ever our brother." I would like to mention here that the rabbi's sentiment is not without objection within the Jewish community. There are certainly debates among non-Christian Jews about Jesus' identity, origin, and even existence. I won't go too deep into Jesus' Jewishness, except to say that there are those on all sides of the debate that affirm or deny Jesus' Jewish heritage.

His teachings, manner of life, and testimony all point to Him being Jewish. That meant that when He spoke, the people heard Jesus as they would listen to a Jewish rabbi. His references to God as His own Father was and still are a point of contention among unbelieving Jews, but His Jewishness was not really an issue, at least not until much later in history. Two of the gospels, Matthew and Luke, both attest to His lineage going all the way back to Abraham and Adam respectively. Therefore, it should come as no surprise if Jesus' own teaching about God would be in perfect harmony with ancient Hebrew theology. The initial disciples and apostles who followed Him were all Jewish and would have been at home with all the Jewish sensibilities about the God of Abraham, Isaac, and Jacob.

All of Jesus' claims were rooted in the Old Testament. It might come as a shock to some that there was no New Testament from which He could read. The New Testament came after the fact. More likely than not, on every Sabbath, He would read from the Law of Moses, the Prophets, and the Writings (Psalms, Proverbs, etc.). No doubt He would also have had access to contemporary second-temple-era documents that expounded on Jewish law, theology, and way of life.

Furthermore, we must take into consideration the world that eventually produced the New Testament. Theologian and author Dr. Michael Heiser wrote:

> "The New Testament writers, being predominantly Jewish and products of the Second Temple Period, more often than not telegraphed the same outlook. We just can't see it because, frankly, we don't have second temple Jewish eyes. We miss what the original audience would have seen." [4]

---

[4] Michael S. Heiser, *Reversing Hermon: Enoch, the Watchers & the Forgotten Mission of Jesus Christ* (Crane, MO: Defender Publishing, 2017).

In order to peer into the New Testament correctly, we must exchange our westernized Christian glasses with biblical-era ones instead. By casting off our deeply held traditions and dogma in favor of scripture, we will be free to put on a pair of biblical glasses to enable us to more clearly perceive God as He really is according to scripture.

In the constant war of ideas, we should not make the mistake of fighting the wrong battles. As a body, we have exhausted so much effort by arguing for things and terms that the early church did not really bother with, thereby making us inefficient in our mission to preach the Kingdom of God, and to promote His truth. I spent a considerable amount of time defending ideas created and defined by men. Unfortunately, our definitions do not always reflect accuracy to the biblical text. This is not about being divisive over a single point of doctrine. It's really about accuracy in a fundamental segment of Christian theology.

We should seek to find some common ground, while not placing our security on wrong concepts about God. Then, after laying aside all those traditions with no basis in biblical semantics, we will then be able to take a more honest look at the Godhead to make sense of the Trinity in proper context. I am aware that you may feel a sense of obligation to keep the traditional model in the forefront of your theology. I totally get it. Having the backing of the majority of the Christian church and its history in your corner is a considerable support. The idea of going against the grain can be intimidating. But if the goal of your pursuit is truth, then at a minimum you ought to be open to making whatever adjustments are needed so as to better align what you believe to what is true, regardless of the argument.

Take into consideration that if you are wrong about this, the responsibility still rests on your shoulders to get it right ... especially if you are wanting to be an effective witness for Christ. Whether or not you hold to the more traditional model, or you are unsure and on the fence, or perhaps never even gave it a thought, I believe you will come away from this book with a fresh perspective on the nature and reality of the God of the Bible; one that will fill you with awe and wonder. Get ready for an exciting ride because what you think you know may not be so.

CHAPTER 3
A Different Perspective

While on a carrier deployment in 2019, part of my daily routine was strolling into the chapel on my free time to quiet myself and pray. The ship had been out to sea for about six months when a shared sense of frustration came over the crew as it became painfully obvious it was going to be a longer deployment than anticipated. When your world consists of 1,092 feet of steel, carrying a mixed crew of over 5,600 souls,[5] rumors of deployment extensions abound. Anyone who has served in the Navy can tell you, changes in schedule are almost an absolute certainty. Going to the chapel was my way of escape, and I was certain that God had a purpose for me to be there. I knew there were Sailors aboard whom God was calling me to reach with the good news of the Kingdom.

I had established a good working relationship with some of the Chaplains. I was entrusted with teaching some Bible studies, and tasked with helping out with other evangelistic efforts in the hopes of leading shipmates to Christ. I was in my element. Though deployment seemed

---

[5] "USS Abraham Lincoln - Nimitz Class Aircraft Carrier." Naval Technology. Accessed May 16, 2020. https://www.naval-technology.com/projects/abraham-lincoln-nimitz-class-aircraft-carrier/.

cumbersome at times, I can wholeheartedly say that serving the Lord was, and still is, my greatest joy. I revel in being about our Father's business, though I did not like being on deployment. Yet, from the point of view of the Kingdom, I basically had a captive audience. What more could I ask for? As time passed, more and more people experienced the need to ask questions on spiritual matters, seeking answers to existential questions. Essentially, that is my bread and butter. I could not ask for a better harvest field.

During one of those long days out at sea, I happened to be sitting in the chapel when Omar, a young officer (an Egyptian/American Muslim) walked in to conduct his daily prayers. As a show of respect, I sat quietly while I observed him go through his normal routine of laying down a prayer mat, removing his shoes, going to his knees, bowing down and offering his litany of prayers in a systematic fashion. When he was finished, he put his shoes back on, sat near me, and picked up the Quran (the Muslim holy book) to read.

After a few minutes, he closed the book. It was then that I strategically decided to engage in some friendly conversation about spiritual things. I just could not help myself. He was very gracious and cordial, and he was also appreciative of the respect I showed him by allowing him to do his thing without disturbance, distraction, or incident. He had apparently been apprehensive seeing me there. We struck up a friendship that may never have happened under different circumstances. Though our worlds were somewhat different and our beliefs went in completely different directions, it was still a privilege to get to know him and learn more about him.

Being confined to the same ship day in and day out in close quarters makes us more keenly aware of each other's daily routines. We had run into each other in the passageways regularly during the hustle and bustle of the work day. Even though we were not yet acquainted, we would always give each other a brief compliment in the passageway. There in the chapel was the first time we officially introduced ourselves to each other. I could tell he had a rudimentary knowledge of the Bible, so I quickly assessed that I was not the first Christian he had interacted with. Still, we were glad to engage in some intelligent and stimulating conversation not relating to our work.

The topic of the nature of God came up almost immediately. He made it clear to me in no uncertain terms, that he had some difficulty understanding the traditional Christian concept of God. In times past, he had lively conversations with other Christians about this very topic. In his mind, the Christian idea of the Trinity gave him the impression that Christians believe in three separate gods. The Trinitarian model seemed to have more contradictions than common sense, in his mind. He had difficulty reconciling some conflicting statements like "God in three persons, yet they are one." As he and I delved further into the discussion, it was clear to me that if I attempted to use any traditional formula in my approach, it would only confuse him and push him farther away.

He found deep solace in what he considered his more "simplistic" view of God without having to complicate it with Trinitarian formulas, like "God in three separate and distinct persons, co-equal, co-eternal, God the Father, God the Son, and God the Holy Spirit." He explained, "The Christian idea of God is just too complicated. At least in Islam I can understand what I believe, and I can also better explain it than Christians can of their own beliefs. It's just simpler." From his perspective simplicity was king.

He proceeded to relay back to me much of what others had told him about the Christian faith. I did notice the earmarks of textbook answers in his responses to my own questions. Though, at the time, I had not really gotten too deep into the subject with him, I did attempt to simplify the discussion. Nevertheless, he was adamant on what he considered pagan overtones of the Christian understanding of the Trinity. I pondered that in my mind. He perceived something pagan in what Christians understand to be diametrically opposed to pagan ideas; it's an interesting dichotomy. After about an hour or so, we left the conversation to get back to our responsibilities on the ship.

Later that week, I met another Sailor who happened to meander into the Chapel. Again, as was my custom, I was sitting down reading my Bible when the thin-framed young man introduced himself as Edward. Actually, I had heard about this young man from some of the other brothers onboard who spoke with him on occasion whenever he showed up in the chapel. The week I arrived on board, the brothers had also mentioned me to him.

What made our encounter more interesting was the fact that both of us were Brazilian-Americans. This one detail alone made us look forward to meeting each other. It's always exciting to meet another Brazilian in any context.

I was able to gather some of his background prior to meeting him. I discovered that back in our homeport in Norfolk, he was affiliated with the same church ministry I had originally been involved with when I first became a believer. Since I had left that church a few years after my conversion, they considered me apostate to the faith according to their doctrine, and speaking with me was now something to be avoided. In all honesty, I was a bit concerned that he might not want to meet with me at all if he found out about my history with that ministry.

Fortunately, he was open to dialogue. As I anticipated, he immediately began with the doctrine of baptism and the Godhead as the first topics of discussion. Now, while I no longer hold a King James-only position, I still read from the KJV, and regularly teach using that translation. I now use other versions for additional emphasis and study. Since I was comfortable with using the KJV, Edward seemed totally open for conversation and even Bible study with me.

I asked him if he wouldn't mind meeting up with me daily so we could talk, as his schedule would be open at the same hour of the day. This way we could have plenty of time for discussion without it being cut short. He excitedly agreed, and for about four hours a day over the next three days, we proceeded to go over every verse on the topic of the Godhead, addressing his underlying assumptions. Surprisingly, after the third day, with a light-hearted demeanor, he stopped me in the middle of my lesson and soberly commented, "Stan ... wow ... seriously ... it's ok ... you've convinced me! I am officially converted!" Through our time of discussing the scriptures, he came to understand that a number of the things he believed about the Godhead were either flat out wrong or grossly inaccurate.

These two conversations coalesced in my mind later in the week, bringing to my attention some reasons as to why Christians have so much difficulty explaining the nature of God. It occurred to me that the details of the traditional Trinitarian formula actually spilled over into other areas of

Christian theology, making it less clear in the minds of people, including Christians. I found that this confusion resulted in some disunity among different believers, and even serious dissent about other topics between ministries on spiritual matters. It was also during this time that I received the inspiration to write this book.

The doctrine of the Trinity is a subject imbued with its own list of assumptions. These shape our worldview on multiple fronts. Additionally, our own values and assumptions do not always translate over from the multiplicity of our different Bible translations[6].

E. Randolph Richards once said:

> "If we fail to recognize this—and we very often do—we risk misreading the Bible by reading foreign assumptions into it. Like Procrustes of Greek Mythology, who shortened or stretched his guests to fit his bed, our unconscious assumptions about language encourage us to reshape the biblical narrative to fit our framework."[7]

Our westernized assumptions may be a greater hindrance to our beliefs and theology than we think, especially with regards to the truth. Of course, that also depends on the accuracy of our assumptions. As I see it, the doctrine of the Trinity unwittingly falls into this category with a number of false assumptions. Don't misunderstand what I am trying to say here. I am in no way against the traditional approach. As I mentioned before, I am not against using the word *Trinity* itself in reference to God.

However, I do believe the reason for the daunting nature of our explanation is due to our propensity to take what we have been taught and simply mimic or parrot what prominent theologians and Bible teachers have said without considering for ourselves what is actually written in the Bible. The over-dependance on the traditions we have built over time have become our Achilles' heel. If we are unwilling to at least admit our traditions

---

[6] The use of different translations by the author is intended to reflect a broad consensus of understanding from the translators' perspectives on the text to provide as cohesive a context as possible in spite of any loss in translation from the original languages.

[7] Brandon J. O'Brien and E. Randolph. Richards, *Misreading Scripture with Western Eyes* (Downers Grove, IL: IVP Books, 2012), p.72)

might get in the way of our reading and interpretation of the Bible, it isn't much of a stretch to say we may never get over the hump.

I have had numerous discussions with both Jews and Muslims over the years on the nature of God. Both religions are monotheistic in their theology, and yet, what I have found is that their prevailing perspective on the Christian interpretation of the traditional view (that is, God in three persons) always comes across as tri-theism (three different Gods). It does not matter if we tell them that the three are one; our explanation is insufficient to clarify. I believe the root cause is that we approach the divine nature of God (or Godhead) solely from the traditional point of view. Now, I know what you might be thinking, "He's going off the deep end." Again, hear me out, and allow me to make my case before you make the judgment call and label me a heretic.

When a Jewish or Muslim person listens to the Christian's explanation of the Godhead, they cannot help but see three separate individuals based on our own description. I am particularly interested in the Jewish response to our claims, seeing that the early church was predominantly made up of believing Jews who did not see a problem with God's divine nature, nor with the revelation of the Messiah as the Son of God.

In the end, after having exhausted every effort to make our answers clear, some of us might just surrender with the cliché, "Well … you just have to accept it by faith." Personally, I think it is a cop out. Not only should we always be ready to provide a reason for the hope we have, but we also ought to possess a clearer understanding for our own selves of our beliefs in order to convey it. We must communicate easily enough that even a child can understand without resorting to clichés.

Unfortunately, there's an enormous amount of red tape to cut through stemming from our church traditions, academia, favorite preachers and teachers, and even the many books we read. We find ourselves at a loss trying to explain something as lofty as the nature of the Infinite God. Part of the problem is that the majority of Christians today were not brought up with the same worldview about God as the early church was. Remember, at first the early church was predominantly comprised of Jews who adamantly held to certain particulars about God, particulars that, in my opinion, are not currently prevalent within church doctrine. I believe the dilemma begins with the undergirding assumptions to our defense of the Trinity.

Allow me to elaborate. By using the word "trinity" we already bring to the table a biased picture of what God is supposedly like. Being visual creatures by nature, we create images in our minds of what we think about and cultivate. We formulate our thoughts into conceptualizations of whatever it is we are trying to understand or explain. Dr. Lera Boroditsky, a cognitive scientist, gave a TED talk in 2017 where she described how language impacts thought. She said, "Does the language we speak shape the way we think? Now, this is an ancient question. People have been speculating about this question forever. Charlemagne, the Holy Roman emperor, said, 'To have a second language is to have a second soul'—strong statement that language crafts reality."[8]

When we speak the word "trinity" we inadvertently create an image or "template" of God in our minds, in which the three "persons" of the Trinity (God the Father, God the Son, and God the Holy Spirit) become the primary "model" by which we understand and perceive God. It is what He "looks like" in our minds. That self-created image acts like a "middleman" in order for us to understand a complex Creator.

Unfortunately, as a habit, we then superimpose that same image we have created in our own minds onto our descriptions of God. Believers can be notorious for being loose with their terminology, especially when it comes to the Bible. Contrary to the opinion of some, our concepts about the Godhead are not immune from what I consider a contamination of foreign ideas.

This is where I digress from the common approach. I believe we should not begin with the traditional view of God, but rather with the essence of who and what God is by using that essence as the basis by which to explain the Trinity, thus eliminating the "middle-man" of the image. My approach differs in that the traditional model is NOT the basis for explaining the true nature of God. We ought to ask ourselves the following question,

---

[8] Lera Boroditsky, "How Language Shapes the Way We Think," TED (TEDWomen, 2017), https://www.ted.com/talks/lera_boroditsky_how_language_shapes_the_way_we_think?utm_campaign=tedspread&utm_medium=referral&utm_source=tedcomshare, Min. 1:35).

"Why doesn't the Old Testament ever use the traditional model of the Trinity to describe God?" Sure, we can make some inference to certain passages where you see some variation of the plurality of God, but you won't find anything explicitly stated in the traditional format to describe God, whether in the Old or New Testaments alike. You might say, "That's a bold claim!" Just you wait and see where the rabbit hole goes.

CHAPTER 4
The Trinity and Church Doctrine

Have you ever thought to ask yourself where we get our descriptions about God? Seeing that I am now bringing it into focus, are you sure it is even biblical? Or perhaps ... are you doubting yourself yet? Well, the following is a list of terms that Christians generally use to describe God, taken directly from conservative Christian literature and reference libraries:

- The Triune God
- Co-Equal
- Co-Eternal
- The Holy Trinity
- One substance in three persons
- God the Father, God the Son, and God the Holy Spirit

This might not come as obvious, but the descriptions mentioned above are merely human constructs,[9] interpretations from well-meaning theologians on passages in the scriptures that do not use these terms to describe

---

[9] "constructs" – This author recognizes that the implementations of "constructs" are unavoidable and practically impossible to omit if there is to be any understanding due to language and cultural constraints. Constructs must be in place to grasp those concepts foreign to one's culture. However, to solely rely on these constructs without the overall context is problematic in that it may convey something contradictory or unintended to the original content from those who penned the scriptures.

the God of the Bible. Consider that even the word *trinity* is not found anywhere in scripture. Sure, you could say that is a moot point because, after all, it's how it's always been.

Well, we might extrapolate from the biblical text some concepts that may sound Trinitarian. I'll give you that. But what I am stipulating is that this is where we can make the fundamental mistake. If you look at almost any article, or read any book by a Christian authority on the subject of God's divine nature, it more often than not becomes a defense of the *trinity*. In fact, there are conservative Christian authors who emphatically declare they love the Trinity as what they consider a proper Christian response.[10]

The church father Augustine once said that anyone who denies the Trinity is in danger of losing his/her salvation, but anyone who tries to understand the Trinity is in danger of losing his/her mind.[11] There are certainly strong opinions on the matter. But, where do we ever see any of the disciples defending this tradition? Furthermore, why isn't it explicitly stated in the New Testament narrative? What we do see, however, are deliberate references to God as the Father and Creator. It also directly references Jesus Christ as the Son of God (Yeshua Hamoshiach, Ben Adonai), and/or God manifested in flesh. The Holy Spirit is consistently addressed as God who is always at work in and among believers, also called the Spirit (Ruach) of God and of Messiah.[12]

Yet, you cannot find a single reference showing the Apostles ever trying to defend Jesus' divinity as the "Second Person of the Godhead." Nor do we see them making a case for the Father, the Son, and the Holy Spirit

---

[10] White, James R. *The Forgotten Trinity: Recovering the Heart of Christian Belief*. Minneapolis, MN: Bethany House, a division of Baker Publishing Group, 2019. Ch. 1, Pg. 1.

[11] Roger E. Olson and Christopher A. Hall, *The Trinity, Guides to Theology* (Grand Rapids, MI: W.B. Eerdmans, 2002), 1.

[12] One fascinating detail in the structure of scripture is how the Lord God always has attributed to Himself the initial reference as "God" who has the title of Father and Creator. However, when it comes to the Son and Spirit, their titles tend to come first, recognizing to their divinity by association. However, their order is not the other way around. As an analogy, imagine a hand with a finger pointing in a specific direction where the core of the essence as God points toward the Father (God > Father), while the Son and Holy Spirit point back to the core essence of God (Son/Spirit > God). In other words, God IS the Father, while the Son/Spirit ARE God. This is a consistent pattern in scripture where God the Father is always presented as the Supreme centric being, with the Son and Spirit always pointing back to Him.

each being co-equal/co-eternal with one another. This is language borrowed from either the church fathers and/or theologians over the centuries of church history. That is not to say they only believed Jesus was a mere man. To the contrary, it was the way in which they described those unique differences between the Father, Son, and Holy Spirit explaining the divinity of God as revealed in Christ that confirmed Christ's divinity, while maintaining the integrity of Divine order.

How then should we approach this? Let me offer a brief solution. We must remind ourselves again that the majority of the early church was primarily Jewish, and held to a Hebraic biblical worldview derived from the Torah narrative. As the Christian church grew and expanded over time, more and more Gentiles (that is ... non-Jews) were incorporated into the church body. So much so that by the end of the first century, the majority of the Christian church was comprised of predominantly Gentile believers.

Prior to believing in Christ, these Gentile believers did not grow up with a biblical worldview. They mostly originated from pagan religion and were later converted to the Christian faith. As the number of Gentile believers increased in the church, the knowledge and Hebraic understanding of the Godhead also diminished resulting in nearly 1,700 years of severe persecution of the Jewish people, ironically by Christians.. Over time, the old ways were overshadowed by new foreign perspectives. I do not believe this was intentional, but it's just the way things worked themselves out.

With the passing of time, the overwhelming majority of theologians, Bible teachers, and church leaders hailed primarily from Gentile backgrounds. Their commentaries on the Godhead were not immune to the influences of their former pagan worldviews, even though they certainly tried to define it scripturally. According to the *Pocket Dictionary of Theological Terms*, Tertullian, an early church father (from 160-220 AD), was ...

> "Next to Augustine, perhaps the greatest Western theologian of the patristic period. Tertullian was one of the first major Christian theologians to write in Latin (the language of Western theology) and authored many apologetic, theological and controversial works in defense of Christianity. Tertullian is often credited as being the first important theologian to coin the term Trinity,

describing God as 'one substance in three persons.'"[13]

Consequently, numerous debates ensued over the centuries, resulting in a number of variations of expression within the Christian faith. Simplistically speaking, today we refer to many of these variations as denominations, among other things. Without going too deeply into it, some things were definitely lost along the way. The formulaic language used today by Christians to describe the nature of God is typically not found anywhere in the Bible and was not even used in the church until the second or third century.

This expression in the infamous hymn, "... God in three persons, blessed Trinity," is really not biblical. Yet, this is the way we understand and teach others about what God is supposedly like. It is even celebrated in song. How can we possibly claim *sola-scriptura* (that is, scripture alone) when our vocabulary is laced with so much non-biblical terminology, especially when it comes to our theology of God? Therein lies the contradiction in our rhetoric. It is no wonder unbelievers who are outside the Christian faith experience a disconnect when we try to explain our Creator to them.

We have built entire libraries of books dedicated to this theology. Unfortunately, the more we try explaining God through the lens of the traditional model, and even more so, trying to defend it, we are forced to come up with new and more complicated terms to explain exactly what it is we believe. Don't misunderstand me, I have a great deal of respect for the academic community. There are numerous theologians and authors that I look to for information on a variety of different topics. I have pastoral friends in active ministry whom I also look to for guidance. Still, what is it that makes us believe it is right to claim biblical authority, all the while using non-biblical, so-called theological, and philosophical language alien to the Bible? Furthermore, if we have to resort to using language that is foreign to the biblical text in order to explain the things of God while calling it "biblical theology," isn't it nothing short of arrogance to assume

---

[13] Brandon J. O'Brien and E. Randolph Richards, *Misreading Scripture with Western Eyes* (Downers Grove, IL : IVP Books, 2012)

the scriptures are not enough on their own?

The point I am making is that too much effort is lost on explaining biblical truths while using concocted ideas rather than the text itself. It's like using the wrong tools to fix a broken item. We cannot assume the truth of God's word will do its job of setting people free if it is interwoven with human constructs, which in many cases end up replacing the text. Take into consideration that explanations provided for us in scripture are the very words that God inspired and ordained to be His written witness. To elaborate on the text is one thing. It is quite another to formulate our theology with deficient substitutes.[14] This is dangerous,[15] and I believe we can already see the effects of this practice.

If you take a step back to look at the state of affairs of the church, things are certainly not what they ought to be. Even though we have access to information, more so than any generation in human history, we are still greatly misinformed about a vast array of topics. For example: Even by taking a glance at the diversity of thought in our recent elections, it baffles me how little discernment exists among professing Christians who vote for candidates that promote platforms antithetical to the gospel and the Kingdom of God. Far too many professing Christians have no problem voting for a candidate whose policies are just plan evil from a biblical worldview, all for the sake of recovering the economy.

You could say that the evidence suggests a large number of church goers trivialize the claims of scripture, at the expense of the truth itself. The problem appears to be systemic. I believe the reasons for this downward spiral stem directly from believing the wrong things about God, and we therefore don't really know what it is we claim to believe. I don't mean to sound pessimistic, but we should be able to honestly assess the condition we are in if we are to see any real change. The scripture is clear, *"For it is time for judgment to begin at the household of God; and if it begins with us,*

---

[14] "replacements" – This term is intended to convey the idea of human "constructs" infused within the interpretations of scriptural passages that completely change the context and overall message of the text. Not all constructs do this, but it does happen.

[15] Replacement theology is one of the many evils infiltrating the church because of the inaccurate use of terms, and misappropriation of theological concepts.

what will be the outcome for those who do not obey the gospel[16] of God?" (1 Peter 4:17 ESV).

The world itself needs the church to step up its game, and carry its burden of the truth. I believe this begins with the most fundamental aspect of our faith, the one true God; the One we claim to believe and have faith in. If we get this one thing wrong, everything else that follows will eventually fall into the same categorical error. We cannot afford to be wrong about this. I am not saying that if you get wrong the doctrine of God's nature that you will end up condemned in hell. That is NOT what I am saying. However, what I am claiming is that the truth of scripture has the power to make us free to the same degree that Christ was free. If we want to experience His freedom, His power, His glory, then we have no choice but to understand the one who give us all those things.

As we progress deeper into the rabbit hole, you will discover that what you understand and believe about God's true nature will ultimately affect how you live out your Christian faith. There is much more to this, and I fully intend to unravel this mystery. By going beyond just a simple surface level view of God's reality, your paradigm will drastically shift, and the deeper meaning of your own life and purpose will come into clearer view. That is why understanding the Godhead is so paramount. Our very purpose in existence depends on it. If you think I'm just trying to hype you up, think again.

In the following chapters we will see the scripture for what they say about the God we serve. There will be some serious mic drop moments along the way. I promise that if you stick with me where we are going, you will not be disappointed. I believe your faith will become reinvigorated and renewed. You will begin to see the world around you differently from what you could have imagined. You will see God where others do not. You will better understand the promises of the New Testament as a believer, and will experience

---

[16] The term gospel tends to have an anecdotal meaning to most English-speaking people. To the non-believing and unchurched, it often carries an overly religious connotation bearing little resemblance to its true meaning. The Greek term is evangelion which literally means good news, while the Hebrew term is Besorah with the same definition. However, the Hebrew use of Besorah has an additional meaning from Israel's historical as a term used to describe good news that comes from victory in battle. The good news, or gospel of God is the message of God's absolute triumph over every adversary in setting every soul free from oppression and sin.

those promises in new fashion. Of these things I am absolutely confident.

There is light at the end of the tunnel. One way we can avoid the trappings is going to the Bible itself as our number one source. I have taken the liberty to list some key verses, pointing out a major theme that the Bible consistently makes about the nature of God. I believe as we read these passages, our paradigm will shift. Since we are New Testament believers, we ought to begin with looking at what the New Testament has to say about what God is really like. But, we will also contrast what the New Testament says with what the Old Testament reveals about God's nature, and compare notes. You'll be surprised by what you'll find. Now would a good time to open up your Bible and see for yourself the magnificent and wonderful truth about the God of Israel!

CHAPTER 5
Persons and Pronouns

Having the Bible in our possession truly is a gift from Heaven. We can always point to the Bible as our reference for spiritual truth. We can trust in its authenticity, reliability, veracity, as well as the entire scope of its message. Looking back into history provides us with a great deal of benefit. Yet, when we read the Bible, we often assume things, among which is that this ancient document we call the Bible was supposedly written in the same communication style of the present day, simply because we have a translation on our lap.

When we read the passages of scripture, we come across certain terms that have been translated to communicate whatever language and to whatever culture it is translated into. Our approach to reading can often skew our understanding of the text because of the language barriers that exist. The Bible was written in a culture and language that is different in scope from what we know in the West. Scholars make it a point to write numerous academic works explaining these differences. Unless you attend seminary or some other Bible school, chances are you never get the training they provide to look into these things, barring the purchase of expensive software specializing in the area of theology.

I bring this up because certain terms carry a host of different assumptions when we read the Bible. Some of those terms provide us with grammar and structure so that we can understand what it is we are reading. The use of pronouns, for example, plays a major role in this aspect. There are terms that, depending on the language, are spelled in such a way that it implies a feminine or masculine context to that term without the use of pronouns. However, in the English language we often have to add the pronouns where the pronouns are not provided because English grammar dictates that we do so.

For this reason, we cannot simply ignore those passages mentioning pronouns whenever it attributes God. The presence of these pronouns are necessary for us to understand the role God plays in the creation. The Bible does in fact use pronouns with respect to God, both in the Old and New Testaments. This brings up an important observation. When we address the topic of the Godhead, the Trinity as we know it has at its core the use of pronouns that identify each of the three *persons* of the Godhead. When you read the following passages, you will see what I mean.

> *"And Miriam answered them, Sing ye to the LORD, for* **he** *hath triumphed gloriously; the horse and his rider hath* **he** *thrown into the sea."* (Exodus 15:21 KJV) [emphasis added].

> *"Unto thee it was shewed, that thou mightest know that the LORD* **he** *is God; there is none else beside* **him***."* (Deuteronomy 4:35 KJV) [emphasis added].

> *"Know that the LORD,* **he** *is God! It is* **he** *who made us, and we are* **his***; we are* **his** *people, and the sheep of* **his** *pasture."* (Psalm 100:3 ESV) [emphasis added].

> *"For as the Father has life in* **himself***, so* **he** *has granted the Son also to have life in* **himself***."* (John 5:26 ESV) [emphasis added].

I bring up these verses to demonstrate that when we read these passages, we understand the pronouns imply that God is addressed as and understood to be masculine. Here is where the crux of the matter truly is. While the Bible builds on the concept of persons because of the grammar, we should not assume that the writers of the Bible placed as much emphasis into the use of those pronouns the same way we do.

We read passages that utilize pronouns like he, his, him, himself, and we automatically impose gender because our grammar demands that we do so. Yet, the Bible doesn't do this in the way our Western culture does, at least not all the time. I will demonstrate what I mean. Paul wrote to the Corinthian church saying,

> *"For since, in the wisdom of God, the world did not know God through wisdom, it pleased God through the folly of what we preach to save those who believe. For Jews demand signs and Greeks seek wisdom, but we preach Christ crucified, a stumbling block to Jews and folly to Gentiles, but to those who are called, both Jews and Greeks,* **Christ the power of God and the wisdom of God**.*"* (1 Corinthians 1:21-24 ESV)

The Apostle Paul clearly says about Christ, he is both the power of God and the wisdom of God. There is no ambiguity as to what Jesus is. Christ is a man and plays the masculine role in his humanity. However, if we look at other passages where wisdom is mentioned, we get a different picture, or different gender role altogether:

> *"Wisdom cries aloud in the street, in the markets* **she** *raises* **her** *voice; at the head of the noisy streets* **she** *cries out; at the entrance of the city gates* **she** *speaks:"* (Proverbs 1:20-21 ESV)

> *"Wisdom has built* **her** *house; she has hewn* **her** *seven pillars. She has slaughtered* **her** *beasts;* **she** *has mixed her wine;* **she** *has also set* **her** *table.* **She** *has sent out* **her** *young women to call from the highest places in the town,"* (Proverbs 9:1-3 ESV)

On the other hand, while there is no specific verse that addresses God's power as a person (other than in 1 Corinthians 1:24), the Bible mostly correlates the power of God to an "it" more than it does a "he," because it highlights God's ability. The point I am making is that our use of pronouns forces us to place the Trinity in a context of three distinct persons, yet the Bible itself does not specifically define the Trinity using a "three persons" terminology as the absolute unquestionable template for understanding the Godhead. We would have to extrapolate that from various textual passages in order to conclude that God is one, yet also three persons. The Bible does use pronouns that indicate the complexity of God's unity, while also retaining the simplicity of His revelation.

When we read about the Father, and the Bible mentions Him in a masculine context, we cannot think of it as though God is Himself a male. God is not referred to as a Father because He is imbued with male reproductive organs like His creation. God does not have anything between a pair of legs that identifies Him as a male, nor a female for that matter. The role of Father is attributed to God because He is the Creator, and He made all things that exist. Just as the biological sex of a baby is determined by the genetics of the father of the child, the Bible uses the term Father as a reference to God in the masculine because God is the Source of all creation. The masculine traits associated with God have nothing at all to do with Him having male private parts. It has only to do with the role He plays as The Creator.

The Trinity concept is in fact in the Bible, but it is not presented as "three distinct persons" in the way we have come to understand it (more on this in later chapters). It should not be considered heresy to look to reconcile the passages of scripture with what we claim to believe. I do believe there is an overuse of the concept of "persons" when it comes to the Trinity, especially in the absence of such overt language in scripture. However, we can conclude from the biblical text that the Trinity is real, but it is still unclear for many people how to explain that. In the following pages we will endeavor to unveil some of this mystery.

The gender issue is not even the problematic one. It is the references to the multiplicity of persons beyond that of three. For example: Jesus openly admitted to being the Son of Man. Yet, he would often refer to the title as though the Son of Man was separate and distinct from Himself. There are many passages where Jesus Christ often refers to himself in a third person context,[17] so much so that the Jews of Jesus' day had to ask Him who the Son of Man really was.[18] Even then, Jesus does not change or alter His rhetoric. The point is that our fixation on the use of pronouns to emphasize a three-person template for the Godhead is not textually consistent all the time. What am I saying then …? Even though the Bible uses pronouns with respect to the Godhead, the verses that use these same pronouns do not use specific language of the traditional expression of "God in three persons."

Discussions and debates on the nature of the Godhead began as early as the second century when questions were presented to explain or define it. From Irenaeus to Tertullian to the Arian controversy, there was no official formulation explaining the Godhead in specific language by Church leadership until the beginning of the fourth century around 325 AD. Anyone who disagreed with the establishment from that point forward were considered heretics. To appropriate any interpretation other than the establishment was viewed as heretical … even though questions still lingered. The need to establish closure in this area also shut out all those who dissented with the language that was used to define the Trinity. That approach is still used today. If you question the use of the "three persons" language, you will most likely be relegated to being labeled a heretic.

But this does not have to be the case. The Trinity is in fact real, and there is an approach to understanding it in a way that this author believes is in closer alignment with the language of the biblical text, rather than the tradition. Our efforts will be to realign what we believe about the Trinity more closely to the language we find in the Bible. This is where the early attempts to explain the Trinity may have gone off into a tangent. As we move forward in this, just take a step back, take a deep breath, and take the next step to see exactly what I mean.

---

[17] Matthew 17:9, Mark 8:38, Luke 12:8, John 3:13
[18] John 12:34

CHAPTER 6
The Essence of God

As I mentioned at the end of an earlier chapter, it is time to open up your Bibles. If we are to grasp what is presented here, we will need to have our Bible open in hand, and actually read what is says. The following verses will provide you with what I believe to be the absolute essential characteristic of God's nature with emphasis added to each verse in order to highlight my point. I took the liberty to quote from different English versions primarily to make the observation that regardless of the translation, the Bible is consistent in the motif. Here we go:

> "<u>No man hath seen God at any time</u>; the only begotten Son, which is in the bosom of the Father, he hath declared him." (John 1:18 KJV *emphasis added*)

> "<u>Not that anyone has seen the Father</u> except the One who is from God—He has seen the Father." (John 6:46 TLV *emphasis added*)

> "He (Jesus) is the image of <u>the invisible God</u>, the firstborn of all creation." (Colossians 1:15 ESV *emphasis added*)

> *"Now to the <u>King eternal, immortal, invisible</u>, the only God, be honor and glory for ever and ever. Amen."* (1 Timothy 1:17 TLV emphasis added)
>
> *"By faith he left Egypt, not being afraid of the anger of the king: for he endured <u>as seeing him who is invisible.</u>"* (Hebrews 11:27 ESV emphasis added)
>
> *"<u>No man hath seen God at any time</u>. If we love one another, God dwelleth in us, and his love is perfected in us."* (1 John 4:12 KJV emphasis added)

Now let's just ponder on these verses for a few moments, and draw your attention to what they imply. According to the above passages, God is portrayed as being INVISIBLE! In other words, God has no visible form whatsoever ... at all. He is completely and utterly unseeable to the extent that He has no physicality. It isn't just about being imperceptible to the eye. God's invisibility implies that He is formless in His essence, which means He does not take up physical space as though He were like one of His creations.

Simply put, God has no body. Location is not a factor of His own existence because space itself is His creation. He is literally everywhere at all times, including inside and outside of space. He is by essence and nature completely and thoroughly other than His creation. He is unlike any other being that exists, and is Himself unseen not only to us humans, but also to any other being in every other realm that exists for that matter.

I must reiterate this to you again. No one; not man, nor angels, nor even any other supernatural created being has ever seen God ... ever! The verses we just read absolutely affirm this truth. This is still absolutely true *even though* there are passages in the Bible where God is described as having appeared throughout human history in some of the following ways: an Angel (Exodus 23:20-22), a burning bush (Exodus 3:2-3), pillars of cloud and pillars of fire (Exodus 13:21-22 and Deuteronomy 1:31-33), and even the Shekinah[19] (Exodus 25:22)

Now, I know this might seem a bit confusing, but it will become clearer as we move along. Theologians refer to these physical appearances of God

---

[19] This is a term referring to the manifest glory of God usually in the form of some illumination such as supernatural fire or divine light that was visible to both Israelites and Gentiles alike.

in scripture as *theophanies*. These are unique moments in time that God chooses to reveal Himself and make Himself known to His creation in a physical manifestation.

Yet, in spite of these appearances, and while both the Old and New Testaments unequivocally assert and affirm that no one has ever seen God. When the verse says "ever," it means at any time in the past, or at any point in time. Both testaments agree on this. This should not be overlooked and cannot be overstated. There are a number of biblical passages that appear as paradoxical statements. These are statements that give the appearance of being contradictory. They don't actually contradict. It only appears that way. Our misunderstanding of God's nature is what causes us to presume there is a contradiction. Such statements can easily be reconciled with God's invisible characteristic as the main undergirding foundation for understanding why. Look at the following account in the book of Exodus as an example:

> *"Then Moses and Aaron, Nadab, and Abihu, and seventy of the elders of Israel went up, and <u>they saw the God of Israel.</u> There was <u>under his feet</u> as it were a pavement of sapphire stone, like the very heaven for clearness. And he did not lay <u>his hand</u> on the chief men of the people of Israel; <u>they beheld God</u>, and ate and drank."* (Exodus 24:9-11 ESV *emphasis added*)

At the outset, that seems pretty cut and dry, doesn't it? However, if we investigate this just a little further, we find that Moses was actually being generic in his assertion. To prove this, let us see how Moses recalls this same incident later in the book of Deuteronomy in a more specified way:

> *"How on the day that you stood before the LORD your God at Horeb, the LORD said to me, 'Gather the people to me, that I may let them hear my words, so that they may learn to fear me all the days that they live on the earth, and that they may teach their children so.' And you came near and stood at the foot of the mountain, while the mountain burned with fire to the heart of heaven, wrapped in darkness, cloud, and gloom. Then the LORD spoke to you out of the midst of the fire. <u>You heard the sound of words, but saw no form; there was only a voice.</u>"* (Deuteronomy 4:10-12 ESV *emphasis added*)

Now, there seems to be an apparent contradiction here! Deuteronomy is recalling the identical event mentioned in Exodus. It explicitly states in Deuteronomy that they did not see any form, yet Exodus implicitly says they "saw" God. This is one of those apparent contradictions we talked about. In the KJV, the term *form* is translated as "similitude." A similitude is defined as a likeness, resemblance, or image. Seems confusing, right? However, this apparent contradiction is not so much an issue as it is a "mystery" that is being revealed to us, since God is indeed making some aspect of Himself known to Moses and the children of Israel.

Remember, even if God makes Himself visible somewhere on earth (or even in heaven), whatever is seen of Him there does not account for the rest of God's unseen reality everywhere else at once. Even if He is seen in one context, He is still unseen in another context. If He makes Himself visible in one location, He doesn't cease to be God in another location where He is still unseen. God maintains His invisible quality in every way in which He is not physically revealed. So, let us delve in a bit deeper here.

When the scriptures provide us with an instance of God's appearance in a particular form, He is in fact revealing some aspect of Himself to His creation. We can emphatically say it would be impossible to know or understand Him otherwise. The Apostle[20] Paul said, *"... the things which are seen are temporal; but the things which are not seen are eternal"* (2 Corinthians 4:18 KJV). The most revealing part of Paul's comment is the nature of the unseen as being "eternal." Though Paul may not have been speaking specifically about God in this particular passage, he is nevertheless stating a theological principle. While Paul was referring to the hope of the resurrection and our heavenly abode, the principal remains the same for God. Furthermore, Paul doesn't actually name any specific thing as eternal in the passage. He is simply making the point ... that which is unseen is eternal.

If we are to take seriously Paul's comment, then we should also ask what follows after we become resurrected and then arrive in heaven. Will

---

[20] One important observation in using terms such as "Apostle" before individual names such as Paul, Peter, etc., may cause believers to forget that Jesus and His disciples were in fact Jews, and that most of the new covenant was written by Jews, and that gospel (besorah) is a Jewish message of redemption.

we actually see heaven? The answer is obviously yes! We will see our heavenly home, and the multitude of the redeemed alongside us among an innumerable company of angels. Everything in Heaven that is not visible to us here in this life will eventually become seen at some point down the road on the other side. Remember, that which is seen is still temporal, *including the things in heaven*. Recall Jesus' own words, *"Heaven and earth shall pass away, but my words shall never pass away"* (Matthew 24:35, Mark 13:31, Luke 21:33 KJV).

Remember, it isn't just the earth that is made new; it is heaven as well. *"Then I saw a new heaven and a new earth, for the first heaven and the first earth had passed away, and the sea was no more"* (Rev 2:1 ESV). The fact that heaven itself will pass demonstrates that it is not as eternal as we might have assumed. If heaven itself must be changed, then it cannot be eternal.

Still, another question we ought to consider is, what makes heaven our "eternal" home to begin with? Is it only because it is *heaven*? Certainly not! It is our eternal dwelling because it is where God's manifested presence resides. It is where He is; His dwelling place … where we go *to be with Him forever*. Wouldn't Paul's statement about that which is unseen as eternal apply there just as well? Of course it would, since in essence God still remains unseen even after we enter into our heavenly inheritance.

Just think about it. If we see any manifestation of Him somewhere in heaven, that appearance is itself limited to that moment in that specific location. That appearance does not account for the rest of His presence that is still unseen in the rest of creation, whether it's in the highest heaven, the lowest part of the earth, and everything in between. It can be stipulated that King David understood God's invisible reality along this same vein of thought when he wrote, *"If I ascend up into heaven, thou art there: if I make my bed in hell, behold, thou art there"* (Psalm 139:8 KJV).

There is another revelation we can also glean from Paul's statement. He shows that only that which is invisible bears the status of eternal. This is a principle that goes well beyond the idea of us humans simply waiting for a future home called heaven. In fact, God is the ONLY being implicitly referred to as the Eternal in the Bible. No other being or creature is ever given such a title, label, or status, and to do so would be considered blasphemy.

For the most part, being eternal is implied as having no beginning and no end, with a perpetuity of being. However, even though we are given eternal life (that is, we are given His life, His Spirit, His presence, etc. to be with Him), we do not become "eternal" by osmosis when we go to heaven; nor do we become "eternal" when we are born again. This is due to the one fact that we have an origin of existence.

By receiving His eternal life we will have no end of days existing in His presence. But at the end of the day, we still have an origin, and a point of beginning. God's "eternal" status is restricted to Him and Him alone, and it stems directly from His incorporeal-invisible state. By virtue of having no physical form or body inherent in His nature, He is in essence unseen and is by that same virtue Eternal. Therefore, wherever He resides, everything that exists in that place shares in His perpetual existence.

The Creation

> "His invisible attributes—His eternal power and His divine nature—have been clearly seen ever since the creation of the world, being understood through the things that have been made. So people are without excuse—" (Romans 1:20 TLV)

According to Paul, God's own divine nature can be understood by everything that has been made, *beginning with the premise* of God's invisibility as the basis for our understanding. Every single thing ever *created*, whether seen or unseen to us in this life or the next, was not made from anything that was seen within creation. In other words, everything was *created* from the non-material, non-visible existence of God. Everything that is made (that is, everything created whether in heaven or in earth) comes out of God's personal essence of reality, and unlimited ability for expression. The moment something of Him becomes visible to anything in creation, that visible manifestation then also becomes limited, definable, measurable, knowable, accessible, and able to be experienced by the creation. God Himself has no discernable dimensions that can be measured. He has no point of origin, nor finality to His existence.

What I am proposing is that if we use the traditional template as the primary model by which we can "see" God in our collective imagination, then we risk falling into constant error because God is in fact unseeable; He CANNOT be seen. If we take the traditional template of the "three in one," then superimpose that concept onto the invisible God, we end up making Him out to be lesser than what He really is. However, if we first begin with the biblical premise that God is invisible and formless, then use that aspect as our lens to look forward to understanding the Trinity, it then makes better sense of the text. Instead of looking at the model from tradition as the lens through which we see God, we ought to first begin at His invisibility and bodiless essence as our absolute foundation and initial place for understanding the Trinity. Remember, this has always been the basic premise of the Jewish faith that all Jews have had about the nature of God, including Jesus and the disciples from the Old Testament straight to the New.

Another way to put it is, while we can truly affirm that God is the Trinity, we cannot simultaneously say that the Trinity is God; much in the same way that we can say God is love, but it is also incorrect to say that love is God. Why? Mainly because while love is a concept in itself, God is Himself so much more than that. He is not limited to only being love. God is also Holy, among other things. While God's love accepts us into His presence, it is His holiness that separates Him from His creation. Love by itself cannot be God. But by saying that God is love, He becomes the Source of love. Yet, if we say that love is God, then we are making love as the source of God. That is backward thinking. The same goes for applying the concept of the Trinity.

While God has indeed revealed Himself in the triune concept of what we call the Trinity, He is still far beyond that. Keep in mind that *any form* that God chooses to manifest to us originates from a *non-material, non-physical* spiritual reality. Therefore, by making the claim that the Trinity is God, we limit and restrict God to a number and a form. The Bible never describes God in terms that diminish Him down to a human concept. It's the other way around. Humans are then elevated to be the image of God. When it comes to revealing Himself to us, the Most High willfully chooses to lower Himself from His lofty place down to where the creation can perceive and understand Him. He does this out of love for His creation. That is precisely why the scriptures are consistently precise with how God is revealed.

He *has* to manifest something in order to reveal His invisible attributes, and to make Himself relatable to His creation. We could not know or understanding Him in any other way. When I say we, I mean humans as well as angels and all other created beings. Just as parables are given to communicate spiritual truths about God, we can also say that any manifestation of God is akin to a parable that reveals His invisible qualities. Therefore, God is not composed of any physical, visible, or created substance. Since He has no particular form (including the Trinitarian one), God Himself has no substance because He is not made from anything. Albeit, He must create in order to reveal, communicate, translate, and display the unsearchable riches of His own person to the creation. While the triune revelation is predominant in the New Testament, He is still not limited to that expression of who He is. That is just simply the starting point given for our sake.

When God created the universe in Genesis 1, He brought it forth *ex-nihilo* (out of nothing). He literally *spoke* everything into existence. This is a testament to His power and greatness! There was no physical or spiritually created being, object, or even an atom in existence prior to God speaking it into reality. Before and after He created everything, He was, is, and has always been unseen and formless. But, all created things are *visual* creatures. Whether human or otherwise … everything has a *visible* existence. Does that surprise you? Even if we cannot *see* the angels, demons, or any other spiritual beings residing in the spiritual realm, they can still see us and/or each other. But even these spiritual beings in their domain still cannot see God.

CHAPTER 7
The Mystery Revealed

As humans, we all have difficulty comprehending the Most High because we don't have the capacity of being everywhere at once. Due to our physical composition, we are restricted to the form we are created with and are limited in our ability to process someone like Him. In order for us to see the invisible God as He truly is, we would essentially have to become invisible just like Himself by default. Here is the caveat though: if that were to happen, we would necessarily cease to exist, since God alone is God who does not share His glory with another (Isaiah 42:8).

We are of a particular kind. We are created beings that share similar physical characteristics with other created beings. Having been created in God's image and after His likeness in no way implies that God is a man, nor does it mean He has physicality as we do. It does mean that we are created in a unique manner in which we can project God's invisible qualities moreso than any other creature that is not made in His image within the creation. As Dr. Michael Heiser would put it, we are in effect "imagers" of God.

When it comes to God, He is a different kind of being altogether, unique and self-existent, uninhibited by space, matter, time, or any combination of these. We humans are created beings, which means we have a beginning, a point of origin. God, on the other hand, has no beginning nor end, with no boundaries to His existence. We are incapable of grasping such concepts perfectly because we don't share in God's invisible nature. We can, however, experience Him when He makes Himself known to us through some creative process, when He chooses to reveal Himself in a manner that we can understand, thereby making difficult and even impossible concepts attainable, that is to say, tangible. God is so far high above and beyond what we are that we just simply cannot grasp Him in His true essence.

Have you ever wondered about some of the paradoxes of scripture, like when God says, *"You cannot see my face, for man shall not see me and live"* (Exodus 33:20 ESV). Yet, we are still called by Him to "seek" His face: *"If my people who are called by my name humble themselves, and pray and seek my face and turn from their wicked ways, then will I hear from heaven and will forgive their sin and will heal their land"* (2 Chronicles 7:14 ESV). God's invisibleness makes Him completely beyond us. Yet, God had a plan from the beginning to make Himself relatable for love's sake. Let us take a look at how the Eternal One chooses to make Himself known to His creation.

The Mystery

No one can ever see God, UNLESS God does (or creates) *something* in order for us to behold and/or experience Him. If we take into consideration every Bible passage that reinforces God's essential nature, it ought to really shock us when we come across passages in which He becomes *visible*. The Bible clearly establishes that God is an unseen/invisible/formless being. Therefore, we must also remember that when the Bible refers to anthropomorphic attributes attributed to God (i.e., body parts, such as a face, mouth, arm, hand, feet, etc.), these are merely tokens derived from human features to provide us with clarity on the functional aspects of God. A Judaism 101 article on the nature of God stipulated as much when it said:

> "Although many places in scripture and Talmud speak of various parts of G-d's body (the Hand of G-d, G-d's wings, etc.) or speak of G-d in anthropo-

morphic terms (G-d walking in the garden of Eden, G-d laying tefillin, etc.), Judaism firmly maintains that G-d has no body. Any reference to G-d's body is simply a figure of speech, a means of making G-d's actions more comprehensible to beings living in a material world."[21]

Any references to physical features of God in the scripture are there to communicate, in human terms, certain realities of an infinitely superior unseen Being. We must be careful not to limit our understanding of God to merely human terms, while simultaneously using physical characteristics within the creation to assist us in understanding how we ought to perceive the invisible Creator. This is the same methodology of scripture.

Complications arise when we try to explain God by beginning primarily from some physical attribute, then superimposing that physicality onto their understanding of God. The traditional approach of The Trinity does this very thing. However, if we are to have a more faithful understanding of the Godhead, we MUST learn to accept Him as He truly is in His most profound essence, as unseen, formless, without substance, immaterial, boundless, and utterly limitless.

When the scriptures present physical components describing God's attributes, we must take into account that the biblical authors *knew* they were doing so in order to describe a Being that CANNOT be seen with such attributes. Physical terms such as face, hand, arm, feet, eyes, wings, and such are conceptual terms used as training aids to assist us in understanding Someone who is not at all like His creation.

God is incomprehensible to us in His true nature, which is why we need the visual aids. Such physical components are used with a functional purpose with respect to God. It has nothing to do with God having a physical body. Therefore, anytime physical characteristics are communicated in scripture with respect to God, the writer's express purpose and intent is to communicate by revelation a mystery of the Unseen One.

Whenever the invisible God chooses to manifest His presence in some conceptual form, that form is made of a substance that is by its very nature

---

[21] "Jewish Concepts." *The Nature of G-d.* Judaism 101, n.d. Accessed January 18, 2022. https://www.jewishvirtuallibrary.org/the-nature-of-g-d.)

inferior to God's eternal divine essence. In other words, the invisible, eternal, unlimited, superior, Most High God is revealing some aspect of Himself in a limited form with a singular purpose in mind: to communicate with His creation.

If God has to produce something that can be seen or heard, it is by *nature* lesser than His true essence. Anything that is made visible or audible is simply lesser than its Creator. In other words, God has to dumb it down for us in order for the creation to even come close to experiencing Him, or understanding Him with any degree of coherence. He does it in order to establish a relationship to connect with His creation.[22]

In His infinite wisdom, God chose to design creation with signatory characteristics of His own person. Since He cannot be approached or related to in His purest essence, He chooses to provide within the creation itself certain earmarks that enable us to recognize Him. I believe the Bible gives us a hint of this when it says, *"By faith we understand that the universe was created by the word of God, so that what is seen did not come from anything visible"* (Hebrews 11:3 TLV). The creation bears the mark of its Creator.

By observing the creation—its order, mathematical precision, immutable laws, etc.—we are given glimpses into the reality of God's own existence and incorruptible nature. The entire universe speaks to us of a Creator by virtue of its own existence. If the universe exists, then God also must exist by necessity as the initial first cause behind the creation. He has infused His creation with certain visual ques of His own attributes making it possible for us to perceive the "invisible things" of Himself.

These attributes are projected through His creation with the intent to

---

[22] We are taught to emphasize in Trinitarian theology that the Father, the Son, and the Holy Spirit are separate and distinct persons of the Godhead. This is mostly because of the logic we follow in our own common language. If a being thinks and feels, that being is therefore his/her own distinct person. We end up reading that into the text and come up with the Trinitarian model of God in three persons, even though the Bible itself does not use this formula. What we often overlook in our rhetoric is that any time God has to manifest Himself in any form or capacity, that manifestation is not fully in the context of who and what the Father is truly like. Since the manifestation itself is lesser than the Father's essence, that manifestation is addressed in a "third person" context without there actually being three separate and distinct beings that make up the one God. If God wanted, He could manifest in 20 different ways, from a human to a dog to a bird, to a burning bush, but it doesn't mean He is 20 different persons or things because of those manifestations.

demonstrate His qualities as God through everything that has been made. When we look at creation, we can infer to the existence of God. Take "wind" for example. Though it is unseen, the effect it gives when it moves reveals that it is there, causing something to happen like rustling leaves, waves in the ocean, etc. Point in fact, wind is probably one of the most useful elements at our disposal used to help us understand the true nature of God. It is precisely why wind is often used in the Bible as a euphemism for and identified with the very Spirit of God. (More on that later.)

These communicable traits are utilized as a witness to the world of its Creator. As far as the physical creation is concerned, humankind is its crown. We are uniquely designed and put together by God as the most efficient models of His image and likeness. However, the fall of man and the subsequent corruption that followed have contributed to our distorted perceptions of God. Far too many people make the grave error of confusing the created things with the Creator. This is how false religions hold divergent and even strange ideas about what they perceive as deities worthy of worship. The distortions and confusion have led to a host of different and often contradictory ideas that can even deny the Creator Himself. It is a kind of willful blindness in plain sight.

The Elephant in the Room

There are various erroneous doctrines floating around today that directly contradict biblical theology and its narrative. I am referring to New Age religion, including also other non-biblical "pagan" beliefs. According to June Hunt, "New Age Spirituality is made up of a large, loosely structured network of individuals and organizations bound together by a worldview that chiefly consists of the central belief of *pantheism*."[23] Pantheism is defined as "the belief that God and the universe are identical and that God is not a personality but the expression of the physical forces of nature. God is in nature, therefore, nature is God. God is in man, therefore, man

---

[23] June Hunt, *Biblical Counseling Keys on New Age Spirituality: A New Mask for an Old Message* (Dallas, TX: Hope For The Heart, 2008), Pg. 1.

is God.[24] Biblical theology is diametrically opposed to these concepts:

> *For his invisible attributes, namely, his eternal power and divine nature, have been clearly perceived, ever since the creation of the world, in the things that have been made. So they are without excuse. For although they knew God, they did not honor him as God or give thanks to him, but they became futile in their thinking, and their foolish hearts were darkened. Claiming to be wise, they became fools, and exchanged the glory of the immortal God for images resembling mortal man and birds and animals and creeping things. ... because they exchanged the truth about God for a lie and worshiped and served the creature rather than the Creator, who is blessed forever! Amen.* (Romans 1:20-23, 25 ESV)

I am convinced that anyone who ascribes to a New Age, or pantheistic worldview has, in fact, "exchanged the truth of God for a lie," and confuse the inferior creation with the infinitely superior Creator. Therefore, by first establishing that God is invisible, it should go without saying that any visible (or created) thing simply CANNOT be God. The knowledge of God's true nature diametrically opposes any belief system that accepts the worship of any created thing that can be seen.

This was a major motivation behind the commandment in the Mosaic Law to reject idols. This includes images of all kinds of beings, whether angelic or human, or material ones such as wood, stone, etc.. Having a proper perspective of the distinction between what God is really like in contrast to His creation protects us from the barrage of false teachings consistently vying for our devotion.

While pagan ideas are foreign to the biblical concept of God, our traditional views have also contributed to the problem of unbelief in or misunderstanding about God. While Trinitarian doctrine affirms to be non-pagan, it nevertheless utilized pagan ideology in its definitions. Traditional Christianity rejects the idea the Trinity has any pagan roots. However, I think such a statement too simplistic and is just as ignorant as our pagan counterparts.

---

[24] Ibid, Pg.4

Dogma and Dogmatism

In light of what we have covered so far, let us revisit the concept of the traditional approach to Christian doctrine. According to the *Oxford Dictionary of the Christian Church*, the Trinity is understood to be:

> "The central dogma of Christian theology, that the one God exists in three Persons and one substance, Father, Son, and Holy Spirit. God is one, yet self-differentiated; the God who reveals Himself to mankind is one God equally in three distinct modes of existence, yet remains one through all eternity."[25]

Whoa! We ought to consider that perhaps our confusion lies in our "dogma" of Trinitarian theology. Is it any wonder how the modern Christian apologist always finds it necessary to defend the doctrine of the Trinity, while the New Testament defends a different narrative altogether?

F.L. Cross once said, "The goal of apologetics is the defense of Christian belief and of the Christian way against alternatives and against criticism."[26] However, what if the focus of our defense has been for the dogmatism of our own traditions, rather than for the actual biblical language of the Godhead? Now, some folks might be tempted to cast off the Trinity altogether. I disagree with this approach, and I believe it to be an error to do so, as you will see. To avoid this, we ought to acknowledge that the traditional model was merely a human attempt at defining what is practically incomprehensible.

Therefore, we should not look at the Trinitarian concept with contempt, respecting the church fathers' meager attempt at comprehending the eternal God. We should cut them some slack. However, as I see it, we also should not be so dogmatic about defending the traditional approach either, having resulted in the doctrine being correlated with pagan ideas in the manner in which it is commonly taught. We will explore that further in the next chapter.

---

[25] F. L. Cross and Elizabeth A. Livingstone, eds., *The Oxford Dictionary of the Christian Church* (Oxford; New York: Oxford University Press, 2005), 1652.

[26] Ibid, 87.

CHAPTER 8
The Stubbornness of Dogma

There is a huge schism between the Christian church and the Jewish community. The traditional Christian view of God is not compatible with Jewish theology in the mind of most Jews. Of course, I disagree with that, but then again, I believe my approach to the subject is much more in line with the biblical narrative. While Messianic Jews do believe in Jesus as the Messiah, the acceptance of Trinitarian doctrine can be somewhat complicated for many Jews who initially come to faith in Christ. This is largely due to the great divide in the schools of thought on the subject. The believing Jew either has to accommodate a rather foreign concept about God, or the other option is to simply accept and believe what both Testaments have to say on the matter.

In any case, the orthodox (or non-Christian) Jew is generally opposed to Trinitarian theology. They view it as heretical. Recently, there have been objections from Jewish and Muslim scholars alike postulating that Christians detract from the Old Testament narrative on the divine nature:

"The New Testament continues the Old Testament emphasis on the oneness of God, and they sometimes criticize Trinitarianism as simple Tritheism on the grounds that a 'fully divine person' must be a god. Both sometimes allege that the New Testament is inconsistent, some parts affirming Christ to be God, while others teach things inconsistent with his deity."[27]

Offering similar observation, Messianic believer Arnold Fruchtenbaum states the following:

> "Whether Christians are accused of being polytheists or Tritheists or whether it is admitted that the Christian concept of the Tri-unity is a form of monotheism, one element always appears: one cannot believe in the Trinity and be Jewish. Even if what Christians believe is monotheistic, it still does not seem to be monotheistic enough to qualify as true Jewishness."[28]

Jews have a difficult time reconciling the traditional explanations because of the overt denial of the basic and historically Jewish understanding of God's nature. There are serious Jewish scholars like Gerald Sigal who argue that:

> "The allegation of a triune deity cannot be established even from the New Testament (despite some Trinitarian interpolations). Careful examination of the evidence presented to prove the existence of a triune deity based on Jewish or Christian Scriptures is found to be without substance."[29]

There are scores of different authors on either side, but that is not the point. The issue is that, as Christians, we want to claim biblical authority to correct error, but we compromise our argumentation with language that is inherently traditional and not truly biblical. While I disagree with some aspects of Sigal's assertion, He makes a valid point. If a non-believing critic

---

[27] Dale Tuggy, "Judaic and Islamic Objections," *Stanford Encyclopedia of Philosophy* (Stanford University, 2016), last modified 2016, accessed May 21, 2020, https://plato.stanford.edu/entries/trinity/judaic-islamic-trinity.html.

[28] Arnold Fruchtenbaum, "Jewishness and the Trinity," *Jewishness and the Trinity* (Jews for Jesus, April 23, 2018), last modified April 23, 2018, accessed May 21, 2020, https://jewsforjesus.org/publications/issues/issues-v01-n08/jewishness-and-the-trinity.

[29] Sigal, G. (2006). *Trinity doctrine error: A Jewish analysis.* Bloomington, IN: Xlibris. Kindle Reader, location 471.

like Sigal can read our own New Testament, and still come away concluding that our own scriptures do not support a traditional Trinitarian formula for understanding God, then what are we actually trying to defend?

Let me be clear. I am not advocating for the anathematizing of Trinitarian doctrine. I am advocating for reform and the believer's return to being faithful to biblical semantics drawing solely from the language of scripture without resorting to traditional language. The concept of the Trinity is a construct resulting from theological debates between scholars and theologians since the New Testament was written; but it is not the same as nor should it carry the same weight of scriptural authority. If we maintain the overly aggressive position of clinging to the traditional formula, we may as well find ourselves spending too much energy on Christianeez that borders on heresy. Even if we do not cross the line while teetering by it, it is still far too close for comfort.

I know this might go against the grain of what many faithful believers cherish as inherently Christian, but that is exactly what I am aiming to reform. I believe we need to rethink our approach and move away from the typical model of the traditional formula, and begin with the premise of God's incorporeal invisibility as His primary characteristic. From there we can approach the Trinitarian model more circumspectly in light of every passage in scripture where God is described.

So, what do I mean, really? Even though the Trinity is not a term found in the Bible, it ought not to be a point of contention among believers. Up until now, I have emphasized how God has marked the creation with His signature by infusing it with aspects that directly communicate His invisible attributes. However, we now must also consider that the very things God intended to be used to reveal Himself to us more clearly have, in a sense, also become a hindrance through a fully developed, yet faulty, theological view.

We have made the mistake of limiting God to those forms He used to reveal Himself to us, when in reality, He is still so much more. One of the names God gives of Himself is "I AM." It is a name given to disclose to us that He is whatever we need Him to be, whether He is our Healer, our Righteousness, or our Savior. He is what He is. He is God. He can meet every need and has no limit in His power to redeem. He can be anything that anyone needs, so that He can by all means save those who believe in Him.

That being said, God cannot and will not contradict Himself. It is literally impossible for Him to lie. Therefore, He would never present Himself to be worshipped in a manner that contradicts His nature and character.

> *"The God who made the world and everything in it, being Lord of heaven and earth, does not live in temples made by man, nor is he served by human hands, as though he needed anything, since he himself gives to all mankind life and breath and everything."* (Acts 17:24-25 ESV)

God is not worshipped with "men's hands" because He is Himself NOT human. God is NOT a man. He does not need to be handled as though He were a human being. If we subscribe only to a traditional view of God, we are indeed limiting Him to an image of humanity. In reality, we are made in His image, and after His likeness, not the other way around.

> *"God is not a man who lies, or a son of man who changes his mind! Does he speak and then not do it? or promise and not fulfill it?"* (Numbers 23:19 TLV)

I would like to again re-emphasize a major point here. I do not intend to utterly remove the concept of the Trinity from our religious expression. Instead, I propose it is best to place the Triunity of the Father, the Son, and the Holy Spirit in a more cohesive and appropriate context that is faithful to the biblical text. I also want to highlight at this point that this "Triunity" is not a contradiction to the Old Testament revelation of God. Traditionally, however, the Christian church has emphasized the Trinity as the sole means by which God is to be perceived and the benchmark by which He is to be understood in Christian doctrine. I believe this is a hindrance to our theology, and it is not an accurate portrayal of the God we claim to worship.

However, to deny the plurality of God's own revelation is equally disingenuous. Many in the Jewish faith do not ever talk about, or even know, that the Old Testament is chock-full of examples where God is revealed in plurality. There are numerous instances where God, who is invisible, is blurred with someone called "The Angel of the Lord," who is a visible being. The blurring occurs in such a manner as to make them both the same, yet distinct one from another.

It is understandable that we run the risk of accentuating God's invisibility almost ad nauseam at this point. But there is still much we have to undo in order to reinstitute this aspect of God's nature back to prominence within Christian theology, making it more widely accepted than the traditional view. In the chapters to come, we will explore what I perceive to be a more accurate application of the Godhead that does not alienate the majority of Christians who vigorously adhere to the traditional model. We will also analyze more closely the sayings of Jesus in the gospels, as well as the rest of the New Testament narrative, with God's invisible nature as the fundamental backdrop used to understand the Godhead in both testaments.

A more concerted effort is warranted here. Consider the fact that the narrative of the New Testament does not consist of the defense of the Trinity as its main point of theology. By simply reading the book of Acts alone, we can easily conclude that there is no mention of any argument or discussion between the disciples of the church in its infancy and the Jewish leadership concerning the Trinity, nor even the deity of Jesus for that matter.

In the various debates between Paul and the Sanhedrin, they are never hung up on the notion of Jesus being God as their major point of contention. Instead, the discussion centers around Jesus as the Jewish Messiah and as God's unique Son. The debate is never about His status as deity. Rather, it tends to be centered around Jesus' claims of Messiahship as God's one and only Son. If we try to go beyond the language of scripture, we will always end up with the same problem. The goal is to reconcile those parts of scripture that have not made sense primarily because of our traditions.

Our Stubborn Dilemma

By being so dogmatic in the traditional view, we are in effect being unfaithful to the biblical text. Using traditional expressions to describe God's nature betrays our ignorance and reveals an argumentative independence from scripture. That being said, I am not denying Jesus' divinity; He IS divine. But everything has its proper context. The divinity of Christ is something we will delve into further. This is a perfect opportunity to analyze Jesus' own commentary about God, as recorded in the gospels. We will also make allowance for how His statements were interpreted by those who heard Him, especially when some of Jesus' statements were of an indirect nature.

In the next chapter we will also look at the Old Testament narrative that describes the roles God played in Israel's history. You might be surprised to discover that the plurality aspect of God is not limited to the New Testament. The language of Scripture is specific enough to provide the framework we need to understand why the New Testament describes God the way it does.

By using this approach, it will help us to clearly understand what Jesus meant by what He said about Himself in relation to the Father, statements that would certainly imply His divine origin, while simultaneously maintaining the integrity of God's invisible nature. The question of Jesus' divine origin is addressed in greater detail in the following chapters. However, if you want the quick and simple answer to the question of whether or not Jesus is God, then the answer is as follows … Yes, He is … and … He isn't … all at the same time.

CHAPTER 9
The Father

Even though the New Testament primarily refers to God as "the Father," this title role is not limited to the New Testament narrative, nor is it uncommon in biblical Judaism to relate to God as the Father. God was always known to Israel as "the Father." But I would like to mention here that this term "Father" has a specific application in both testaments, and it denotes a particular kind of relationship between God and His people. The following verses should be sufficient to make my point:

> *"Do you thus repay the LORD, you foolish and senseless people? <u>Is not he your father</u>, who created you, who made you and established you?"* (Deuteronomy 32:6 ESV) [emphasis added].

> *"Therefore David blessed the LORD in the presence of all the assembly. And David said: "Blessed are you, O LORD, <u>the God of Israel our father, forever and ever</u>."* (1 Chronicles 29:10 ESV) [emphasis added].

> *"<u>As a father</u> shows compassion to his children, so the LORD shows compassion to those who fear him."* (Psalm 103:13 ESV) [emphasis added].

"For Adonai loves those He reproves, even as a father, the son in whom He delights." (Proverbs 3:12 TLV) [emphasis added].

"For You are our Father—even if Abraham would not know us or Israel not recognize us. You, Adonai, are our Father, our Redeemer —from everlasting is Your name." (Isaiah 63:16 TLV) [emphasis added].

"But now, Adonai, you are our Father. We are the clay and you are our potter, we are all the work of Your hand." (Isaiah 64:7 TLV) [emphasis added].

"But I said, How shall I put thee among the children, and give thee a pleasant land, a goodly heritage of the hosts of nations? and I said, Thou shalt call me, My father; and shalt not turn away from me." (Jeremiah 3:19 KJV) [emphasis added].

"They shall come with weeping, and with supplications will I lead them: I will cause them to walk by the rivers of waters in a straight way, wherein they shall not stumble: for I am a father to Israel, and Ephraim is my firstborn." (Jeremiah 31:9 KJV) [emphasis added].

"Have we not all one father? hath not one God created us? why do we deal treacherously every man against his brother, by profaning the covenant of our fathers?" (Malachi 2:10 KJV) [emphasis added].

As we have just read, God was known to Israel as their Father. This title role is primarily drawn from His role as Creator. However, calling Himself Father wasn't the only way in which God related to Israel. Other passages also present Him as Israel's Lord (meaning owner or master) all throughout scripture. Additionally, in other passages, He is also portrayed as Israel's husband (Isaiah 54:1, Jeremiah 3:1, 8, 14-20, Jeremiah 31:31-33, Hosea 2:2, 7, 16, 19-20).

Now, what may not be so obvious is how even the Old Testament presents God in a trinity of sorts (Father, Lord, and Husband). Furthermore, I should point out that each one of these individual titles applies to a unique role of God's varying approach toward his relationship with Israel at particular moments in Israel's history. Therefore, God is NOT advocating some form of incest by being both Israel's Father and Husband, nor a convoluted totalitarian dictator by being a Master and Husband. Here is a clue: These titles are applied to God when it brings attention to an aspect of His relationship toward His people. In one sense, He is Israel's Father, while in another sense, He is also their Husband, and as Lord or Master in another sense.

This can be true of God's relationship to Israel because He is not a human like us. His incorporeality allows Him to express Himself in any way He deems necessary in order to establish an intentional relationship with humanity. His non-physicality is a hindrance to us because we cannot relate to Him in that way, but when God chooses to reveal Himself with a specific title role (such as husband or father), He is taking the initiative and making a necessary step toward establishing a specific relationship to express His intentions with us who could not know Him otherwise.

It is a matter of function for the sake of relationship to help us understand and relate to Him. Seeing that He is invisible, the title that He takes to Himself in a time appointed indicates His desired approach within that relationship. That is why God seems to change in His titles whenever He addresses Israel under different circumstances.

Interestingly, Israel's response to God is also indicative of their role in that relationship. Look at the details in the following verse:

> *"A son honors his father, and a servant his master. If then I am a father, where is my honor? And if I am a master, where is my fear? says the LORD of hosts to you, O priests, who despise my name. But you say, 'How have we despised your name?'"* (Malachi 1:6 ESV)

God is drawing attention to Israel's disobedience and disregard, and begs the question that if He is their father, then why doesn't He receive honor as a father should. He isn't saying that He isn't a Father, for we have seen from previous passages that He Himself affirms to be their Father. It's in their disobedience, their wicked works, that they deny Him His right as their Father. Conversely, Israel's disposition in their attitude toward God shifts the focus of the relationship from Father to Master.

Likewise, when the focus changes from obedience as sons and shifts toward Israel's faithfulness, whether it's brought into question or recognition, the relationship then changes from that of Father/Son to Husband/Wife. When faithfulness to God is highlighted, Israel is referred to as His wife. When it's their obedience that is highlighted, then Israel's title changes back to children to reflect that aspect of their relationship toward God as sons.

As long as we continually make the mistake of making the temporal title role the default universal template for God, we risk falling into error because, even if He reveals Himself in that way, He is not restricted to only that revelation. Keeping the invisible nature in the forefront makes it simpler to understand the roles that God plays.[30]

Israel's relationship to God in the Old Testament was largely dependent on keeping the Law of Moses and loyalty to Yahweh alone. Ironically, Israel's name was often changed to Jacob as a reflection of Israel's attitude toward God. The name Jacob means "he who supplants." Whenever this name is applied to Israel, it's indicative of the nation's posture toward God, thereby indicting the nation for its rebellion.

Likewise, the undergirding nature of their relationship was also that of Master and Servant. This is also fully supported by the Old Testament:

> *"Thus says <u>the Lord GOD</u>: When I gather the house of Israel from the peoples among whom they are scattered, and manifest my holiness in them in the sight*

---

[30] The main difference between a covenant and a testament is this: A covenant refers to the relationship itself, whereas the testament refers to the document that defines said relationship. To illustrate, we can use marriage for our example: The ceremonial union of the man and woman is representative of the covenant, whereas the testament is represented by the marriage certificate. The Old Covenant is the relationship between God and the Nation of Israel as prescribed in Mosaic Law. The New Covenant is a relationship established between God and the House of Israel under the auspices of Israel's Messiah. The covenants reflect the nature of the different relationships as they are described by those written testaments. In the same manner, the changing of names and titles is a biblical method of communication often used to convey a particular nature of something. In the Bible, God establishes all His relationships by way of covenant. Covenants were confirmed and ratified by the sacrifices offered by the people as prescribed. When covenants were made in ancient Israel, the parties involved would kill an animal and divide the parts. The parties would then walk between those parts reciting the words of the covenant. This process was referred to as cutting a covenant.

of the nations, then they shall dwell in their own land that I gave to <u>my servant Jacob</u>." (Ezekiel 28:25 ESV) [emphasis added].

"They shall dwell in the land that I gave to <u>my servant Jacob</u>, where your fathers lived. They and their children and their children's children shall dwell there forever, and David my servant shall be their prince forever." (Ezekiel 37:25 ESV) [emphasis added].

"So now, do not fear, <u>Jacob my servant</u>, says Adonai, nor be dismayed, O Israel, for behold, I will save you from afar, your seed from the land of their exile. Jacob will again be quiet and at ease, and no one will make him afraid." (Jeremiah 30:10 TLV) [emphasis added].

"But you, <u>Israel, My servant, Jacob whom I have chosen</u>, descendant of Abraham, My friend." (Isaiah 41:8 TLV) [emphasis added].

However, having been under the Mosaic Law, Israel's relationship to God was dependent on how she kept the terms of the Old Covenant. The nation's response dictated how God would relate to Israel as a whole. While the Old Covenant defined the nature of their relationship, it was also the *basis for their righteousness: "Ye shall therefore keep my statutes, and my judgments: which if a man do, he shall live in them: I am the LORD"* (Leviticus 18:5 KJV). The point being is that God's relationship toward Israel was exemplified in the titles used.

When Israel's obedience or disobedience is in view, the emphasis of the relationship between God and Israel was that of Father and son respectively. If the nation's faithfulness or infidelity were highlighted, then the relationship would shift from Father and son to Husband and wife. Then again, when the people's works are bought to light, the relationship would shift again to Master and servant. The change in titles was always indicative of the nation's posture in its relationship toward God at any given time.

What I am aiming to demonstrate here is that the New Covenant inaugurates the establishment of a new kind of relationship, one that is different from that which was under the Old Covenant. It is of a different nature, one that is not dependent on Israel's faithfulness, works, or obedience according to the Law of Moses (Torah). The nature of this new relationship between God and His people is now permanently that of Father and child. This means that the relationship no longer shifts from one kind to another as it was under the Law of Moses.

Via this New Covenant, a new relationship is being revealed with the Messiah Himself as the primary catalyst (see Jeremiah 31:31-33, Isaiah 42:5-9, and 2 Corinthians 6:17-18).[31] While all of creation serves God, the nature of the relationship that God intends to have with the creation as revealed in the New Testament is a permanent one as our Father. Through the New Covenant, He seeks to establish an immutable relationship that sets the tone for what is to come. That tone is the very core of this New Covenant relationship.

JESUS' OWN SAYINGS

After having defined what the New Covenant relationship looks like, we can now explore the sayings of Jesus in greater detail. Seeing that the nature of God's relationship with humanity has changed to a perpetual one of Father and Child, we will need to analyze Jesus' views about the realities of that relationship. His words provide us with a wealth of information, not only about His own identity, but also that of His origin, and the nature of His relationship to the Father. Keep all this in mind as we read the following account:

---

[31] The New Covenant God mentioned in Jeremiah was never made with the church, as some may presume. God made it specifically with the House of Israel and the House of Judah. He made this Covenant with the Nation of Israel as a whole. However, aside from Jeremiah, there is no record of God ever officially making this Covenant with the people of Israel, as in the event of the giving of the Law by the hand of Moses, other than the New Testament. Nevertheless, He does stipulate that even though the Covenant was made with Israel, He confirms it would be accomplished by the Messiah when he says, "… I will give you for a Covenant of the people …" The Messiah is Himself the representative of the entire nation with whom God makes this new Covenant. He is also the embodiment of the Covenant itself. Besides this, He is also the One who carries out the terms of the Covenant; He is the Priest who offers the sacrifice, and also the Sacrifice itself. The entire New Covenant begins and ends with the Messiah! Hence, the catalyst.

> *"Jesus said to him, 'I am the way, and the truth, and the life. No one comes to the Father except through me. If you had known me, you would have known my Father also. From now on you do know him and have seen him.' Philip said to him, 'Lord, show us the Father, and it is enough for us.' Jesus said to him, 'Have I been with you so long, and you still do not know me, Philip? Whoever has seen me has seen the Father. How can you say, 'Show us the Father'? Do you not believe that I am in the Father and the Father is in me? The words that I say to you I do not speak on my own authority, but the Father who dwells in me does his works. Believe me that I am in the Father and the Father is in me, or else believe on account of the works themselves' "* (John 14:6-11 ESV).

In prior chapters, we have purposely beaten a dead horse with the notion that God (the Father) is invisible. This was the default belief and understanding about the nature of God among Jewish people throughout history. Now we see Phillip making a request for Jesus to show them the Father. His question implies that even until that point in Jesus' ministry, the disciples still had never seen the Father. But Jesus' response gives us the insight we need because His statement to Phillip was specific.

When Jesus says that they saw the Father, Jesus was not referring to His own physical body ... not exactly. Jesus makes it abundantly clear that what actually revealed the Father to His disciples, that is what they actually saw of the Father, were the works He performed. The preaching, the miracles, signs, and wonders Jesus performed, they are what revealed the invisible Father, and it is always in this context that the Father is "seen." The body of Jesus was only incidental to the works. There is no other context ever given in scripture where the Father is seen. Here is another example:

> *"He that hateth me hateth my Father also. <u>If I had not done among them the works</u> which none other man did, they had not had sin: <u>but now have they both seen and hated both me and my Father</u>"* (John 15:23-24 KJV) [emphasis added].

Again, we see that Jesus Himself is not claiming to be the Father. The things that were actually made visible of the Father were the works Christ performed through His preaching while in a physical body. By Jesus speaking the Father's words and doing the Father's works, He was showing them the Father who remains unseen, while simultaneously being revealed. This is a consistent pattern with Jesus. He never deviates from it. On a prior occasion, Jesus engaged in somewhat of a heated discussion with the religious leaders. See below:

> "So the Jews gathered around him and said to him, 'How long will you keep us in suspense? If you are the Christ, tell us plainly.' Jesus answered them, 'I told you, and you do not believe. <u>The works that I do in my Father's name bear witness about me</u>, but you do not believe because you are not among my sheep. My sheep hear my voice, and I know them, and they follow me. I give them eternal life, and they will never perish, and no one will snatch them out of my hand. My Father, who has given them to me, is greater than all, and no one is able to snatch them out of the Father's hand. I and the Father are one.' The Jews picked up stones again to stone him. Jesus answered them, '<u>I have shown you many good works from the Father; for which of them are you going to stone me?</u>' The Jews answered him, 'It is not for a good work that we are going to stone you but for blasphemy, because you, being a man, make yourself God.'" (John 10:24-33 ESVI) [emphasis added].

We clearly see that it was the works that He did as the visual evidence of the Father. This time, however, there is some more information provided to us. Contrary to "oneness" doctrine, all these accounts give no indication that Jesus ever claimed to be the Father. This passage is no different. Note that what He actually said was, "I and the Father are one." Again, Jesus is not claiming to be the Father here, but He is in fact claiming divinity by the *inference* of His statement. Jesus *knows* the Father is invisible, as does His audience. If Jesus were to simply flat out say, "I *am* the Father," then Jesus would be caught in a bold-faced *lie*. If Jesus ever made such a claim, every Jew present would have been fully justified in stoning Him as a heretic according to Old Testament theology. But that is NOT what Jesus said at all.

By carefully choosing his words, Jesus could lay claim to divinity without actually saying it directly. His admission to being one with the Father was understood by the people to mean that He was making Himself God.

Yet, Jesus' specific use of semantics could not be used to accuse Him of admitting to a lie. Follow the logic: If the Father is invisible, then it goes without saying that Jesus cannot be the Father because Jesus is in a visible physical body. The people did not accuse Him of saying He was God; they accused Him of *making* Himself out to be God because of the things He did through His admission of being one with the Father.

CHAPTER 10
The Father Revealed

All gospel accounts, including the rest of the New Testament, emphasize this same aspect of Jesus' identity. The post-resurrection encounter of Jesus with His disciples is equally revealing. The following passage demonstrates this consistent theme:

> "Eight days later, his disciples were inside again, and Thomas was with them. Although the doors were locked, Jesus came and stood among them and said, 'Peace be with you.' Then he said to Thomas, 'Put your finger here, and see my hands; and put out your hand, and place it in my side. Do not disbelieve, but believe.' Thomas answered him, 'My Lord and my God!' Jesus said to him, 'Have you believed because you have seen me? Blessed are those who have not seen and yet have believed.' " (John 20:26-29 ESV)

In the above passage, Thomas IS in fact referring to Jesus as God by his comment, "My Lord and my God." One remarkable detail is that prior to the resurrection, there is no record of anyone ever directly referring to Jesus as God in the same manner as Thomas. However, it must also be pointed out that Thomas does NOT refer to Jesus as "Father" either. Even so, the following statement from Jesus confirms that Thomas was NOT out of line in his affirmation, and Jesus does not rebuke Thomas for it.

Jesus did not turn to Thomas saying, "Thomas! That is blasphemy! You should never say that about me!" To the contrary, point of fact: Jesus never wastes His breath correcting Thomas for his assertion. If anything, Jesus goes out of His way to attest to Thomas' boast. Yet, even within these verses, Jesus never admits to saying anything akin to, "I am God," or "I am the Father." For Him to do so would have been a violation of the Mosaic Law and would rightly have been construed as blasphemy.

So how do we process all this in a way that makes sense? There is a passage I need to bring to your attention. It provides us with some key information that helps us understand the rationale behind Jesus' approach as to why he would not just come out and overtly say He is God. Jesus always spoke with a set purpose. He was never careless with His words, as so many of us may be today. To maintain proper order, He had to abide by certain restrictions due to His human nature. The following passage is taken from three different English versions offering a perspective on the reasoning behind Jesus' method:

"Let this mind be in you, which was also in Christ Jesus: Who, being in the form of God, thought it not robbery to be equal with God: But made himself of no reputation, and took upon him the form of a servant, and was made in the likeness of men: And being found in fashion as a man, he humbled himself, and became obedient unto death, even the death of the cross." Philippians 2:5-8 KJV)

"Have this mind among yourselves, which is yours in Christ Jesus, who, though he was in the form of God, did not count equality with God a thing to be grasped, but emptied himself, by taking the form of a servant, being born in the likeness of men. And being found in human form, he humbled himself by becoming obedient to the point of death, even death on a cross." (Philippians 2:5-8 ESV)

"Have this attitude in yourselves, which also was in Messiah Yeshua, Who, though existing in the form of God, did not consider being equal with God a thing to be grasped. But He emptied Himself—taking on the form of a slave,

becoming in the likeness of men and being found in appearance as a man. He Humbled Himself—becoming obedient to the point of death, even death on a cross." (Philippians 2:5-8 TLV)

The main reason He never overtly admitted to being God was simply because He shouldn't. Yes, that's right! He shouldn't, and if He did so, He would have been violating the most fundamental aspect of God's true nature and essence. Jesus knows that while the Father is invisible, being a human with a physical body excludes Himself from that attribute. In other words, by virtue of His humanity, He is a lower state of being, and is lesser than the Father who is greater than all. Therefore, He must have had to use precise language distinguishing between Himself and the Father.

It's pretty simple really. Jesus' rhetoric is such that He always alludes to His own divinity indirectly without overtly claiming to be God. Jesus always alludes to His divinity with veiled indirect statements, and never directly admits to it. Although others can and do affirm Christ to be God, as in the case with Thomas, Jesus points to it indirectly, yet he would never deny it. That is how the scripture portrays the divinity of Christ. It is the only way we can broach the topic if we are to maintain biblical accuracy, *"If we are faithless, He remains faithful,* <u>for He cannot deny Himself</u>*"* (2 Timothy 2:11-13 TLV) [emphasis added].

We have already established that no one can ever see God, UNLESS God does or creates something in order for us to interact with Him. We ought not to think of God's attributes in the same way we think of ourselves, as though He were one of us. When the Creator is portrayed as having a face, mouth, hands, voice, eyes, etc., these are all invisible with no form to them, and they are more than just figures of speech.

They are actually the very things of Him, part of His essence that perform a function within the creation while having no form whatsoever. Regardless of the body part mentioned, these are all non-physical, unseen characteristics of God's essence. These attributes are not merely expressions of His mind. They are in fact Him, His very person and presence in the context of function, not physicality.

Everything the invisible God does is first accomplished by what He says, His Word. We see biblical precedent for this in the creation account itself, and it is also the first time we see God in action. By speaking everything into existence, He sets everything into motion. That precedent is the consistent thread throughout both testaments. The following verses provide us insight:

> "As they were going down toward the edge of town, Samuel said to Saul, 'Tell your servant to go ahead of us and pass on, but as for you, stand still awhile, so that I may <u>proclaim to you the word of God</u>.'" (1 Samuel 9:27 TLV) [emphasis added].

> "But that same night <u>the word of God came to Nathan, saying</u>," (1 Chronicles 17:3 TLV) [emphasis added].

> "After these things the <u>word of Adonai came to Abram in a vision saying</u>, 'Do not fear, Abram. I am your shield, your very great reward.'" (Genesis 15:1 TLV) [emphasis added].

> "<u>Adonai started to appear</u> once more in Shiloh, for <u>ADONAI revealed Himself</u> to Samuel in Shiloh <u>by the word of Adonai</u>." (1 Samuel 3:21 TLV) [emphasis added].

> "Then the <u>word of Adonai came to him saying</u>:" (1 Kings 17:2 TLV) [emphasis added].

Draw your attention to how the Word of the Lord is portrayed. In some cases, the Word of God *came* to someone in a *vision*. Other times, the Word of the Lord is said to have *appeared* to a prophet. In other instances, it was a *spoken* word. The point I want to make is that the Word of God is always that aspect of God that is revealing something to demonstrate His intent. The Word of God is that part of God that communicates the will of the Father in order to make Himself knowable and relatable to His creation. What we actually "see" are the effects of the invisible God by His Word, the result being the fulfillment of His will.

When God speaks, He is not using a mouth as you and I do. He has no physical mouth. Therefore His Word comes from God's own bodiless existence and essence. His Word is actually Himself in the non-physical form of *communication*. Anything that He does is accomplished by what He says. Whether it is creation from nothing, keeping promises, or giving prophecy, all of it is accomplished by His Word. The Word of God is the very person of God in a type of expression. Sometimes the Word takes a form *(came, or appeared)*. At other times, it is words that are spoken *(saying)*. God's invisible quality makes His Word open to convey God's will in whatever manner the Father deems necessary. The major point here is that an action must take place, resulting in what can be seen of Him.

> *"So shall my word be that goeth forth out of my mouth: it shall not return unto me void, but it shall accomplish that which I please, and it shall prosper [in the thing] whereto I sent it."* (Isaiah 55:11 KJV)

Anytime the INVISIBLE GOD speaks, He is in fact doing something. There is always an action that is taking place when God speaks. To the creation, the only evidence the invisible God spoke is when an action of substance is made visible or revealed to us. That action may come in the form of His voice by the words He uses to communicate His intent. Remember, His voice comes out of the non-physical, non-visible reality of the Father. The voice does not come from a larynx. It is an audible manifestation of His Presence. What God speaks is what is referred to in the Bible as *His Word*, or *the Word of the Lord*, or *the Word of God*, or *God*.

Now, let's take a look at what the New Testament says about the Word. Again, I want to include three different Bible versions to get as broad a perspective as possible:

> *"In the beginning was the Word, and the Word was with God, and the Word was God. He was in the beginning with God. All things were made through him, and without him was not anything made that was made."* (John 1:1-3 ESV)

> *"In the beginning was the Word. The Word was with God, and the Word was God. He was with God in the beginning. All things were made through Him, and apart from Him nothing was made that has come into being."* (John 1:1-3 TLV)

"In the beginning was the Word, and the Word was with God, and the Word was God. The same was in the beginning with God. All things were made by him; and without him was not anything made that was made." (John 1:1-3 KJV)

Note the verbiage here. The Word (LOGOS) is WHO was in the beginning (at creation). The LOGOS was WITH and IS God all at the same time. This makes much better sense when we keep in mind that everything about God is essentially invisible ... including His WORD, which is Himself who is unseen *until* an action takes place.

I would like to draw your attention to a brief analysis of the first three verses in John's Gospel. Notice what the verbiage *does not* mention. It *does not* say that Jesus was in the beginning. It *does not* say that *Jesus* was with God. And it *does not* say that *Jesus* is God. However, IT DOES say all these things about **THE WORD**. I am deliberately placing a difference between the Word who is God, and the man Jesus who is the Son. The nature of the Word who is God is not the same nature of Jesus who is a man. The Word is invisible, but Jesus is a man who can be seen.

So please understand the context. I am *not* denying Jesus' divinity. I absolutely affirm that Jesus is, in fact, God. I am only making an analysis of the Apostle's use of specific terms. In the beginning of John's gospel, the Apostle could have written the word "Jesus" in the place of "the Word," but he didn't. It simply is not what he recorded. He makes this distinction on purpose. This is not a denial of Jesus' divinity. Rather, the passage actually demonstrates that Jesus is not a mere man; He is, in fact, the Word of God (who is God) made flesh. The contrasts provided in the text are there to highlight the main differences between the invisible Word and the visible Son.

Jesus the man is the Word made flesh. The major difference between Jesus and the Word is a matter of composition. The Word was made visible after He took on flesh. That flesh is the body, which is manifested in order for the invisible God to be seen. The Word (who is God) became visible through a physical body that He made in order to fulfill the will of the Father. Consider the following verses:

> *"Wherefore when he cometh into the world, he saith, Sacrifice and offering thou wouldest not, but a body hast thou prepared me: In burnt offerings and sacrifices for sin thou hast had no pleasure. Then said I, Lo, I come (in the volume of the book it is written of me,) to do thy will, O God."* (Hebrews 10:5-7 KJV)

As the Word, He is God. Yet, as a man, He is the Son. Jesus is the perfect marriage of both humanity and divinity in one. Jesus IS God … as revealed through a human body. This is what is referred to as the "Hypostatic Union." What often results in confusion is our lack of differentiation between the flesh that is seen, and the Spirit that is invisible, in relation to Jesus' incarnation. As long as we fail to make these distinctions, we will always attribute divinity to that which the Bible emphasizes as humanity. However, if we differentiate between the two, we then can see the harmony of the biblical text from the Old Testament directly into the New Testament. There is no break in understanding who God is from one testament to the other.

Remember, every person in the New Testament that Jesus ministered to was Jewish. They all had an understanding of the nature of God, which they all inherited from the Tanach, including Jesus Himself. The Old Testament understanding of God's nature was not altered through Jesus' incarnation. Rather, it was exemplified in the way in which He was revealed to the world. The Apostles, the early church, and those who came to believe in Him thereafter, all bet their lives on it, and so should we.

CHAPTER 11
The Word and The Son

I would like to draw your attention to John 1:3. It states that ALL things were MADE by THE WORD. The language is specific here. They were not made by Jesus. All "things" were made by THE WORD. It goes on to say that without Him (that is, THE WORD) there was not anything made that has been made. Everything that has been made was done so by THE WORD who is God. Now let's look at verse 14 in the same three versions:

"And the Word became flesh and dwelt among us, and we have seen his glory, glory as of the only Son from the Father, full of grace and truth." (John 1:14 ESV)

"And the Word became flesh and tabernacled among us. We looked upon His glory, the glory of the one and only from the Father, full of grace and truth." (John 1:14 TLV)

"And the Word was made flesh, and dwelt among us, and we beheld his glory, the glory as of the only begotten of the Father, full of grace and truth." (John 1:14 KJV)

Everything that is ever made is made by THE WORD. In verse 14, we see something else uniquely being "made." The Word was MADE (or became) "FLESH" and dwelled among us. The Word comes into the world as a SON by being given a BODY that is made. The Word of God was "made flesh" … that flesh that was made is who we refer to as the man Jesus. It says that Jesus' glory is regarded as that of the only begotten (or unique) Son of the Father.

The glory of Jesus is that of a Son, but the glory of The Word is that of God. The glory of the Son is NOT attributed to the Word. Instead, it is attributed to the man (Jesus) being in human form. It is attributed to the physicality of the "begotten-ness" of Christ; The Word become flesh. The glory of the Word is actually that of God who is invisible. However, the man Jesus is the visible Son.

BREAKING IT DOWN

There is an important purpose behind Jesus' approach to alluding to His own divinity in relation to the Father. Jesus, His disciples, the Sanhedrin, and all the children of Israel always understood God to be unseen in the purest sense (without a body). Philippians 2:6-8 sheds light into the mystery surrounding Jesus' methodology for revealing His divinity. There are seven points of interest given in Philippians that we ought to observe. Take a look at the following list from Philippians 2:6-8:

1. Who, being in the form of God
2. Thought it not robbery to be equal with God
3. Made himself of no reputation
4. Took upon Him the form of a servant
5. Was made in the likeness of men
6. Found in fashion as a man, He humbled Himself
7. Became obedient unto death, even death on a cross

The main difference in the description between The Word and Jesus is simply a matter of function. The Word of the Father, who is God, is the

Father's intent that is itself also invisible until it is revealed. In the case of the New Testament record, when the Father revealed His Word, He did it by making a body to communicate His will, to reveal His works, His purpose, and His intent. Take a look again at the short list. If we transpose what we've covered so far in PHILIPPIANS 2:6-8 onto the verses in JOHN 1:1-3, 14 we find an interesting parallel of ideas:

PHILIPPIANS 2:6-8	JOHN 1:1-3, 14
Who, being in the form of God	In the beginning was the Word
Thought it not robbery to be equal with God	The Word was with God
But Made Himself of no reputation	And the Word Was God
Took upon Him the form of a servant	And the Word was made Flesh
Was made in the likeness of men	And dwelt among us
Found in fashion as a man, He humbled Himself	We beheld His glory, as the only begotten of the Father
Became obedient unto death, even death on a cross	Full of grace and truth

This chart is not some major secret theological revelation. I admit to doing some cherry-picking here, and I admit I am just having fun with it. Still, the more I look at certain patterns of scripture, the more I am convinced that we read too much of our own presuppositions onto the Bible. Christians across the board, from academics to pastors, layman to theologians, have all been guilty of it. We do it at times even by generalizing too much of what we read.

One example of this is when we make the mistake of reading a passage in one gospel where Jesus makes some comment about a topic, and then we assume the same thing is simply repeated in another gospel account. When we lump everything together like that, we take it all to mean the same thing. I believe this is a grave mistake. The specifics matter. Likewise, our approach to the Trinity makes a similar kind of mistake.

We read the words "Father, Son, and Holy Spirit," and there is an automatic association being made with The Trinity without differentiating between them. We just lump it all together to mean the same thing when, in reality, they don't. "Oneness" doctrine proponents are notorious for doing this very thing. They always claim that Jesus is the Father, Son, and Holy Spirit in bodily form. Unfortunately, that is how they and other segments of Christianity are trained to think about these things.

Another example is when we look at passages mentioning the Angel of the Lord. We might hear things like, "That is an early appearance of Jesus in the Old Testament." Here is a tidbit of information people often ignore. Prior to the incarnation, the Lord was never known by nor referred to as "Jesus," whether on earth or in heaven, not among humans or angels. None of the Hebrews in the Old Testament ever referred to Him as *Jesus*.

However, He was always known to them as The WORD of the Lord who came, spoke, and/or appeared to them. We make the mistake of reading "Jesus" into the Old Testament text, when "Jesus" is not there. The Word is the One they recognized as being there. When we make overly generalized statements about Christ, we end up ignoring the importance of the specificity highlighted in certain passages. This makes the obscure Bible passages even more ambiguous to us.

To be clear, I am NOT denying the divinity of Jesus. What I am saying is that we ought not to interpret passages to mean one thing when they are actually saying something different. We ought to accept the passages as they are written and utilize the infrastructure of scripture as our glossary.

For example, earlier in this book, the question was posed of whether Jesus is God. Most evangelical Christians will answer with an emphatic yes, and rightly so. Yet, the answers Jesus consistently gives about Himself are only admissions to being the Son of God. In the meantime, He does not stop anyone from worshipping Him as God, while never denying what they profess, as in the case with Thomas. He does it this way for the following reasons:

- As the Word, He pre-existed His birth in the flesh. He was there in the beginning as God.

- He came down from heaven out of God the Father as The Word. He proceeded from God, therefore making Him Divine.

- For the carnation, The Word (who is God) was made (or put on) flesh, sharing the constraints of humanity.

- Once The Word was made flesh (that is, within a human body), He is in a limited *form*, and therefore restricts Himself from making specific admissions to being God. Within those restrictions, He acted and spoke as a Son of God.

As a man, Jesus faithfully kept the Mosaic Law. He preserved the integrity of His claims by speaking only what was needed to maintain proper order and balance between humanity, seen without, and Deity, veiled within. As we read in Philippians, the Lord could not personally lay claim to being God because He took on a human form. The moment The Word took on a visible human body, His role changed, and His status became that of a Son, not that of The Word who is God.

The following statement may illicit anger in some, but everything that Jesus did on earth, He did not accomplish any of those things as God. He did them as Christ, the Son of God. As I said it before, I say it again. Everything that Jesus Christ accomplished on earth, whether teaching and preaching about the Kingdom, healing the sick, raising the dead, feeding the poor, defending sinners, protecting the weak, walking on water, calming storms, casting out demons, giving sight to the blind, making cripples walk, being judged and condemned, dying and rising from the dead, He did it all as a man, not as God.

The scripture attributes the responsibility for accomplishing all the things mentioned above to God as having done them by Christ.

"And all things are of God, who hath reconciled us to himself by Jesus Christ, and hath given to us the ministry of reconciliation; To wit, that God was in Christ, reconciling the world unto himself, not imputing their trespasses unto them; and hath committed unto us the word of reconciliation." (2 Corinthians 5:18-19 KJV)

As a man, Jesus mediated between deity and humanity, *"For there is one*

God, and one mediator between God and men, the man Christ Jesus" (1 Timothy 2:5 KJV). We should never forget that it is the scripture itself that makes the distinction between the Father and the Son (2 Corinthians 5:19).

All the Apostles' writings affirm that it was the Son of God who actually did those things; it was God who is in Christ that receives the credit for accomplishing them. The Bible says that, *"God was in Christ, reconciling the world to Himself"* (2 Corinthians 5:19 KJV). The scripture does not emphatically say, "Christ is God who reconciled the world," even if that may be implied by the text. The fact remains that the wording is such that the distinctions between the Father and the Son are consistent. Therefore, we must be consistent with the words we use by remaining true to the biblical text. We must rely on the infrastructure provided by scripture in order for us to explain our theology. We ought not offer an interpretation just because it doesn't make immediate sense. If we confuse the two and lump it all together, we not only water down our message, but we also weaken our position because we end up changing the truth of God into a lie. That is definitely not good.

When the New Testament refers to Jesus' ministry, His humanity is what is in focus, NOT His deity. The language shifts when it talks of the divine nature of God. The Bible makes zero reference to Jesus' humanity ever being God, except to say that the Father dwelt in the Son in that body that proceeded from (or was made by) Him. That body was a man. The Presence that resides in that body is God. The Apostle Paul wrote:

> *"And without controversy great is the mystery of godliness: God was* **manifest (revealed)** *in the flesh, justified in the Spirit, seen of angels, preached unto the Gentiles, believed on in the world, received up into glory"* (1 Timothy 3:16 KJV) [emphasis added].

Notice how the above passage directly associates the incarnation of Christ with angels having seen God, implying the angels had not seen Him prior to the incarnation of Christ. This passage also is in perfect alignment with Jesus' own statement about His own works as the mechanism that revealed the Father. This follows the same pattern for all the passages that affirm God has never been seen at any given time (including Jesus' own words), while simultaneously affirming God manifested Himself throughout human history. Take into consideration the wording of the following verses and note their specificity. See if you can recognize a pattern:

> *"Concerning his Son Jesus Christ our Lord, which was made of the seed of David according to the flesh …"* (Romans 1:3)

> *"But when the fulness of the time was come, God sent forth his Son, made of a woman, made under the law …"* (Galatians 4:4)

> *"Who being the brightness of his glory, and the express image of his person, and upholding all things by the word of his power, when he had by himself purged our sins, sat down on the right hand of the Majesty on high: Being made so much better than the angels, as he hath by inheritance obtained a more excellent name than they. For unto which of the angels said he at any time, Thou art my Son, this day have I begotten thee? And again, I will be to him a Father, and he shall be to me a Son? And again, when he bringeth in the first begotten into the world, he saith, And let all the angels of God worship him."* (Hebrews 1:3-6)

> *"For verily he took not on <u>him the nature</u> of angels; but he took on <u>him</u> the seed of Abraham. Wherefore in all things it behooved him to be made like unto his brethren, that he might be a merciful and faithful high priest in things <u>pertaining</u> to God, to make reconciliation for the sins of the people."* (Hebrews 2:16-17) [emphasis added].

All of these passages, and others that are not mentioned here, have a consistent theme. The Sonship aspect of Jesus is intimately linked to His human body. The physicality of Christ IS the basis of His title as God's Son. In Romans 1:3-4, the verses highlight Christ as the Son of God in the context of being *made* of the seed of David *according to the flesh*. He then points to the exalting declaration of His title as a Son of God. There is still much more to this verse that we have not covered here. The emphasis on His Sonship in Galatians 4:4 is even more overt than that of Romans. It directly associates Jesus' Sonship with the fact that He is made of a woman.

The book of Hebrews, on the other hand, gives attention to the difference that exists between angels and the Son of God, citing Jesus' *earthly role* as "the express image of His (God's) person." His physical body is the catalyst for His exaltation as the Son of God above the angels. In fact, the writer in Hebrews makes some interesting connections. Jesus is consistently presented as being made from the stuff of humanity, and the declaration of His status as a Son is in direct *response* to His incarnation, ministry, death, burial, resurrection, and ascension to the Heavenly throne. His "Sonship" is associated with and related to His humanity and earthly ministry.

Isaiah's prophecy of Messiah's birth also makes this connection between the body of Christ and His status as a Son:

> *"For unto us a child is born, unto us a son is given: and the government shall be upon his shoulder: and his name shall be called Wonderful, Counsellor, The mighty God, The everlasting Father, The Prince of Peace."* (Isaiah 9:6)

I would like to draw your attention again to the first part of the verse. It says, *"For unto us a CHILD is born, unto us a SON is given."* Can you see how that we are GIVEN a son because a child is BORN? The sonship is directly related to His coming into the world as a human child. Sound familiar? This theme is thoroughly woven into the New Testament narrative. Moreover, when we arrive at the New Testament, we see Mary receiving a visitation from the Angel Gabriel who announces she is being chosen to bring the Messiah into the world, thereby fulfilling the long awaited prophecy of Isaiah. The passage clearly exhibits continuity of thought from Isaiah's prognostication of the child's birth, with His body in particular as the catalyst to His Sonship:

> *"And the angel answered and said unto her, The Holy Ghost shall come upon thee, and the power of the Highest shall overshadow thee: therefore also that holy thing which shall be born of thee shall be called the Son of God."* (Luke 1:35)

According to the KJV, the angel specifies the object by saying, *"... that holy thing ..."* He articulates the body of the Messiah as the "holy thing" correlating it with His Sonship. Admittedly, some other translations render it differently, with the angels saying either "holy child" or "holy one" or "holy baby," rather than as a "thing." Regardless, in any case, it still does not change the association of the body with His Sonship. The book of Hebrews provides us with a glimpse into Messiah's priestly mission, and the significance of that role. You should take the time and read the chapter in its entirety, but for now see verses 5-10:

> "*Consequently, when Christ came into the world, he said, 'Sacrifices and offerings you have not desired,* but a body have you prepared for me; *in burnt offerings and sin offerings you have taken no pleasure. Then I said, 'Behold, I have come to do your will, O God, as it is written of me in the scroll of the book.'* When he said above, 'You have neither desired nor taken pleasure in sacrifices and offerings and burnt offerings and sin offerings' (these are offered according to the law), *then he added, 'Behold, I have come to do your will.' He does away with the first in order to establish the second. And by that will we have been sanctified through the* offering of the body of Jesus Christ *once for all.*" (Hebrews 10:5-10 ESV)

Before we go any farther, it is important for us to point out that the focus of the book of Hebrews is the human priestly role of the Son of God and self-sacrifice. The book of Hebrews, especially here in chapter 10, accentuates Messiah's incarnation, humanity, and more precisely, His physical presence in the natural world. The preparation of a body is particularly noteworthy for this discussion. (Re-read Hebrews 10:5-10 as needed.)

A quick thought: Our traditions have a nasty habit of getting in the way of us seeing this connection of Jesus' body with Him being called a Son. I believe this is because our traditional Trinitarian approach simply overlaps the "Son" title with "God" in places where the Bible doesn't. Again, I'm not denying Jesus' divinity. What I am saying is that the precise language of the Bible is drawing attention to those specifics that remain faithful to the rest of scripture. These passages in Hebrews are no exception. When we read "Son of God" in the text, by our traditions we become blind to the man, and instead, we see only God in the passage. It is a grave mistake to filter the writer's intent through the reader's bias. We read and misread the roles because of the traditional approach.

I would be remiss if I did not mention that the Bible also speaks of other "sons of God." The Old Testament clearly makes mention of them. However, Jesus is God's unique Son. It does not matter if the sons of God mentioned in the Old Testament already existed. The fact is that God declared Messiah to be His Son and exalted Him to a position of worship, which is quite revealing. When the writer of the book of Hebrews quotes from Psalm 97:7, he says, *"Thy throne, O God, is forever and ever,"* he is, in fact, referring to the Son.

What may not be obvious is that he is quoting an Old Testament verse that does not use the term *Son* in that passage. The author of Hebrews is deliberately making the connection between the two. He is clearly referring to the deity of Messiah by making that association. At the same time, the "Son" aspect remains directly linked to His coming into the world as a human. That is the whole point of Hebrews.

Lastly, the author of Hebrews provides us with another important detail. Actually, when you read it, it is almost like the author gave it as an afterthought. Here's the verse in question:

"Being made so much better than the angels, as he hath by inheritance obtained a more excellent name than they." (Hebrews 1:4)

Now, have you ever stopped to ask yourself what he meant by *"... he hath ... obtained a more excellent* **name** *than they"*? Chances are that you've probably let the autopilot take over, and the name of "J.E.S.U.S." popped up somewhere in your head. If you have, then you may have unwittingly just made another common blunder. From the outset, I will just tell you that he wasn't talking about speaking the name JESUS, or even the Hebrew YESHUA. The proper name is not the point in Hebrews. I believe our ideas and applications of Jesus' name are more often than not crude stereotypes.

For example, it's like when people use His name like a lucky charm thinking that by repeating it over and over, it magically does something, like when some folks feel that if they don't say the words, "In the name of JESUS," to end every prayer, then they might not be heard at all. Of course, I am being flippant, but that is how many people feel about it, and how they treat His name. In the same way, we tend to misread that passage in Hebrews and simply assume it is referring to JESUS, but it isn't, not really.

The name of JESUS was common in Israel. If I were to ask you to open your Bible to the book of Jesus, most people would be stumped because they will not find it, at least not in the way they expect. You are probably looking in your Bible, and I'm sure you may not see it, at least not yet anyway. However, if I told you it is the sixth book of the Old Testament, you still might not be sure. Well, it is because the name of JESUS is an English translation of the Greek IESOUS, which is translated from the Hebrew YESHUA.

If you did a bit of digging as if you were searching for a treasure, you would discover that YESHUA is the short version of YEHOSHUA, which if translated directly to English from Hebrew, you get JOSHUA, the sixth book of the Old Testament. Sounds weird now that you may have come to realize that there is in fact the book of Jesus in your Bible, or rather the book of Joshua. Now, before I go too far off script, I did this little "digging" exercise to show that what we assume about a name is not always so. There is much more to His name than meets the eye. And where we're going with this next may just about blow your mind!

CHAPTER 12
The Name and Presence

Before I got married, my then fiancé (now wife) expressed her desire to have children. While sitting in the living room talking about our future as a married couple, the topic of children came up. As though she had made the determination well before we ever met, she simply blurted out, "I want five kids!" To her, it was the magic number! Yeah, it almost felt like I didn't really have a choice in the matter. Of course, I knew I had a choice, but her excitement only intensified my affections for her. So, with a warm and somewhat quizzical look, I gazed at her and said, "Tell you what, babe, let's start with one. Then we'll see about working our way up to five." Now, eighteen years later, we have four children … and two dogs, if you count them as the fifth and sixth additions to the family.

Before any of them were born, my wife and I had the pleasure of sharing in the excitement of choosing a name for each of them. We were deliberate in our choices. For our first child, we came up with different variations of then popular dual-name combinations. Since our first child was going to be a boy, we finally decided on "Benjamin Grant." I knew Benjamin meant "son of strength," or "son of my right hand." As for adding "Grant," well, together they just sounded *Presidential*.

I wanted my first-born son to spearhead my family name. At the time, I understood that his name could also be a foretelling, both of his character and also of his destiny. In my eyes, I see him as strong and driven with purpose. So I gave him a name that reflected my deepest hopes for him. I mean, isn't it what every father wants for his son?

It was during that time that I asked myself, *What's in a name?* Pondering the question brought to mind how biblical patriarchs would always name their children with a purpose. Their names would reflect their character and/or destiny. It was meant as a constant reminder of what their mission, life, and, on occasion, even what their nature would be like. It was not just about having a name that sounded nice. Knowing that I felt like I was contributing to the legacy of holy men, I followed suit.

There is much we can tell by a name. God would often customize a name for Himself intended as a reminder to the people of His ever-present provision. Many times in scripture, God presented Himself in a certain light that revealed how He wanted to be perceived, a name indicative of His character toward His people in order to meet their need. I know what you might be thinking. Right about now, you might be anticipating a typical list of all the Old Testament names of God, such as Jehovah-Jireh (the Lord our provider), or Jehovah-Tsidkenu (the Lord our righteousness), or even Jehovah-Rapha (the Lord who heals). Well, there's your list.

Those are fascinating names, for sure. As much as all those names had tremendous impact on Jewish theology and culture, that is not really going to be the focus of our study here. Our attention will be elsewhere. While the different names of God are indeed important for understanding God's character, I prefer a different route by concentrating on the concept of *The Name* in order to better understand *His nature*. You see, in human terms, when we speak a particular name, it evokes an image into our minds of whoever it is that we assigned that name. So, if I were to say the name "Albert Einstein" aloud to you, you will probably find the following picture floating somewhere in your head.

However, when it comes to the God of Israel, they wouldn't have had any image pop up in their mind. The different names of God described the roles He played when He interacted with His people, but these never would

Albert Einstein
(1879-1955)

evoke an image in their mind because their theology was adamantly clear: God has no body! The God of Israel was nothing like the gods of the neighboring nations. The counterfeit gods of those nations had set up idols in order to localize their deity. In the gentile or pagan world, they would pay homage to their gods by worshipping images made of wood and stone.

Israel, however, had no such proclivity. They did not have any frame of reference from which they could produce an image. Of course, that was the plan all along. God made it that way by design. Every name He gave of Himself communicated the idea that He could not and would not be contained in an object made by men's hands. It was intended to distinguish Himself from all the other gods, so-called. His invisible nature is what demonstrated His superiority to those other gods, since He was not limited to matter, time, or space.

As I have mentioned before, keep in mind that we are going to focus on God's nature, not necessarily His character. That will come later. For now, take a look at the following verses referencing God's nature, and let's see where we end up:

> And the LORD said to Moses, "Thus you shall say to the people of Israel: 'You have seen for yourselves that I have talked with you from heaven. You shall not make gods of silver to be with me, nor shall you make for yourselves gods of gold. An altar of earth you shall make for me and sacrifice on it your burnt offerings and your peace offerings, your sheep and your oxen. In every place where I cause my name to be remembered I will come to you and bless you.' "
> (Exodus 20:22-24 ESV)

It is pretty clear that the revelation Israel received of God meant that making any image was understood to be an affront to the true God, demeaning His superior nature by making Him comparable to the idol gods of other nations. Israel did not just worship any god. Israel worshipped THE God, the only true, living, and eternal God. The nation of Israel was the only one with the knowledge of the true God. By the time they arrived in the Promised Land after the exodus, Israel's God had garnered a reputation among the surrounding nations. While Israel wandered in the desert, the fear of Him had spread abroad with stories of what God did in Egypt and the other nations Israel encountered along the way. The God of Israel was not to be trifled with because He is not like those "other gods." He is greater, superior, and higher than all of them.

No Competition Here

The gods of those nations also had names, like Baal, Ashtoreth, or Dagon (among others) with their corresponding idols. But when it came to the God of Israel, His name was different. In ancient Semitic culture, to even speak the name of a deity was akin to calling on them. God understood this and gave command to the Israelites to not even mention the name of other gods saying, *"Pay attention to all that I have said to you, and make no mention of the names of other gods, nor let it be heard on your lips"* (Exodus 23:13 ESV).

To the Israelites, the name of God meant much more than just simply saying LORD, or the Hebrew YHWH (supposedly pronounced Yah-Weh). Interestingly, even the Hebrew spelling of God's spoken name YHWH conveyed the reality of His invisible nature. It has been proposed by some that the Tetragrammaton, the four letters YHWH that spelled out God's name, is composed of only consonants with no vowels. Since the Name of God is considered too holy to be spoken aloud, then it would only come out as a faint whisper. Remember that to say the name of a deity in Semitic culture was the same as calling on that deity. But with the LORD, that was not just a mere cultural nuance. Israel connected God's Name with God's very presence. In other words, the Name of God is equated with the Presence and

Person of God. It may sound strange to us in the West, but to the Hebraic mind, this was part of the template they understood of God's nature.

Today, the Orthodox Jewish community refuses to speak the name YHWH because it is considered too Holy to be uttered by sinful men. Therefore, they refer to Him as HaShem, which literally means "the Name." From this logic, you would conclude that the Name of God is God Himself. Indeed, that is the whole point. This brings us to a theological concept known as Name Theology theory. According to Dr. Michael Heiser:

> "Biblical writers often refer to Yahweh, the God of Israel, as 'the Name,' a usage that contemporary conservative Jews practice today—referring to God's special divine name (YHWH, 'Yahweh') without using it. 'YHWH,' however, occurs in the Old Testament nearly 7,000 times, so the biblical writers did not use ha-Shem to avoid using the divine name; rather, it is a supplementary way to refer to Yahweh." [32]

I have taken the liberty at this juncture to list some biblical verses in support of this concept:

> *"Then to the place that the LORD your God will choose, <u>to make his name dwell there</u>, there you shall bring all that I command you: your burnt offerings and your sacrifices, your tithes and the contribution that you present, and all your finest vow offerings that you vow to the LORD." (Deuteronomy 12:11 ESV emphasis added)*

> *"And ministers <u>in the Name of the LORD his God</u>, like all his fellow Levites who stand to minister there <u>before the LORD</u> ..." (Deuteronomy 18:7 ESV emphasis added)*

> *"To the choirmaster. A Psalm of David. May the LORD answer you in the day of trouble! <u>May the Name of the God of Jacob protect you</u>!" (Psalm 20:1 ESV emphasis added)*

> *"Behold, <u>the Name of the LORD comes from afar, burning with his anger,</u> and in thick rising smoke; his lips are full of fury, and his tongue is like a devouring fire." (Isaiah 30:27 ESV emphasis added)*

---

[32] Michael S. Heiser, "The Name Theology of the Old Testament," in *Faithlife Study Bible* (Bellingham, WA: Lexham Press, 2012, 2016).

The New Testament uses this same pattern of associating the Name with the Presence of God. Ironically, it is Jesus who does the talking:

"And now, Father, glorify me <u>in your own presence</u> with the glory that I had with you before the world existed. <u>I have manifested your name</u> to the people whom you gave me out of the world. Yours they were, and you gave them to me, and they have kept your word." (John 17:5-6 ESV) [emphasis added].

"While I was with them, I kept them in your Name, which you have given me. I have guarded them, and not one of them has been lost except the son of destruction, that the Scripture might be fulfilled. ... I made known to them your Name, and I will continue to make it known, that the love with which you have loved me may be in them, and I in them." (John 17:6, 12, 26 ESV)

The words of Christ are especially revealing. When we read it, certain questions might begin to formulate in our minds, but we should not get ahead of ourselves. Jesus asks the Father to glorify Him with His own self, that is to say, His own presence. Then Jesus proceeds to declare how He manifested the Father's "Name" to the disciples. This is where we should be asking ourselves the obvious questions, "In the gospels, when is it ever recorded that Jesus declared 'YHWH' to His disciples?" Or you might ask, "Since the disciples were all Jewish, did they not already know God's name was YHWH by way of the Old Testament?"

By answering these questions, we can clearly see, if we just give it some thought, that it makes little to no sense to assume Jesus referred to YHWH. Perhaps the more pertinent question we should ask is, "Did Jesus think 'The Name' was synonymous with the Father's presence?" The answer, "Yes, … absolutely!" Living in the first century, the disciples would have already known that God's name was Yahweh.[33]

---

[33] Michael S. Heiser, *"The Name Theology of the Old Testament,"* in *Faithlife Study Bible* (Bellingham, WA: Lexham Press, 2012, 2016).

CHAPTER 13
The Name

We maintain in the forefront of our minds, since God is INVISIBLE, the concept that God's Name takes on a completely different dimension by virtue of His unseen nature. The problem crops up when we become so hung up on our dogmatism that we fail to capture the multitude of gems in the treasure chest of scripture. There is such a wealth of information, but we become blinded to it because of our presuppositions, assumptions, traditions, and biases.

If we generalize a passage when we read it, our perceptions become cluttered, making it almost impossible to see what the scriptures actually give us in the specifics. This is true of all passages in the Old and New Testaments alike. This is particularly true of prophecy, and especially true of Messianic prophecy. Since we are on this train of thought, let's take a look at the prophet's take on the coming Messiah and see if we can discover other hidden treasures concerning The Name. Isaiah said:

> "For to us a child is born, to us a son is given; and the government shall be upon his shoulder, and his name shall be called Wonderful Counselor, Mighty God, Everlasting Father, Prince of Peace." (Isaiah 9:6 ESV)

Isaiah 9:6 is one of those verses that can bring some confusion. It is often used by traditional Christians to point out Jesus' divinity, primarily because of the reference to "Mighty God" (El-Gibbor) within the verse. Ironically, this is also a key verse used by non-Trinitarian and Oneness-Doctrine groups to justify claiming that Jesus is the Father, namely because of the reference to "Everlasting Father" within the same verse. But let's try reading it again with different eyes.

The prophet did not actually say that Jesus would be called "Everlasting Father" or "Mighty God," did he? In fact, the child in question is not called anything in that passage! By simply looking at what the text *actually* says, and applying just a little bit of scrutiny, what we actually read is *"... and his Name shall be called ..."* all those things. Not *Him*, but *His Name* is called "Mighty God." *His Name* is called "Everlasting Father" (other translations might render it, "the Father of Eternity"). If you have never noticed this little gem before, it should provoke you to beg the question, why? I am sure the answers you come up with will be enough to keep you preoccupied for a while.

Still, for the time being, we need to address this issue if we are to maintain a coherent perspective of God's nature. It isn't normal to say, "So and so's name is called ..." The normal way of saying it would be, "So and so is called ..." or "He is called ..." That is because the person is the object of the name. But when you say, "His Name shall be called ..." then it implies that his Name is the object, something independent from the person.

Though I am not a Hebrew scholar, I would bet that if Isaiah had been referring to the actual child, he would have been using poor Hebrew grammar, just like it would be in English. In truth, he used correct grammar because the object of the passage IS the Name, not the human child being born. That human child could not be called "Mighty God," nor could he be called "Everlasting Father." But His *name* certainly could.

If we go two chapters earlier, we can see a similar phraseology of this very pattern. In the fourteenth verse of the seventh chapter, the infamous prophecy of Isaiah is often ignored or overlooked in terms of details of this peculiar phraseology, *"Therefore the Lord himself shall give you a sign; Behold, a virgin shall conceive, and bear a son, and shall call his name*

Immanuel" (Isaiah 7:14 KJV). The interpretation of this name is given to us in the New Testament to be *"God with us."* This is a prophecy of the Messiah's virgin birth. The often overlooked major detail of this passage is that it does *not* say *the Messiah* will be called *Immanuel*.

Again, the details matter. We know Messiah's name is actually *Jesus*, not *Immanuel*. But the name *Immanuel* itself has a meaning, and it is accurately given to us in the New Testament:

> *"But while he thought on these things, behold, the angel of the Lord appeared unto him in a dream, saying, Joseph, thou son of David, fear not to take unto thee Mary thy wife: for that which is conceived in her is of the Holy Ghost. And she shall bring forth a son, and thou shalt call his name JESUS: for he shall save his people from their sins. Now all this was done, that it might be fulfilled which was spoken of the Lord by the prophet, saying, Behold, a virgin shall be with child, and shall bring forth a son, and they shall call his name Emmanuel, which being interpreted is, God with us."* (Matthew 1:20-23)

What makes this passage even more illustrating is the fact that two names are mentioned in Matthew's gospel. The name "Jesus" is attributed directly to the Messiah because of the salvation He was to attain for us, which is why His *name* was called *Jesus*. The name "Jesus" means *savior*. It uses this phraseology primarily because it is referencing His mission. This act was done with the express intent of fulfilling Isaiah's prophecy where His *name* would be called *Immanuel*. When it comes to Jesus' own name, it uses this phraseology to highlight His purpose to save. The phraseology used in Isaiah is incidental to His identity and the implication of the life He is to live. In both contexts, the use of this phrase is functional in nature, even if it doesn't seem clear at first glance.

The point made in these passages is that the phraseology of *"shall call his name"* is functional in that the details point to something other than the assumed object. If you think I'm stretching, you may find the following passage far more compelling. We are about to go deeper into the rabbit hole, so keep your eyes open by taking another close look at the following scripture:

> *"And I saw heaven opened, and behold a white horse; and he that sat upon him was called Faithful and True, and in righteousness he doth judge and make war. His eyes were as a flame of fire, and on his head were many crowns; and he had a name written, that no man knew, but he himself. And he was clothed with a vesture dipped in blood: and his name is called The Word of God."* (Revelation 19:11-13 KJV)

If you have been keeping up, then you may have already noticed it. In verse 11, he refers directly to Christ, the man himself, as *Faithful and True*. But when you get to verse 13, it is not *Christ* who is being referenced as *The Word of God*. Rather, it is *His Name* that is called *The Word of God*. Read it for yourself and think about it for a few moments. The entire passage depicts Christ as a man, riding on a horse, coming to "tread the winepress ... of God's wrath." The author is careful to distinguish between the humanity of Christ who is a man, and His Name, which is called *The Word*, who is God. The mystery of Jesus' own divinity is almost always revealed in this way.

ONE LAST THOUGHT

After His resurrection and shortly before His ascension, the Lord Jesus gave His disciples what is famously known as The Great Commission. This event is recorded in the gospel of Matthew:

> *"Go therefore and make disciples of all nations, baptizing them in the name of the Father and of the Son and of the Holy Spirit ..."* (Matthew 28:19 ESV)

Jesus' commission was for them to baptize *"in the Name of the Father and of the Son and of the Holy Spirit."* Baptism is intended to be understood as a declaration to the world and the powers that be that you have changed sides. When Jesus was baptized and coming up from the water, the Father spoke out of heaven, *"This is my beloved Son, in whom I am well pleased"* (Matthew 3:17; 17:5). Jesus' baptism was witnessed by the Father at the moment it happened. This was testified by the voice of the Father and confirmed by the presence of His Spirit in the form of a dove.

Now fast forward to the end of the gospel account, and you come to Jesus' command for us to baptize. When He says to baptize in the Name of the Father and of the Son and of the Holy Ghost, He is not thinking about a formula. To be baptized in His Name is to be immersed in His Presence. It is a play on words used to legitimize the act. Not only are you changing sides, but you are pledging your loyalty to the One who is present with you as a witness.

The disciples took to heart Jesus' command. Fast forward again to the book of Acts. When we see them again in Acts Chapter 2, they were baptized in the Holy Spirit and receiving a fresh dose of the Holy Presence of God. Let's read what happened after Peter addresses the crowd:

"Now when they heard this, they were pricked in their heart, and said unto Peter and to the rest of the apostles, Men [and] brethren, what shall we do? Then Peter said unto them, Repent, and be baptized every one of you in the Name of Jesus Christ for the remission of sins, and ye shall receive the gift of the Holy Ghost. For the promise is unto you, and to your children, and to all that are afar off, even as many as the Lord our God shall call." (Acts 2:37-39 KJV)

The question you might ask is why the change? Why does Peter say, *"in the Name of Jesus Christ"* instead of *"in the Name of the Father and of the Son and of the Ghost"*? Again, they are not trying to follow a formula. Think of it this way. They are keenly aware that they were plunged into the Presence by the Spirit of God that manifested to them in the form of cloven tongues of fire on the Day of Pentecost, also called the Feast of Weeks. They were there in direct obedience to Jesus' instructions. He told them they would receive the promise of the Father, which is the permanently abiding Presence of God upon them. When Peter says, "Be baptized in the Name of Jesus Christ," he is not thinking, *I must say the name 'JESUS.'* He is referring to the Presence of God that resides in Jesus Christ, the Name.

Finally, let's look at one more passage that connects the idea of God's Presence in Christ. Since it speaks for itself, I will close with it here:

"For though I be absent in the flesh, yet am I with you in the spirit, joying and beholding your order, and the stedfastness of your faith in Christ. As ye have therefore received Christ Jesus the Lord, so walk ye in him: Rooted and built up in him, and stablished in the faith, as ye have been taught, abounding therein with thanksgiving. Beware lest any man spoil you through philosophy and vain deceit, after the tradition of men, after the rudiments of the world, and not after Christ. <u>For in him dwelleth all the fulness of the Godhead bodily.</u> And ye are complete in him, which is the head of all principality and power: In whom also ye are circumcised with the circumcision made without hands, in putting off the body of the sins of the flesh by the circumcision of Christ: Buried with him in baptism, wherein also ye are risen with him through the faith of the operation of God, who hath raised him from the dead." (Colossians 2:5-12 KJV) [emphasis added]

CHAPTER 14
The Divine Profile

We all have our favorite movies and TV shows. If you are anything like me, *Lord of the Rings*, *Chronicles of Narnia*, and *Ben Hur* (the Charlton Heston version, of course) come to mind as my personal all-time favorites. Spiritually based movies can be particularly impactful on how we perceive spiritual matters. So much of our world and culture is being influenced by entertainment, and I dare say that through this medium, much of our theological positions may have been hijacked to a considerable degree. I will elaborate to illustrate my point.

In the year 2000, the movie *Hollow Man* hit theaters, doing relatively well at the box office. It is a typical horror flick that tells the story of a team of scientists led by Sebastian Caine (played by Kevin Bacon) doing research in an effort to achieve human invisibility. As the story goes, things take a dark turn when Sebastian decides to become a human test subject. The experiment is purportedly successful much to the team's surprise. Against all odds they finally achieve human invisibility!

However, there is one major drawback. The problem that gives rise to the plot is they did not plan ahead to figure out how to turn him back to normal again if and when they succeeded. The plot thickens. Sebastian is unable to sleep because he sees through his eyelids and becomes increasingly restless. They resolve to paint his transparent body with a rubber latex concoction in order for him to have some semblance of normalcy. Over time, he begins to lose hope that he will ever be normal again. He eventually succumbs to madness, resulting in a rampage of rape, murder, and mayhem. Like I said, typical horror.

You may not have realized it, but you may have unwittingly accepted the undergirding assumption for the movie. The plot presupposes that the character who is made invisible exists in some *substance*, hence the painting of his body. In other words, even though his body is not seen, it is still assumed that the invisibility just means he is a see-through or transparent kind of person. That is at the heart of the problem. When we say God is invisible, we tend to think of Him to be more like the antagonist of the movie. We assume God has a kind of "hollow man" type of substance complete with all the human, yet unseen, features to help us "see" the Almighty in our mind's eye. But, in truth, God is nothing like that at all. He does not have a human looking body floating around somewhere as the essence of His eternal being and self-existence.[34] It simply doesn't exist. He is completely and utterly *without* substance to His being.

Unlike the *Hollow Man*, God does not have a body that takes up space or is localized in some way, even though we can't see Him. Many times, we do not think through the reality of what God is truly like and often fail to differentiate Him from the creation itself on the most fundamental level. By being overly committed to the traditional model, we conjure up images in our minds whenever we think of God in these terms without realizing it. If you were to type "Trinity" in the search section of any browser, you will come up with all kinds of artistic renditions. On the next page are a few images that illustrate what I mean.

Look at these images and consider what these paintings are communicating to us. They depict two *men* sitting on *something*, with a *bird* flying

---

[34] The idea of God existing as a human, or with human features as the very essence of His being is in agreement with Mormon beliefs about God, and is fundamentally not Christian.

around between them, typically with light either surrounding from above it or beaming directly from it. That image is not what we actually believe, but it is the image most of us see in our minds. Anyone looking at these pictures would conclude that they represent the Trinity of Christian doctrine. The artists simply painted onto canvas the very images that we all think.

Jesus is evidently on the left by virtue of the cross he bears in some images or with visible scars. On the right is the "Old Man" we automatically assume to be the Father, which by the way, is where we also get our cultural idiom, "The Old Man in the Sky." The Holy Spirit is usually represented by the white dove shining with brilliance in the background referencing the manifestation of the Spirit at the baptism of Christ. It is no wonder why the Jewish community rejects the doctrine of the Trinity as heretical and pagan. Two human-looking men and a bird; that is what the Trinity "looks like" to them. Three created things being viewed as God. Now *that* certainly *IS* pagan!

However, since God has no physicality or form, we must take into account what that implies, and what it means for us who are created in His image and after His likeness. If He doesn't take up space like a created being, that also means He doesn't get up and move around from place to place. God is by Himself the boundary for all things created. In other words, God doesn't occupy a chair in a room in a building as though He took up residence in some heavenly palace.

That imagery is what the ancient Babylonians, Assyrians, Greeks, and Romans held of their own pantheon of so-called gods. The biblical depiction of Jesus sitting at the right hand of the Father is conceptual in nature, not a physical one like those of pagan idols. The right hand or arm of the Father is always an association with God's power and authority; it is not the physical attribute of a right arm or hand like that of a human. Jesus clearly alluded to the power of God when he said, *"Hereafter shall the Son of man sit on the <u>right hand of the power</u> of God"* (Luke 22:69 KJV).

All of creation is the realm wherein the pantheon of gods from other nations. They all have a finite presence within the realm of their existence. They live in and are subject to the universe in which they reside, whether physical or spiritual for that matter. These so-called deities are limited to the conditions of their environments. However, when it comes to Yahweh, the God of Israel, all of creation, including these so-called gods, have their existence within Him, just as we do. Absolutely everything, all of space, time, matter, created things of every sort, whether spiritual or otherwise, or anything else that has ever been made has always had its existence within the true God.

> *"God that made the world and all things therein, seeing that he is Lord of heaven and earth, dwelleth not in temples made with hands; Neither is worshipped with men's hands, as though he needed any thing, seeing he giveth to all life, and breath, and all things; And hath made of one blood all nations of men for to dwell on all the face of the earth, and hath determined the times before appointed, and the bounds of their habitation; That they should seek the Lord, if haply they might feel after him, and find him, though he be not far from every one of us: For in him we live, and move, and have our being; as certain also of your own poets have said, For we are also his offspring."* (Acts 17:24-28 KJV)

All of reality finds source from Him and by Him. God is singularly separate from His creation in that even though it all came into existence by His sovereign will, He is not made, nor does He consist of any of those things that are created. All reality from any dimension, every bit of it, is found in Him alone. To imply that there is some form of existence outside of God is to imply that there is something that transcends Him. This is impossible because He alone is God, and it is by Him that all things consist (Colossians 1:17 KJV). This brings me to an important point. Traditional language of the Trinity describing God as having "one substance" is actually foreign to the biblical text. By using words like "substance," we are actually applying a "Hollow Man" concept onto the God of the Bible without even realizing it. Substance is a quality of *creation*, not of the Creator Himself. It simply is not a part of the Divine profile.

He is not "sitting" on a chair or a throne in a room somewhere where he simply stands up and walks around as though He is occupying some space. Those are human characteristics we apply to God. In reality, God has no such boundaries. There is no such thing as space outside of God in which He can move around. There is no such place. Everything that exists, even space, matter, time, angelic beings (good or evil), the universe, or heaven itself, all of it exists only within Himself. Consider the implications of the following verse:

> *"Thus saith the LORD, The heaven is my throne, and the earth is my footstool: where is the house that ye build unto me? and where is the place of my rest? For all those things hath mine hand made, and all those things have been, saith the LORD: but to this man will I look, even to him that is poor and of a contrite spirit, and trembleth at my word."* (Isaiah 66:1-2 KJV)

The place we call Heaven is what God refers to as His throne, and the earth we live on is what He deems His footstool. Now, I don't wish to sound disrespectful or blasphemous by any stretch of the imagination, but just think about this for a moment. We don't see any toes when we look up into the sky, nor do we live in a world that smells like feet. We are not going to see massively divine buttocks above us when we get to heaven.

God does not have a conventional body like we do. These concepts about God are functional in nature, and are not associated with any real physical attribute. Heaven is called His Throne because it is the place from which He reigns supreme, and the earth is the place where He chooses to establish His peace. This passage in Isaiah reveals how God relates to His physical creation. He gives to us certain facets of His being in the context of function so that we can recognize Him in the physical universe.

When it comes down to it, God wants us to know Him as He is. He desires for us to draw near to Him, and along the way, he leaves clues for us to follow until we behold that part of Him that is kept secret. The Bible uses specific language to convey those clues to us in a coherent way. Since God is unknowable in His true nature, He casts a visualization of Himself by referring to human features, helping us grasp things about Himself that have no substance in and of themselves in the creative sense. We are being used as models to illustrate His invisible qualities. When He does this, He is revealing His Presence in a unique way. If God is everywhere at the same time, then it is obvious that most of the time either we are not aware of Him, or at the very least, we don't live like He is even there. God is always present. Look at the following Psalm:

> "Such knowledge is too wonderful for me; it is high; I cannot attain it. Where shall I go from your Spirit? Or where shall I flee from your presence? If I ascend to heaven, you are there! If I make my bed in Sheol, you are there! If I take the wings of the morning and dwell in the uttermost parts of the sea, even there your hand shall lead me, and your right hand shall hold me." (Psalm 139:6-10 ESV)

God is always present, whether or not we see Him or feel Him. If you were to look back at your own life, can you say without reservation that you have lived your life as though God was always there, present at every passing moment of your life? Can you say that when you were doing something questionable, did you really … I mean really … act as though God were right there watching? If we are honest, during our moments of weakness, we act more like He is an afterthought. It does not matter that you did not feel His Presence. He was still there. He was simply ignored.

Yet, he was indeed there. He may not have stopped you from committing your sin, but He was there, beholding all that you did. Generally speaking, we refrain from doing the wrong things when someone else is physically there with us. We are conscious of their presence because they can see us, and we can see them. The worst part about getting caught is the look on the face of the one we don't want to disappoint. That's why we are more careful when others are there with us. If they can see us, and we know it, then we won't do it.

The Bible tells us what God is like. God in His wisdom saw fit to provide us with impressions of His unseen reality in the Word by spotlighting certain "features" of His being that reside within Himself. In this case, I would like to highlight one particular feature, His Face. There are many items that can be gleaned from these two facets alone.

THE FACE

Look at the following verses:

"But," he said, "you cannot see my face, for man shall not see me and live." (Exodus 33:20 ESV)

"Seek the LORD and his strength, seek his face continually." (1 Chronicles 16:11)

"... when my people, over whom My Name is called, humble themselves and pray and seek my face and turn from their evil ways, then I will hear from heaven and will forgive their sin and will heal their land." (2 Chronicles 7:14 TLV)

"Seek the LORD, and his strength: seek his face evermore." (Psalm 105:4)

"I will return again to my place, until they acknowledge their guilt and seek my face, and in their distress earnestly seek me." (Hosea 5:15 ESV)

Do you see the pattern? If not, I will tell you. In every instance, His face is being correlated with His Presence, His very Person. Remember, God is not like you and me. He has no body. When physical features are attributed to God, such as His Face, what goes without saying is that the feature is understood to be invisible, and therefore of the same essence of His Person. In the case of His Face, He is communicating to us by using peculiar language to aid us in our understanding.

We need to be more like Moses who, when he fled from Egypt, he *"...endured as seeing him who is invisible"* (Hebrews 11:27). We need to abandon the kind of language that keeps us imprisoned to our traditions that have no basis in truth, so that we, too, can endure as seeing Him who is invisible. *"And he said, Thou canst not see my face: for there shall no man see me, and live."* (Exodus 33:20 KJV)

According to Exodus 33:20, no one can see His Face and survive the encounter. So when God instructed the Israelites to seek His Face, it was not an invitation to get slaughtered. It was His way of saying, *"Come to me for all your needs. I am your King forever. I am your Provider who continually cares for you. I AM."* The figure of speech is used to convey His presence and sovereignty in every circumstance.

Furthermore, when we say God is sovereign, it does not mean that He just does whatever He wants. His sovereignty is rooted in His Lordship as the King who is able to perfectly govern in spite of everything that is contrary to Him. This is going to take some unpacking, so bear with me here.

God's Face and Name are two distinct characteristics of God passed down to reveal different facets of His Presence and Nature. Both are associated with God's Person, yet each has a different application. God's FACE is what we are called to seek, and therefore it is associated with what is "seen" of Him. On the other hand, His NAME is what we are called to proclaim and is therefore associated with what is "heard" of Him. Experiencing His Presence is always accomplished by what is seen and heard.

You see, what we think about God, about His nature and character, ultimately affects how we live and what we perceive of everything, including what we read in the Bible. It directly impacts how we interpret what we read, resulting in what we believe about God. Our beliefs profoundly dictate our thoughts that tend to direct our behavior. The heart of the New Covenant is in forging a permanent bridge between God and man. The LORD is not just redeeming the human race to bridge a gap; He intends to restore all that was lost.

CHAPTER 15
The Holy Spirit of God

So far, we have mostly addressed those passages that highlight the differences between the Father and the Son. We are now shifting gears and focusing more on the role of the Holy Spirit. My approach to this or any part of our study will be to explore those passages where the Spirit of God is mentioned and to observe how the term is used in those passages. We will be able to determine a consistent theme or context that tells us how the first century writers would have understood the Holy Spirit.

As previously mentioned, the Spirit is often referred to as the third Person of the Trinity, co-eternal with the Father and the Son. We will purposefully avoid this terminology, as it is foreign to the text. Instead, we will take a look at the Old and New Testament narrative and see how the Spirit is revealed.

First Things

There is a concept (or theory) that theologians refer to called "the law of first reference," also known as "the law of first mention." It is the idea that whenever a distinctive word or phrase is used or mentioned the first time in scripture, the meaning and theme contained within its first usage is carried throughout the rest of scripture. To be clear, this is just a theory, albeit a very interesting one, especially for our discussion here. For example, the most revered portion of the Old Testament to the Jewish people is what they call the "AKEDAH." It is the portion in the *Torah* (Law of Moses) in which Abraham is tested when God instructs Abraham to offer his only son Isaac, whom he loves, as a burnt offering sacrifice to the LORD (Genesis 22).

In the story, Abraham wakes up early the following morning and takes his son and two other servants. It takes three days for them to arrive at the location designated by God. When Abraham sees the spot from far away, he then tells his servants to remain behind and takes his son to the spot, giving him the wood to carry. When they get to the specific point on the mountain, Abraham binds up Isaac, and as he is about to offer his son as a sacrifice, the Angel of the Lord stops him and shows him a ram caught in the bush. Abraham offers the ram instead of his son. Abraham then calls that place *Yahweh Yireh*, or *Jehovah Jireh*, which means "the Lord will provide."

There are many parallels between this story and that of Jesus the Messiah, more than I am willing to expound here. However, I will say that the most notable part of the story to me is that when God tells Abraham to offer his only son whom he "loves," it is also the first time we ever see the word "love" used in the Bible. *Love* is first introduced in the Holy Scriptures in the context of a father who is offering his son as a sacrifice to confirm a promise God made to Abraham.

In the same way, there appears to be a similar pattern attached to those references where the Spirit of God is mentioned. The initial use of the word Spirit (*Ruach* in Hebrew) in the Bible is found in the first two verses of the book of Genesis. It says:

"In the beginning God created the heavens and the earth. Now the earth was chaos and waste, darkness was on the surface of the deep, and the **Ruach Elohim** [Spirit of God] *was hovering upon the surface of the water."*
(Genesis 1:1-2 TLV) [emphasis added]

In this passage, we first see the Spirit (*Ruach*) in the unique setting of creation. The spirit is moving over waters, implying the Spirit of God was not only present at creation, but pivotal in the creation account. This gives some insight into the themes associated with the Spirit of God. The Spirit is said to be "moving," and it is not there by accident. The Ruach in the Hebrew language and in thought gives the impression of different euphemisms that are used throughout scripture.

One use representative of this is wind, and another is that of water. Wind is important for a number of reasons, not the least of which is that it is unseen; but that is not really the only underlying concept. It is exemplified by the fact that even though wind itself is non-visible, it produces effects that can be seen. These effects are made visible by the movement of objects affected by the wind. It is how we know that it is there. The presence of the wind is evidenced by movement (animation) and sound. The unseen characteristic of wind might go without saying, but it is the resulting action that brings attention to its existence.

"Living water" also reveals this truth in a similar manner, but with some additional insight. Beside the fact that pure water is essentially transparent, echoing the unseen nature of God, living water also refers to moving (active or animated) water, such as rivers and streams. In an agrarian culture, like that of ancient Israel, living water was commonly known as a source of life that always works to sustain life. It is water you can drink, like from rivers, streams, and even including rain. Only living water can be used for drink. Its properties promote the abundance of life and health.

However, stagnant water, or water that does not move, is understood to be "dead water." Drinking this water could make a person sick and even result in death due to a lack of filtration and stagnation. "Living water" is used as a type of the Spirit because it is the Spirit that gives life and health; it is the Spirit that makes alive and gives animation to that which does not move or is dead. The Spirit is what gives life to the dead.

This is how the Spirit of God is portrayed in the Bible, and all these themes are present throughout. Therefore, to receive the Spirit *is* to be made alive. The Holy Spirit of God is living water that is always bringing life. The Spirit of God is the breath of life in the nostrils of all living things.

At this point we should probably take a look at how these themes are consistently carried through. Take a look at the following verses:

"... *as long as my breath is still in me, the* Ruach *of God in my nostrils."*
(Job 27:3 TLV)

"The Ruach *of God has made me; the breath of* Shaddai *gives me life."*
(Job 33:4 TLV)

Since there is no such thing as a place to which God can move outside of Himself, all movement of God that occurs is therefore accomplished within Himself. Anytime the Bible mentions an event where God is said to be moving in some fashion, it is not like God has His own separate version of a universe where only He resides. No, all of creation has its existence within God's own being.

God is incorporeal, making Him beyond any created thing with a body, whether physical or spiritual. But when He chooses to produce an effect within Himself, He does so in order to help the creation to recognize or behold Him in His omnipresence. That part of Himself that moves is what the Bible refers to as the Holy Spirit. This detail cannot be overlooked. When we say that God is moving, that does not mean He is going from one location to another where he is not. God is omnipresent; which means He is everywhere all at once. He cannot move to a place where He is not because God cannot move in the conventional sense.

When we say God is moving, what we actually mean is that God is doing something of significance. However, our traditional language causes a picture to formulate in our minds that God is moving to some place from some other place. By removing the traditional language from our preconceived notions of God, we can see that He moves by His Spirit in the creation that exists within Himself. No doubt it can be a daunting subject, but understanding this one thing can eliminate so much confusion in the body of Christ.

The absolute nature of the Father is such that all existence in all dimensions throughout all time define their limits by virtue of God's unlimited stature. You can take everything that has ever been created, from eons into the past to eons into the future; all existence is finite within the infinite Creator. The Spirit of God is that part of God that draws the attention of creation to what God is doing. This is how the Spirit is always portrayed. Even Jesus Christ said as much when He said:

"But when the Comforter is come, whom I will send unto you from the Father, even the Spirit of truth, which proceedeth from the Father, he shall testify of me ..." (John 15:26)

The reason for the Spirit being in a "third person" context is because of the diminutive context of the Spirit in relation to the Father being that the Holy Spirit IS the Spirit of the Son and of the Father. There is an interesting verse where Jesus makes a correlation between Himself and the Spirit:

"And I will pray the Father, and he shall give you another Comforter, that he may abide with you forever; Even the Spirit of truth; whom the world cannot receive, because it seeth him not, neither knoweth him: but ye know him; for he dwelleth with you, and shall be in you. I will not leave you comfortless: I will come to you." (John 14:16-18)

This passage clearly demonstrates that Jesus correlates the Spirit that will come to comfort with Himself in a different form. Yet, he refers to Himself in a "third person" because the Spirit who is invisible is different from that of Christ Himself who is in the form of a man. This is not an isolated incident. There are other occasions where Jesus refers to Himself in the third person whenever He relates to the Father:

"Verily, verily, I say unto you, The hour is coming, and now is, when the dead shall hear the voice of the Son of God: and they that hear shall live. For as the Father hath life in himself; so hath he given to the Son to have life in himself; And hath given him authority to execute judgment also, because he is the Son of man. Marvel not at this: for the hour is coming, in the which all that are in the graves shall hear his voice, And shall come forth; they that have done good, unto the resurrection of life; and they that have done evil, unto the resurrection of damnation." (John 5:25-29)

> *"Jesus heard that they had cast him out; and when he had found him, he said unto him, Dost thou believe on the Son of God? He answered and said, Who is he, Lord, that I might believe on him? And Jesus said unto him, Thou hast both seen him, and it is he that talketh with thee. And he said, Lord, I believe. And he worshipped him." (John 9:35-38)*

> *"Say ye of him, whom the Father hath sanctified, and sent into the world, Thou blasphemest; because I said, I am the Son of God?" (John 10:36)*

The Spirit is placed in a similar category in relation to the Father. By using this method, the biblical writers consistently place the Father as far greater, superior, and unequaled is essence and being. Jesus Himself said as much, and we do a disservice to the text when we deny the Father His place in the hierarchy of things. The scriptures never ever place Christ, nor the Holy Spirit, on par with the Father. Neither would they want to. The Father is greatly above all and exercises supremacy over all, even the Son and the Spirit.

The role of the Holy Spirit is to bring attention to the Father *through* the Son. The Spirit never speaks of himself, while always pointing to Christ, as Christ always redirects to the Father. This is how the scriptures break it down. It is wrong to refer to the Holy Spirit as a *separate* and *distinct* person because the Spirit has both the nature of the Father, and the mind of the Son.

CHAPTER 16
Spirit Nature

From creation, the Spirit of God is conferred as God's very Presence in the context of motion and action. If we use the traditional model in our approach to understanding the Holy Spirit, we will always perceive Him as a *separate and distinct* person of the Godhead. However, if we keep in mind that the Father is unseen and that His Spirit is simply that part of His invisible essence that moves within Himself, then we no longer have the need to use traditional language to describe the Holy Spirit as a separate and distinct person. Instead of using traditional language foreign to the Bible, we ought to just stick to the language provided in scripture for us. *"God is Spirit, and those who worship Him must worship in spirit and truth"* (John 4:24 TLV).

The Spirit of God IS God Himself; the Spirit of your Heavenly Father is the same Spirit in and of Christ. This is what is known as the Holy Spirit. These are all terms used to describe this aspect of the one true God.[35] The Father does not move because there is no such thing as a place for Him to

---

[35] The following verses show the relationship within the Godhead: Matthew 10:20; Acts 20:28; Galatians 4:6; 1 Corinthians 6:17; 2 Corinthians 3:17-18; Ephesians 4:4-6.

move to. But within Him, His Spirit moves to accomplish the Father's will for the sake of the creation.

So what is a Spirit anyway? The most simple and rudimentary answer is that the spirit of a thing is the nature and mind of a thing. For example: Whenever someone is said to have a "spirit of fear," we most likely imagine some hulking demon standing over a person using intimidation tactics in order to make a person feel afraid. But that is not what a spirit of fear is really like. A spirit of fear is a spirit that is itself afraid. When a person feels the presence of a spirit of overwhelming fear, that spirit is expressing its own self through that person's emotions. That spiritual entity's true nature is being revealed in the form of the expression. It is the same thing as when Jesus confronted a woman who had a spirit of infirmity. The spirit was imposing itself on the woman, thereby oppressing her with bondage to its will in the form of an ailment. Even Jesus acknowledges that it was the adversary who had bound her all along (see Luke 13:11-17).

As Christians, we receive the Spirit of and from God, who happens to be God Himself living in us. Therefore, the Spirit of God is the nature and mind of God at work within the believer. Once a person is born again, they receive the Spirit of God, and from that point on, they take part in God's divine nature; and why not? God is interested in producing sons and daughters who speak like Him, act like Him, think like Him, and "look" like Him.

It is a common reality that children who come into the world often take on many characteristics of their parents. Likewise, when we receive the Holy Spirit, we are changed from an old carnal nature (the flesh) to a new godly nature (the Spirit), which is created after the image of God as it is revealed in Messiah.

> *"That ye put off concerning the former conversation the old man, which is corrupt according to the deceitful lusts; And be renewed in the spirit of your mind; And that ye put on the new man, which after God is created in righteousness and true holiness."* (Ephesians 4:22-24 KJV)

The Spirit is that part of God that moves, causing an action in alignment with expressing the Father's will. Anytime the Spirit does anything, something happens according to His will as revealed by His Word, drawing attention to God's nature and character. The Spirit of God works and moves to bring fallen men back to and in alignment with God's intent; and He has chosen to do this through His sons and daughters.

> *"Moreover if the Spirit of the one who raised Jesus from the dead lives in you, the one who raised Christ from the dead will also make your mortal bodies alive through his Spirit who lives in you. So then, brothers and sisters, we are under obligation, not to the flesh, to live according to the flesh (for if you live according to the flesh, you will die), but if by the Spirit you put to death the deeds of the body you will live. For all who are led by the Spirit of God are the sons of God. For you did not receive the spirit of slavery leading again to fear, but you received the Spirit of adoption, by whom we cry, 'Abba, Father.' The Spirit himself bears witness to our spirit that we are God's children."* (Romans 8:12-16 ESV)

> *"I can pray this because his divine power has bestowed on us everything necessary for life and godliness through the rich knowledge of the one who called us by his own glory and excellence. Through these things he has bestowed on us his precious and most magnificent promises, so that by means of what was promised you may become partakers of the divine nature, after escaping the worldly corruption that is produced by evil desire."* (2 Peter 1:3-4 ESV)

The Holy Spirit is simply God Himself *when He moves*. The Spirit of God is always presented in the context of motion and action. I mentioned earlier how the triune revelation of God in the New Testament is mostly revealed in a functional context. Take a quick look at the following verse and see in what context the Godhead is presented:

> *"Now there are various kinds of gifts, but the <u>same Ruach</u>. There are various kinds of service, but the <u>same Lord</u>. There are various kinds of working, but the <u>same God</u> who works all things in all people."* (1 Corinthians 12:4-6 TLV)

Take notice of how it is the *Spirit* that is associated with the gifts, not Christ, not the Father, but the Spirit. It is the Spirit that is directly linked to that which brings attention, that which makes noise, that which causes animation. The gifts are those elements that draw attention to something God is doing. The most simple way you can put it is that the Holy Spirit is that part of the Father that moves and *causes* action within Himself. The Lord, who is the Son, is the administrator who carries out the activity by the Spirit that causes it. The Father has the overall responsibility (oversight) for the operation because both the Spirit and the Son are manifestations of Himself through function so that we can understand God's work.

The role of the Holy Spirit is simply that part of God that is the initial cause of bringing everything into motion to fulfill the Father's will. There is a cause and effect paradigm within God's creation. The Spirit is that cause, while the Son is the vehicle through which the effect is caused. The Father is the one behind the entire process because both the Spirit and the Son proceeded from Himself. Therefore, the three are one. The plurality of God is implied because of God's ability to manifest Himself in any way He sees fit to fulfill His will.

The Hebrew Bible refers many times to God as "Elohim," rightly understood as God in plurality. This Hebrew term is often used to justify Old Testament proof texts of Trinitarian doctrinal assertions. However, it is not used solely referring to God alone. In fact, Elohim refers to any being residing or operating within the spiritual realm. Therefore, if we are honest, we cannot infer the Trinity because of a single term. Since the Trinity is never mentioned in either Testaments, we must come to recognize there is no transition to a Trinitarian model during what is known as the intertestamental period (the time between the Old and the New Testaments).

What the Jews believed about the nature of God (Elohim) in the Old Testament is what was carried over into the New Testament era. Jesus did not appear onto the world scene teaching a different version of God, with a new revelation of the Trinity. If you read the New Testament with these assumptions, then you won't have any choice but to see it through that paradigm, even when the scriptures never present it that way. It is always the same God who reveals Himself as the great "I AM." When it comes to the Holy Spirit, we treat it like He has been hiding His true identity, and then without warning, He comes out the separate and distinct third person of the Godhead in the New Testament.

When Jesus refers to the Holy Spirit, He is not using a Trinitarian model, nor is He drawing from a foreign interpretation of God. The core of His mindset and approach is still Jewish. The Hebraic nature of His comments become veiled if we read it with the glasses of our tradition. Again, just take off the glasses for a moment, and take a look at what was said in plain context, this time through the eyes of New Testament Hebrews who only had the Old Testament as a reference for the nature of God. We read:

> *"If you love me, you will keep my commandments. And I will ask the Father, and he will give you another Helper, to be with you forever, even the Spirit of truth, whom the world cannot receive, because it neither sees him nor knows him. You know him, for he dwells with you and will be in you. "I will not leave you as orphans; I will come to you. Yet a little while and the world will see me no more, but you will see me. Because I live, you also will live. In that day you will know that I am in the Father, and you in me, and I in you."*
> (John 14:15-20 ESV)

What may not appear obvious to you is that I have deliberately selected these verses, not just to draw your attention to what they say, but also to what they don't say. You see, before and after this part of the narrative, Jesus explains how He is in the Father, and the Father is in Him. On the surface it would seem that Jesus is making a case to His disciples for being God, and that when the Holy Spirit comes He will reveal that truth. But that is not the context of the passage.

Jesus calls the Holy Spirit the "Helper" and "revealer of Truth" because that is what the Spirit *does*. If you read the very next verse, Jesus says, *"In that day you will know that I am in my Father, and you in me, and I in you"* (John 14:20 ESV). Jesus is making the point that the Spirit is the catalyst bringing us into the same kind of relationship with the Father that Jesus has with the Father. If Jesus were making a case for His deity in this passage, then that would mean that He would imply the pagan idea that we could become gods ourselves. What Jesus is actually saying is that, by the Spirit, we would become sons and daughters of God, just as He is, and with all the benefits that come with that relationship.

Therefore when Jesus says that the Spirit *"dwells with you and will be in you,"* He is pointing out that a transition will take place. In the entire chapter, Jesus drives the point that our relationship to God as His own children will be established as permanent because we can then be *joined* to Him, and *be with* Him forever in the Father's house. Until that day comes, Jesus anticipates us being about our Father's business by doing the same kinds of works that He did while on earth. The role we play assists the world to recognize that we too are in Him, and He is in us just like the Father and the Messiah. Instead of looking at the Holy Spirit as a separate distinct person of the Godhead, it would behoove us to see the Spirit as that part of God acting as the catalyst to move us into proper relationship with the Father.

Jesus goes out of His way to tell us that the Holy Spirit is the Spirit of Truth *unseen* by the world. He also says that the Spirit was *with* them and was going to be *in* them. Up until that point, they did not have the ability to do certain things by their own volition. They were tasked by Messiah to do things as those who were delegated authority for a season, but with the giving of the Spirit, the authority becomes inherent as those who are born again as into a great household.

Since the Spirit of Truth is unseen, then that should also tell you something about the Spirit. He is, in fact, God. Yet, the Holy Ghost does not play the role of the Father because He is causing something to happen. The Spirit is referred to in this way because the function of the Spirit is to transition us into a deeper and more intimate relationship with the Father. Remember, The Father is the One with no boundary, in whom everything exists and consists, and therefore does not move.

So Holy Spirit is the Father's own Spirit that moves to bring animation, giving life to created things. He is the same Spirit that resides within the Son of God, Who *is* a man and *has* a human body. Since the Father is in the Son, and the Son is in the Father, that makes the Spirit the binding factor in the entire equation. The Holy Spirit makes that connection possible between mankind and the Father, thereby confirming our status as sons and daughters.

"For ye have not received the spirit of bondage again to fear; but ye have received the Spirit of adoption, whereby we cry, Abba, Father." (Romans 8:15)

"And because ye are sons, God hath sent forth the Spirit of his Son into your hearts, crying, Abba, Father." (Galatians 4:6)

We cannot live out our purpose, nor fulfill our destiny without the Holy Spirit active in our lives. The end game is that we grow up *into* Jesus ... it is not just to be *like* Him. We are called the "body of Christ" for a reason. We are extensions of Messiah's own person. If we are hated by the world, it is because they hated Him first. If the world touches us, they are touching Him. If they persecute us, they are persecuting Him. This is the case because His Spirit, the Spirit of Truth, is the Father's Spirit that binds us to Him in this unique way. Furthermore, the Lord Himself is that self-same Spirit, and those that are united with Him are one Spirit with Him!

We have been given the Spirit of His Son because the Father has declared us to be His children. That reality comes with many perks, not the least of which are those things that belong to Christ. Unfortunately, more often than not, Christians tend to act as slaves more than they are like sons and daughters of God. It is not about rules for us because we have been born again of the Spirit, and we received a new nature by the Spirit that is now supposed to govern how we are to behave, think, and speak. Jesus gave us the shoes to walk in despite our failures or our propensity to foul up at every turn. You may not realize it yet, but what you have in Christ is so much better than you think!

CHAPTER 17
Function of The Spirit

In an earlier chapter, we briefly touched on the role of the Holy Spirit within the Godhead, and we saw the functional nature of the Spirit as that part of God that moves and gives life. This will play an important part in unraveling our own part to play, including our development in this story. For believers, the Holy Spirit plays an integral role in revealing God's nature, and this is central to our purpose as Christians. When the Spirit of God moves, it is always with a special purpose with humanity's best interests in mind: the revealing of the Most High.

As human beings, we are uniquely fashioned by our Creator to manifest Him. Everything God has created and made speaks to us of God's attributes. However, more than everything else in the created order, we are the ones with the most at stake. We carry something of infinite value as human beings. As those created in the image of God, we are given the extraordinary ability to project God to His creation.

As imaging agents, we display His likeness wherever we go, to everyone and everything that has eyes to see and ears to hear. His Spirit lives within the believer to accentuate God's invisible attributes with the express intent of revealing His unseen characteristics through us. For this reason alone, we are the crown of His creation. This knowledge comes with many advantages.

Our bodies are made entirely to function as those creations particularly designed to reflect God's invisible qualities. For that to happen, we need to look at how those qualities are most efficiently displayed through us. There are certain points of interest we must look at in regards to the Spirit and the role the Spirit plays within the believer.

> *"For it is God who works in you, both to will and to work for his good pleasure."* (Philippians 2:13 ESV)

God is at work within the believer to make Himself known to the rest of the world. Yet, it requires our cooperation for the reality of His presence to be made visible. This cooperation is in fact a prerequisite. As Christians, you and I are called to reveal the Unseen One. We are intentionally created by Him as continuous active manifestations of His Person. Our understanding of the Spirit's activity through us enables the believer to be the vessels of honor we were intended to be.

However, when sin entered the world through Adam's transgression, the image of God in man became marred. The crown became tarnished, as it were. Suddenly, those vessels that were created for displaying His invisible qualities turned into vessels of dishonor by the sin that infected them. As a result, the entire creation became alienated from its Creator. With the rest of creation having lost the ability to see Him clearly, this only served to compound the problem. But God had a plan that would restore all that was lost in paradise. With the coming of the Son of God, His Kingdom would be reintroduced, and all those who thereafter believed in Him would become heirs to His Kingdom.

As Christian believers, we received the Holy Spirit of God to begin the process of rehabilitating us, to remake us into the "habitation of God" for His special purposes. Our contribution to this whole plan is our willingness to surrender to what God has prepared for us. There are certain items unique to the New Testament narrative that we must explore. Each one of these terms addresses a particular application of the Spirit that believers must appropriate to themselves if they are to truly understand the role and function of the Holy Spirit in the believer's life.

It is important for us to understand what it means to live in the Spirit, to be led of the Spirit, walk in the Spirit, and to be filled with the Spirit. Each one of these terms has a specific function that reveals a mystery of God within the believer. I am not referring to demonstrations of power necessarily, but I am referring to laying the foundation of character that is needed for us to be able to walk in that power. One way we become imaging agents is specifically by applying certain character traits. I will elaborate.

There are two main passages that describe the specifics that led to the fall of the adversary from heaven.

> "Son of man, raise a lamentation over the king of Tyre, and say to him, Thus says the Lord GOD: 'You were the signet of perfection, full of wisdom and perfect in beauty. You were in Eden, the garden of God; every precious stone was your covering, sardius, topaz, and diamond, beryl, onyx, and jasper, sapphire, emerald, and carbuncle; and crafted in gold were your settings and your engravings. On the day that you were created they were prepared. ... Your heart was proud because of your beauty; you corrupted your wisdom for the sake of your splendor. I cast you to the ground; I exposed you before kings, to feast their eyes on you." (Ezekiel 28:12-13, 17 ESV)

> "For thou hast said in thine heart, I will ascend into heaven, I will exalt my throne above the stars of God: I will sit also upon the mount of the congregation, in the sides of the north: I will ascend above the heights of the clouds; I will be like the most High." (Isaiah 14:13-14)

The main reason behind the fall of the adversary in these passages is aptly attributed to his pride. Why? Precisely because he was made perfectly beautiful, having coverings made of precious stones that could reflect light from the entire spectrum. He was purposefully built to reflect the light of God's glory to the creation. But instead of directing worship to God, he began to desire the worship for Himself. All of the attention He received became misplaced as his pride grew in his heart. In his pride, he demanded the attention to Himself and desired worship. His pride then became rooted in the one visual aspect of his being: his beauty. It was like a magnet that pulled the eyes of every living being toward him. The more they looked at him, the more he wanted their attention. As a result, he rebelled and fell from his lofty position. His nature became warped, and his character corrupted. Nothing like it had ever been seen before.

Now let us consider ourselves. What does the New Testament say about those who are proud? *"... God opposes the proud but gives grace to the humble"* (1 Peter 5:5b ESV). Think about God's warning here. Our adversary wanted to bring attention to himself by giving in to his pride, thereby becoming distorted within himself. However, God has a different plan for us, a solution for humankind made in His image.

His desire for us is the exact opposite of pride. He desires for us to be humble. God does not want us to be self-absorbed, seeking to draw attention to ourselves. He desires for us to be humble, to seek to remain out of the limelight that draws attention. Essentially, He wants us to be invisible. By exercising humility, we are emulating the invisible nature of God within the visible world. We are literally imaging Him within the creation!

Consider how humble God is. Though being invisible makes Him infinitely superior to everything created, His desire is for us to know Him because of His love for us. To make some part of Himself visible for our sakes means He has to condescend to us for the sake of the relationship. It is similar to a parent stooping down to their child's level. If the child is a newborn baby, he brings it up to look into its eyes. Even though the infant understands nothing in this stage of its development, the parent still loves to blow coos and make other "baby" kinds of sounds to connect with the child. The parents have to bring themselves low for the sake of the relationship. What's fascinating is that it's neither a burden nor an offense to the parent. It is an experience of joy! It's just the way love is.

God is a personal Being. He is not an impersonal force. His very person, His character and nature, are evidenced in the standards He lays out for us because every one of His commandments directly reflects His own character and nature. When God tells us not to lie, it is not because He just wants to prevent us from doing evil. It is because He is Truth. When He says, "You shall not murder," it is because He is Life and the Source of it. His Spirit is the essence of life itself. *"For in him we live and move and have our being ..."* (Acts 17:28a ESV).

While I intend to emphasize the function of the Spirit, I do not believe it is appropriate to refer to the Holy Spirit as simply "the creative force of God" because the Holy Spirit is indeed God Himself. However, referring to the Holy Spirit as a separate, distinct Person is equally erroneous. Instead, we ought to simply accept the Holy Spirit as God "... *who works in you, both to will and to work for his good pleasure"* (Philippians 2:13b ESV).

That being said, I want to point out one significant detail of the New Testament narrative with a question that no one bothers to ask, or hardly ever thinks important enough to bring up. Why is the Spirit of God mostly referred to as the "Holy" Spirit in the New Testament, while in the Old Testament it is only mentioned as a characteristic of God, and that only about three times? This is an important question and deserves consideration.

As I have mentioned before, the titles of Father, Son, and Holy Spirit are more a matter of function for the sake of relationship. When we look at the New Testament, the title of the Holy Spirit is unique to the relationship between the believer and God as our Father. I'll suggest that the key to understanding the reason for this rests in the first word of the title: Holy. Holiness is a characteristic of God that separates Him from everything else He creates. Likewise, we have been separated by the Spirit of God for a purpose. In order for us to fulfill that purpose, a relationship has to be established first, one that is modeled for us in the Father with the Son.

In all of humanity, Jesus the Messiah was the only one who perfectly demonstrated what a faithful Holy Son looks like in the world. He showed us what it means to live in the Spirit, to be led of the Spirit, to walk in the Spirit, and to be filled with the Spirit. Therefore, He is our template for understanding what our purpose and destiny is supposed to look like in the Spirit during this life and the next.

As believers, we have a unique role to play in God's creation, just as Jesus was also unique in His own right.

CHAPTER 18
Living and Led By The Spirit
(Part 1)

LIVING IN THE SPIRIT

When speaking about living in the Spirit, together we might hold varying ideas as to what that could mean. Depending on our church or religious tradition, it could have a wide range of meaning. However, I prefer to have a more restrictive approach. There is only one verse in all of scripture that actually mentions the phrase, with only one other possible exception.[36] Paul wrote, "If we live in the Spirit, let us also walk in the Spirit" (Galatians 5:25). This may get a little technical, but it won't be unbearable.

The primary verse we will look at will be in Galatians because of the precision of the words being used in the phrase. Since we have only one or two verses that mention this construct, we will have to break down the phrase to the use of the word "live" in the context of how it is first used in scripture. The word *life* or *living* is first found in Genesis:

---

[36] The only other person that comes close to using this phraseology is Peter, "For this cause was the gospel preached also to them that are dead, that they might be judged according to men in the flesh, but live according to God in the spirit" (1 Peter 4:6).

> *And God said, "Let the waters swarm with swarms of living creatures, and let birds fly above the earth across the expanse of the heavens." So God created the great sea creatures and every living creature that moves, with which the waters swarm, according to their kinds, and every winged bird according to its kind. And God saw that it was good. And God blessed them, saying, "Be fruitful and multiply and fill the waters in the seas, and let birds multiply on the earth."* (Genesis 1:20-22 ESV)

God created every "living" creature with an express commandment to be fruitful and multiply. This implies one thing: a continued lasting existence. The reproduction of their kind reveals God's intent to ensure their existence in perpetuity. The other time we see the word "live" is in the garden after the first human family has sinned:

> *"Then the LORD God said, 'Behold, the man has become like one of us in knowing good and evil. Now, lest he reach out his hand and take also of the tree of life and eat, and live forever—' "* (Genesis 3:22 ESV)[37]

God says that He would prevent man from eating from the tree of life after the fall to prevent him from living forever. Again we begin to see a pattern emerge. Notice how in this passage God's purpose in passing judgment is to prohibit man from eating of the fruit from tree of *life* to prevent man from *living forever*, that is in a *continual* state of sin. When God pronounces His judgment of death over Adam and Eve, He is in effect offering hope to mankind by confining their corruption to a limited span of life. Death places a time limit and a cap to their sin. The caveat to this tree was that if they were to eat from the tree of life after having committed sin, they would forever live in a perpetual state of corruption with no hope of change.

When the Bible uses the term "live," it implies endurance, persistence,

---

[37] Scholars have long debated the meaning behind God's reference to "us" in Genesis. Historically, the Hebrews understood it to imply God was addressing His divine counsel who witnessed the creation take place (Job 38:4-7). While God addresses the divine counsel, He alone takes credit for the act. Reading the Trinity into those passages was never addressed in the New Testament by any of the Apostles. It was not until after Tertullian introduced Trinitarian concepts that these references became topics of debate.

progression, a maintaining and sustaining, thriving. This is an enlightening detail considering the context of Galatians 5:25. We also begin to see another pattern. To "live" implies to continually exist, and to remain in a perpetual state of constancy. Everything is sustained in that mode of existence. I am of the opinion that to "live" is analogous to abiding without fluctuation, to be unwavering. Life is meant to persist. Therefore, if a person remains consistent in their walk, they experience life in its fullness. But those who are double-minded are really not living because of the instability that comes from being fickle. Staying firm and consistent results in the richness of life. Therefore, to live in the Spirit means to remain steadfast in your walk without wavering or fluctuation. It means to maintain a sustainable mode of operation. This is akin to not moving up and down, forward and backward, but rather maintaining a constant, stable state of renewal and progression:

> *"Count it all joy, my brothers, when you meet trials of various kinds, for you know that the testing of your faith produces steadfastness. And let steadfastness have its full effect, that you may be perfect and complete, lacking in nothing. If any of you lacks wisdom, let him ask God, who gives generously to all without reproach, and it will be given him. But let him ask in faith, with no doubting, for the one who doubts is like a wave of the sea that is driven and tossed by the wind. For that person must not suppose that he will receive anything from the Lord; he is a double-minded man, unstable in all his ways. ... Blessed is the man who remains steadfast under trial, for when he has stood the test he will receive the crown of life, which God has promised to those who love him."*
> (James 1:2-8, 12 ESV)

Notice the context of how a person who does not waiver, that is, who remains steadfast in the midst of temptation, receives the crown of *life*. Living in the Spirit implies that we do not backslide. This means you remain faithful, having a one-track mind. It also means you don't keep falling back into the arms of the world. You remain loyal to your King, even if it means you pay with your life in the process. Not relying on anything of the flesh, the world, or the devil for your sustenance. In other words, you refuse to become dissuaded, and are committed to the one you serve.

When Paul says that they should live in the Spirit, he is referring to a sense of permanence. This too is another aspect of God's nature that we image and project into creation. Since God is unseen, He is therefore eternal. Since everything that is seen is temporal, we can easily understand that by being constant, steadfast, and permanent, we emulate the eternality of God. As He is a perpetually self-existent person. His eternal nature is exemplified by our consistency. We are faithful and steadfast because God is eternal. Even His name "I AM" is in a present tense. He is not the "I WAS," nor is He the "I WILL BE," but He is the ever-present, always-constant "I AM":

"And God said unto Moses, I AM THAT I AM: and he said, Thus shalt thou say unto the children of Israel, I AM hath sent me unto you." (Exodus 3:14)

"For I the LORD do not change; therefore you, O children of Jacob, are not consumed." (Malachi 3:6 ESV)

"Every good gift and every perfect gift is from above, coming down from the Father of lights, with whom there is no variation or shifting shadow." (James 1:17 TLV)

"Jesus Christ the same yesterday, and to day, and for ever." (Hebrews 13:8)

Therefore, we can conclude that living in the spirit is associated with always maintaining a constant state of unwavering faith in the midst of the corruption of carnal influence. To live in the spirit simply means to stand your ground. Constancy. Endurance. Never giving up. Never surrendering to pressure. Living in the Spirit is our commitment to maintain a steady pace in the race that is set for us to run. In other words, we are to adopt a marathon mindset; this is not a sprint. Longevity is what is in view here.

BEING LED OF THE SPIRIT

I believe this to be somewhat of a problematic term. When we think of being led of the spirit, what comes to mind is the idea that God somehow leads us by the hand with some arbitrary voice telling us what to do, what to say, where to go, and how to behave, etc. In the English language, it gives the impression that God is actively directing every choice we make from moment to moment. We get this idea from passages where God may have instructed some prophet here, or some other important figure there. We then take those parts of the Bible and automatically interpret these accounts as "being led" because our English vernacular dictates that logic. When we say "being led," it tends to paint a picture of either someone or something walking ahead of us, holding our hand, as it were, while traversing through some dark passage. They lead, we follow. It makes sense, right?

However, if we look at every biblical passage wherein this term or some variation of it is mentioned, a different theme emerges. The concept of being led takes on a different context from what is conventionally understood about being led. The first time we see it mentioned in the Bible is found in the gospels at the baptism of Christ. It also happens to be the same event where the Spirit descends on Him like a dove to rest on Him. Upon receiving the Spirit, Jesus is then "led" into the desert:

> *"Then was Jesus led up of the Spirit into the wilderness to be tempted of the devil."* (Matthew 4:1)

> *"And Jesus being full of the Holy Ghost returned from Jordan, and was led by the Spirit into the wilderness ..."* (Luke 4:1)

In both gospel accounts, Jesus is being "led" by the Spirit for the purpose of testing. This is a significant detail that should not be overlooked. Jesus had just been baptized by John in the Jordan river, and a voice of God from heaven declared Jesus to be His "Beloved Son" with whom He was "well pleased." Before Jesus had ever stepped into His ministry, He already had a reputation with God who was "well pleased" with him.

That means that before Jesus ever received empowerment of the Spirit to do any miracles, signs, or wonders, He had already been faithfully abiding under the Law of Moses without compromise. Jesus kept the Mosaic Law without any additional "boost" of supernatural power. In other words, Jesus had impeccable character before He ever stepped foot into His ministry. The Law of Moses was the minimum standard of holiness, and Jesus had perfectly maintained that standard.

CHAPTER 19
Led By The Spirit
(Part 2)

Having been faithful under the teachings of Moses, Jesus pleased the Father by submitting to God's will as revealed in the Torah. I will say it again, this was *before* He ever received the empowerment of the Holy Spirit. Jesus' will was forged by God's Holy Law, and His character was molded by His love for God. Before He ever walked in supernatural power, He walked in holy character. The Law of Moses was designed to prepare Israel for the Messiah. When the Messiah came, He maintained all jurisprudence because the nation of Israel was founded as a theocracy with God reigning supreme as King. All legal requirements were met in and by Jesus Christ. He never faltered, never sinned. He *is* the *Holy One* of Israel.

When Jesus received the Holy Spirit, it rested on Him before He was driven into the wilderness to be tempted by the devil. This is also where the theme becomes more obvious in being led of the Spirit. The context given in both gospel accounts of the same event are associated with enduring trials of temptation. The way Jesus handles His temptation in the wilderness provides us with the precedence for dealing with all temptation, and it also demonstrates the primary characteristic of the Son: Holiness.

In the wilderness, every temptation was preceded with the epithet, *"If you are the Son of God ..."* This highlights Jesus' Sonship on purpose as a fundamental element to the theme. Jesus' holiness was being put to the test. I would like to point out here that the temptations Jesus endured did not happen when He left for the wilderness. The first temptation occurred *after* He had already fasted for forty days in the desert.[38] This means Jesus was tempted not because he was hungry but because He was famished. In other words, if Jesus did not eat then, He could potentially die. At that point, eating was a matter of absolute necessity. The first temptation was to turn stones to bread. It was not a temptation simply because the devil came to Him offering something random. It was a temptation because His life depended on it. Even then, Jesus refused to give in. He would rather die for lack of a basic human necessity than to give in to temptation by eating bread from His enemy's hand. What a tremendous example for us to follow.

This human aspect in the trial of Christ demonstrated that supernatural power was not really the prevailing factor in the temptation. Previous to even being baptized, Jesus had already established an iron clad will through His submission to God's Law. However, the temptation itself was more about derailing His status as a Son by getting Him to sin and bring into question His character. The life He lived up to that point had been more than stellar. But when the tempter came to Him at His most vulnerable point, the Son of God chose to risk tarnishing God's reputation as The Provider. What? How?

Think about it. His act of dependence on God in resisting temptation was at the potential expense of God's reputation because God promised to be their Jehovah Jireh. What this entails is that God is not so concerned with His own reputation as He is with our holiness. If we are doing our part to be obedient in pursuing holiness, He will uphold His own reputation in our midst. He can handle the questions that may arise from human blindness to the bigger picture, which is precisely why we must make character our number one priority! King David said:

---

[38] Matthew 4:2 and Luke 4:2

> *"I will worship toward thy holy temple, and praise thy name for thy loving kindness and thy truth: for thou hast magnified thy word above all thy name."* (Psalm 138:2)

Not only is it a necessary step if we want to experience walking in supernatural power, but also to continue in it. Sure, you can say, "Well, He had a divine mission, so He was going to succeed no matter what." Well, I don't necessarily agree with this sentiment. The fact He endured testing like any one of us proves there was a possibility of failure on His part. It is this aspect of His obedience that resulted in His exaltation to the right hand of the Father. This, too, is in God's plan for us.

If we emulate our Heavenly Father in humbling ourselves and depending on Him while also resisting the temptations when they come, in due time we will also be exalted. God's divine power is needed in order for us to step into the purposes God intends for us. But if we are to sustain that, we must make holiness our goal in all things.

Every time we see the term "led," either *by* the Spirit or *of* the Spirit, we find this theme of resisting temptation always present. Resisting temptation is the means by which we maintain and sustain holiness. Look at the following verses and see the connection made between resisting temptation with identifying as a child of God:

> *"So then, brothers, we are debtors, not to the flesh, to live according to the flesh. For if you live according to the flesh you will die, but if by the Spirit you put to death the deeds of the body, you will live. For all who are* **led by the Spirit of God are sons of God.** *For you did not receive the spirit of slavery to fall back into fear, but you have received the Spirit of adoption as sons, by whom we cry, 'Abba! Father!' The Spirit himself bears witness with our spirit that we are children of God, and if children, then heirs—heirs of God and fellow heirs with Christ, provided we suffer with him in order that we may also be glorified with him."* (Romans 8:12-17 ESV) [emphasis added].

Being led of the Spirit does not mean that God has to speak directly to us or say anything to tell us what to do. In other words, being led of the Spirit is not demonstrated in acts of *commission*. Rather, it is better expressed in acts of *omission*. It is not about having good works being augmented by God's direct involvement. Rather, it is in the abstinence of evil. Denying the carnal nature is what it means to be led of the Spirit. The Holy Spirit of God is there to provide us with a new nature that is according to the *"... new man, which after God is created in righteousness and* **true** **holiness***"* (Ephesians 4:24b) [emphasis added]

According to the pattern of how it is consistently used in scripture, being led always means to deny the desires of the flesh or carnal nature. Being led does not mean that we must be told what to do by God. Of all the people who have ever walked with God in history, Jesus was the one person who was the most perfectly led by the Spirit. Yet, there is not a single instance where we ever see the Father telling the Son what to do. Instead, the Son is always led to resist the works of the flesh. We can see this through the examples given of Jesus having been led of the Spirit.[39]

In all instances where being "led by the Spirit" is mentioned, the term is correlated with the status of being a son of God. In order to verify if our interpretation is correct, we should see other passages where the term "sons" or "children of God" are mentioned, with evidence associated with similar concepts. If we pick up from the Romans 8 passage above, we can see the greater context showing the clear connection between *denying the carnal nature* with *having the status of sons*:

> *"For I consider that the sufferings of this present time are not worth comparing with the glory that is to be revealed to us. For the creation waits with eager longing for the revealing of the sons of God. For the creation was subjected to futility, not willingly, but because of him who subjected it, in hope that the creation itself will be set free from its bondage to corruption and obtain the freedom of the glory of the children of God."* (Romans 8:18-21 ESV)

---

[39] NOTE: It has often been said in varying church circles that Jesus received His marching orders everyday whenever He got up to pray. The problem with this view is that it is mere speculation on our part. The Bible never says in any text that Jesus received instructions on what to do when He prayed. We assume that because we are taught to do so, but that is not biblical. If we are to use only the biblical text to interpret Jesus' act of prayer, then He did so because Jesus understood that while the Spirit is willing, he also knew that the flesh is weak (Matthew 26:41 and Mark 14:38). Furthermore, Acts 10:38 indicates that Jesus often wandered about with no set destination, and did all the good He did simply because God was with Him.

"What agreement has the temple of God with idols? For we are the temple of the living God; as God said, "I will make my dwelling among them and walk among them, and I will be their God, and they shall be my people. Therefore go out from their midst, and be separate from them, says the Lord, and touch no unclean thing; then I will welcome you, and I will be a father to you, and you shall be sons and daughters to me, says the Lord Almighty. Since we have these promises, beloved, let us cleanse ourselves from every defilement of body and spirit, bringing holiness to completion in the fear of God."
(2 Corinthians 6:16-7:1 ESV)

"Therefore, preparing your minds for action, and being sober-minded, set your hope fully on the grace that will be brought to you at the revelation of Jesus Christ. As obedient children, do not be conformed to the passions of your former ignorance, but as he who called you is holy, you also be holy in all your conduct, since it is written, 'You shall be holy, for I am holy.' " (1 Peter 1:13-16 ESV)

"See what kind of love the Father has given to us, that we should be called children of God; and so we are. The reason why the world does not know us is that it did not know him. Beloved, we are God's children now, and what we will be has not yet appeared; but we know that when he appears we shall be like him, because we shall see him as he is. And everyone who thus hopes in him purifies himself as he is pure. Everyone who makes a practice of sinning also practices lawlessness; sin is lawlessness. You know that he appeared in order to take away sins, and in him there is no sin. No one who abides in him keeps on sinning; no one who keeps on sinning has either seen him or known him."
(1 John 3:1-6 ESV)

Our status as children of God is directly linked to holiness because God's own divine nature is emulated through our obedience. In another passage where we see being led by the Spirit is mentioned in scripture is in Galatians. There is actually more to this chapter than meets the eye:

"But I say, walk by the Spirit, and you will not gratify the desires of the flesh. For the desires of the flesh are against the Spirit, and the desires of the Spirit are against the flesh, for these are opposed to each other, to keep you from doing the things you want to do. But if you are led by the Spirit, you are not under the law. Now the works of the flesh are evident: sexual immorality, impurity, sen-

suality, idolatry, sorcery, enmity, strife, jealousy, fits of anger, rivalries, dissensions, divisions, envy, drunkenness, orgies, and things like these. I warn you, as I warned you before, that those who do such things will not inherit the kingdom of God." (Galatians 5:16-21 ESV)

Paul lists the works of the flesh, that is *works associated with the carnal nature*, as those things we are to avoid if we are to inherit the Kingdom of God. The Kingdom is our inheritance as sons and daughters of God Who is our King. The carnal nature is that which corresponds solely to the created visible corrupted world. Being led of the Spirit causes us to deduce certain items by taking on the characteristic of God's invisible nature through our character.

In other words, since "being led" is not associated with "being told" by God what to do, what to say, or even where to go, then we can conclude that as long as we are not entertaining any of the works of the flesh, we can rest in the knowledge that we are being led by the Spirit. You can go everywhere, talk to everyone, and do anything as long as none of those things entertain the works of the carnal nature.

The first of the six elementary principles of the doctrine of Christ is repentance from dead works (Hebrews 6:1). If we do not abstain from sin, we cannot fulfill our purpose in God. However, while abstaining from sin is a necessary step in the right direction, it is not the only objective. Abstaining from sin is only one part of the story, and doing the *other* things that identify us as sons is the other part. The Apostle Paul said, *"Nevertheless, the firm foundation of God stands, having this seal: 'The Lord knows those who are His,' and 'Let everyone who names the name of the Lord keep away from unrighteousness'"* (2 Timothy 2:19 TLV). Now that we have somewhat covered what it means to keep away from unrighteousness, we can now look into what it means to live and act more like sons, as those who are known to the Lord.

"I give you a new commandment, that you love one another. Just as I have loved you, so also you must love one another. By this all will know that you are My disciples, if you have love for one another." (John 13:34-35 TLV)

CHAPTER 20
Walking and Being Filled

WALKING IN THE SPIRIT

Paul also adds another important detail in the passage in Galatians. He said, *"If we live in the Spirit, let us also **walk** in the Spirit"* (Galatians 5:25). We can deduce that living in the Spirit and walking in the Spirit are not synonymous terms. In order for us to differentiate between walking in the Spirit and being led of the Spirit, we need to first take a closer look at the entire section and break it down.

> *"This I say then, Walk in the Spirit, and ye shall not fulfil the lust of the flesh. For the flesh lusteth against the Spirit, and the Spirit against the flesh: and these are contrary the one to the other: so that ye cannot do the things that ye would. But if ye be led of the Spirit, ye are not under the law. Now the works of the flesh are manifest, which are these; Adultery, fornication, uncleanness, lasciviousness, Idolatry, witchcraft, hatred, variance, emulations, wrath, strife, seditions, heresies, envying, murders, drunkenness, reveling, and such like: of the which I tell you before, as I have also told you in time past, that they which do such things shall not inherit the kingdom of God. But the fruit of the Spirit is love, joy, peace, longsuffering, gentleness, goodness, faith, Meekness, temperance: against such there is no law. And they that are Christ's have crucified the flesh with the affections and lusts. If we live in the Spirit, let us also walk in the Spirit."* (Galatians 5:16-25)

By looking at the entire passage, we can begin to see some details that might have otherwise escaped our attention in the past. The Apostle Paul begins with *"Walk in the Spirit,"* with a result, *"and you shall not fulfill the lust of the flesh."* Walking in the Spirit implies taking further steps to do what is necessary in preventing the gratification of the carnal nature. Where being led of the Spirit can be akin to starving the carnal nature, walking in the Spirit is a matter of feeding a different nature altogether. It is about fueling different appetites.

If being led of the Spirit is expressed in acts of omission, then walking in the Spirit can be expressed in acts of commission. While being led of the Spirit directs us to *abstain* from the works of the flesh, walking in the Spirit directs us to exercise the *fruit* of the Spirit. When we say *no* to the flesh, we deny the carnal nature that works against us. But this can only take us so far.

While it is a good thing to say no to the flesh, we cannot sustain a mode of inaction for very long; a vacuum is left to us when we remove the works of the flesh. Therefore, we must replace that vacuum with the works of the Spirit. These works are what the scriptures categorize as *fruit* of the spirit. Walking in the Spirit has a different trajectory from that of being led.

Whereas in being led, our focus is inward to ourselves in denying our carnal nature, by walking in the Spirit, our focus is projected outward toward others, beginning with love. While living in the Spirit is associated with persisting in whatever we are doing for God, walking in the Spirit is associated with how to accomplish it. In other words, growing in the fruit of the Spirit is meant to replace the works of the flesh.

When we look at the fruit of the Spirit listed in Galatians, we see a list of qualities that are indicative of the nature of God Himself. The first of the fruit listed is *love*, and that is what sets the precedent for the rest of the fruit that follows. By walking in the Spirit, we demonstrate God's invisible quality in a specific way. By applying the fruit of the Spirit, we project His image. God's deepest desire is for all of creation, especially humanity, to know Him intimately. Consider how the Apostle John connects God's invisible nature with how we love one another:

"Beloved, let us love one another, for love is from God, and whoever loves has been born of God and knows God. Anyone who does not love does not know God, because God is love. In this the love of God was made manifest among us, that God sent his only Son into the world, so that we might live through him. In this is love, not that we have loved God but that he loved us and sent his Son to be the propitiation for our sins. Beloved, if God so loved us, we also ought to love one another. **No one has ever seen God; if we love one another, God abides in us and his love is perfected in us.** By this we know that we abide in him and he in us, because he has given us of his Spirit. And we have seen and testify that the Father has sent his Son to be the Savior of the world. Whoever confesses that Jesus is the Son of God, God abides in him, and he in God. So we have come to know and to believe the love that God has for us. God is love, and whoever abides in love abides in God, and God abides in him. By this is love perfected with us, so that we may have confidence for the day of judgment, because as he is so also are we in this world." (1 John 4:7-17 ESV) [emphasis added].

I want to draw you attention to the very last verse, "*... as He is so also are we in this world.*" This minute detail is at the heart of why the Spirit has been given to us. The Holy Spirit is given to emulate through us those character traits that most accurately reflect God's invisible qualities. Remember, He wants His creation to know Him. He desires for us to understand His ways and to recognize Him when He moves.

The fruit of the Spirit—love, joy, peace, patience, kindness, goodness, faithfulness, gentleness, self-control—are all characteristics of what God is truly like. This is what He wants His creation to know about Him. We are honored with being the chosen vessels, as those best equipped to most effectively display His invisible qualities:

"But God, being rich in mercy, because of the great love with which he loved us, even when we were dead in our trespasses, made us alive together with Christ--by grace you have been saved-- and raised us up with him and seated us with him in the heavenly places in Christ Jesus, so that in the coming ages he might show the immeasurable riches of his grace in kindness toward us in Christ Jesus." (Ephesians 2:4-7 ESV)

Our ultimate destiny is to "show the immeasurable riches of his grace in kindness toward us" for all eternity. We really do not know what that is going to look like, except to say that when we walk in the Spirit, we get a foretaste of the world to come:

> *"For it is impossible, in the case of those who have once been enlightened, who have tasted the heavenly gift, and have shared in the Holy Spirit, and have tasted the goodness of the word of God and the powers of the age to come, and then have fallen away, to restore them again to repentance, since they are crucifying once again the Son of God to their own harm and holding him up to contempt."* (Hebrews 6:4-6 ESV)

Living in the Spirit keeps us steadfastly going strong. Being led by the Spirit keeps us from going to a bad place of no return. Walking in the Spirit enables us to engage with our brethren in the process to reveal our Heavenly Father to the world. We should keep in mind that all we do in obedience is a manifestation of God in the creation, to the creation, and for the creation.

BEING FILLED WITH THE SPIRIT

As we continue exploring these different applications of the Spirit within the believer, we should not lose sight of the main objective of each of these functions: **projecting and imaging the invisible God.** So far, we touched on some basic elements of the relationship between the believer and the Spirit. We have seen the importance of being consistent, of abstaining from sin, and how we treat others. But now we will address one final aspect that benefits and blesses us directly. Being *filled* with the Spirit accomplishes this very thing. The first time a variation of this term is ever mentioned in scripture is actually found in the Old Testament:

> *"Then bring near to you Aaron your brother, and his sons with him, from among the people of Israel, to serve me as priests—Aaron and Aaron's sons, Nadab and Abihu, Eleazar and Ithamar. And you shall make holy garments for Aaron your brother, for glory and for beauty. You shall speak to all the skillful, whom I have filled with a spirit of skill, that they make Aaron's garments to consecrate him for my priesthood."* (Exodus 28:1-3 ESV)

This passage gives us insight into the premise behind being filled. The garments of the priesthood needed to be designed and made to specification so that Aaron and his sons could operate in the office of the priesthood. According to God's assessment, it takes wisdom that is imparted by the Spirit in order to accomplish this task. The garments were to display two particular attributes: glory and beauty. These two attributes of glory and beauty give us some fascinating revelations directly related to being filled.

GLORY

When we think of Glory, we tend to assume the popular notion of some form of illumination. While that does have something to do with it, light is not the major element of the theme. Some have gotten that idea from passages where God is said to appear in His Glory. We assume it is because His appearance was usually accompanied by the brightness of fire. I will suggest at this point that I do not agree with the common view of the Glory being associated with light. Rather, it is primarily associated with something else altogether. If I were to tell you to give God glory, would your first impression be to pull out matches or a lighter, ignite it, and raise it up? Or would it be, perhaps, to turn on a flashlight? Of course not! To give glory to God is not illuminating something with a light emitter.

You give God glory by lifting up your voice in praise and honor to Him. Lifting up the voice is what giving Him glory is associated with. It is no different. In most instances where God's glory is depicted in the Bible, it is almost always accompanied by a voice that speaks. One of the most fascinating moments recorded in scripture is when Moses asks God to show him His Glory. The following account is God's response to Moses' request:

> "And the LORD descended in the cloud, and stood with him there, and proclaimed the name of the LORD. And the LORD passed by before him, and proclaimed, The LORD, The LORD God, merciful and gracious, longsuffering, and abundant in goodness and truth, Keeping mercy for thousands, forgiving iniquity and transgression and sin, and that will by no means clear the guilty; visiting the iniquity of the fathers upon the children, and upon the children's children, unto the third and to the fourth generation. And Moses made haste, and bowed his head toward the earth, and worshipped." (Exodus 34:5-8)

The answer Moses receives is not *light*. God chooses to reveal His Glory to Moses in the *proclamation* He makes about Himself. This is a special moment in history because God is doing something you don't normally see. He is literally *raising His voice* to make a declaration about *Himself*. You would think He does not need to do that, but that is how He chooses to reveal His Glory to Moses. While beholding the moment, Moses reacts to witnessing the Glory by worshipping God. The sound of God's voice when He speaks is how God's Glory is revealed. *It's in the sound of His voice!* Allow me to show you another passage that links the Glory with a voice that declares something about God:

"The heavens declare the glory of God; and the firmament sheweth his handywork. Day unto day uttereth speech, and night unto night sheweth knowledge. There is no speech nor language, where their voice is not heard." (Psalms 19:1-3)

The glory of God is always associated with Him speaking with a voice that can be heard. Remember, God is invisible and has no mouth or larynx from which sound is made. His voice is a manifestation of His invisible essence in the form of *sound*. If you have never looked up the multiple passages where Glory is mentioned, then you should because you will see this theme rather consistently.

There are a couple of other passages I would like to share to drive this home. The New Testament keeps this theme going when Jesus' Glory is in view. John 12:41 quotes Isaiah where he is said to have seen the Glory of the Lord:

"In the year that King Uzziah died I saw the Lord sitting upon a throne, high and lifted up; and the train of his robe filled the temple. Above him stood the seraphim. Each had six wings: with two he covered his face, and with two he covered his feet, and with two he flew. And one called to another and said: "Holy, holy, holy is the LORD *of hosts; the whole earth is full of his glory!" And the foundations of the thresholds shook at the* **voice** *of him who called, and the house was filled with smoke"* (Isaiah 6:1-4 ESV) [emphasis added].

In the same chapter, there is an instance where Jesus prays and asks The Father to glorify Him. Here is that account:

"And Jesus answered them, saying, The hour is come, that the Son of man should be glorified. ... Father, glorify thy name. Then came there a voice from heaven, saying, I have both glorified it, and will glorify it again." (John 12:23, 28)[40]

On another occasion, Jesus' glory is mentioned when He goes to a mountain with Peter, James, and John to pray:

"And it came to pass about an eight days after these sayings, he took Peter and John and James, and went up into a mountain to pray. And as he prayed, the fashion of his countenance was altered, and his raiment was white and glistering. And, behold, there talked with him two men, which were Moses and Elias: Who appeared in glory, and spake of his decease which he should accomplish at Jerusalem. But Peter and they that were with him were heavy with sleep: and when they were awake, they saw his glory, and the two men that stood with him. And it came to pass, as they departed from him, Peter said unto Jesus, Master, it is good for us to be here: and let us make three tabernacles; one for thee, and one for Moses, and one for Elias: not knowing what he said. While he thus spake, there came a cloud, and overshadowed them: and they feared as they entered into the cloud. And there came a voice out of the cloud, saying, This is my beloved Son: hear him. And when the voice was past, Jesus was found alone. And they kept it close, and told no man in those days any of those things which they had seen." (Luke 9:28-36)

While on the mountain, they see Jesus transfigured, and standing next to Him are Moses and Elijah. As they look on, a cloud overshadows them, and they hear a voice from within the cloud that declares, *"This is my Son, my Chosen One, listen to him"* (Luke 9:35b ESV). Years later, when the Apostle Peter recalls the same incident, he comments about the voice saying, *"For he received from God the Father honour and glory, when there came such a voice to him from the excellent glory, This is my beloved Son, in whom*

---

[40] It should be noted that Jesus requests the Father to glorify His name. The Father glorifies it His name not by saying "YHWH" or even "Jesus". Instead, He speaks aloud for everyone present to hear. The sound that the people around Jesus heard was that of thunder. Though the sound was indiscernible to the people, it was in direct response to Jesus' prayer. The glory was in the voice that was heard. The glorification of the Name that was glorified was the evidence of the presence of the Father in their midst speaking to the Son.

I am well pleased. And this voice which came from heaven we heard, when we were with him in the holy mount" (2 Peter 1:17-18).

I believe I have made my point.

CHAPTER 21
The Spirit in Context

BEAUTY

The other detail of Aaron's garment is for beauty. This is a visible aspect that has a particular association, specifically, with worship. Aaron was given a *mitre* (head covering, turban) that had a plate with an engraving that said, "HOLINESS TO THE LORD." The visual beauty of the mitre does not have any of the same connotations that caused the adversary to be lifted with pride. Lucifer's beauty drew attention to himself. However, the beauty of Aaron's garment is related to drawing beauty toward holiness, something that is kept separate from view, so to speak. As a matter of fact, beauty from God's perspective is always associated with quiet holiness in the act of worship:

> "Give unto the LORD the glory due unto his name: bring an offering, and come before him: worship the LORD in the beauty of holiness." (1 Chronicles 16:29)

> "Ascribe to the LORD the glory due his name; worship the LORD in the splendor of holiness." (Psalm 29:2 ESV)

> "O worship the LORD in the beauty of holiness: fear before him, all the earth." (Psalm 96:9)

Being filled with the Spirit is mentioned only once in the New Testament. When we look at being filled, it carries the same themes of speaking in personal devotion of worship. Take a look:

> *"Therefore do not be foolish, but understand what the will of the Lord is. And do not get drunk with wine, for that is debauchery, but be filled with the Spirit, addressing one another in psalms and hymns and spiritual songs, singing and making melody to the Lord with your heart, giving thanks always and for everything to God the Father in the name of our Lord Jesus Christ, submitting to one another out of reverence for Christ."* (Ephesians 5:17-21 ESV)

The verses indicate that being filled is associated with preparation for ministry by first building personal devotion and intimacy with God. This is the main point of being filled. Being filled is to build intimacy between the Father and us. Being filled is how we cultivate this new relationship. The way we do it is explained within these verses. The verbiage is specific. It instructs us to speak to ourselves (and to each other) in psalms, hymns, and spiritual songs. But when it comes to God, we are supposed to sing and make melody within our hearts, that is, unseen by others.

We speak audibly to the human race and sing in silence to God. I am in no way saying that you cannot sing out loud to God. What I am saying is that to be filled with the Spirit, we need to speak aloud regularly to ourselves and others with psalms, hymns, and spiritual songs because we need to hear it to act as a constant reminder for our sake. However, we sing and make melody in our hearts to God as a constant devotion that is hidden from sight. In this way, we can image both His voice and His holiness.

There are things that constantly pull at us from multiple directions, moment to moment, usually in an attempt to draw us away from the very things that conform us into the likeness of the Son of God. They are constantly vying for our loyalty and devotion, always looking to have the preeminence in the midst of humanity. The Holy Spirit of God is come into our hearts to mold us into the image of Christ who is the express image of God's person.

By cooperating with the Spirit, we become conformed more and more into that image that reveals the nature and superiority of God. We become the proxies of His presence. Of those things that stubbornly work against us, these fall into only three categories:

- The desires of flesh
- The desires of the eyes
- The pride of life

"Do not love the world or the things in the world. If anyone loves the world, the love of the Father is not in him. For all that is in the world—the desires of the flesh and the desires of the eyes and pride of life—is not from the Father but is from the world. And the world is passing away along with its desires, but whoever does the will of God abides forever." (1 John 2:15-17 ESV)

These three items are most likely derived from the very first temptation in the history of man. This is found in the third chapter of Genesis:

"Now the serpent was more crafty than any other beast of the field that the LORD *God had made. He said to the woman, 'Did God actually say, "You shall not eat of any tree in the garden?"' And the woman said to the serpent, 'We may eat of the fruit of the trees in the garden, but God said, "You shall not eat of the fruit of the tree that is in the midst of the garden, neither shall you touch it, lest you die."' But the serpent said to the woman, 'You will not surely die. For God knows that when you eat of it your eyes will be opened, and you will be like God, knowing good and evil.' So when the woman saw that the tree was* **good for food***, and that it was a* **delight to the eyes***, and that the tree was to be* **desired to make one wise***, she took of its fruit and ate, and she also gave some to her husband who was with her, and he ate. Then the eyes of both were opened, and they knew that they were naked. And they sewed fig leaves together and made themselves loincloths."* (Genesis 3:1-7 ESV) [emphasis added].

When Eve saw that it was good for food, it corresponded to the desires of the flesh. When she saw that the fruit was a delight to the eyes, this corresponded to the desire of the eyes. When she saw that the fruit was desired to make one wise, that corresponded to the pride of life.

In a similar manner, there are also three influences with which we must contend: The Flesh, The World, and the Devil. All three of the latter correspond to the three things that are in this present age. When Jesus was tempted, there were three temptations, each having a theme:

- Turning stones into bread (The FLESH and the Desire of the Flesh),
- Seeing angels to pick him up from falling, being seen by men in the temple (The World and the Desire of their EYES),
- The worship of the devil (The Adversary and the PRIDE of Life).

I am of the opinion that each of the three influences (Flesh, Eyes, and Pride) are a primary concern to the ministry of the Holy Spirit. For that reason, we have been instructed in the Word on how to be **led of the Spirit**, which contends with the *desires of the flesh*; **walking in the Spirit**, which contends with *desires of the eyes*; and being **filled with the Spirit**, which contends with the *Pride of Life*. Being **led of the Spirit** is the relationship that exists between *me and the flesh*. **Walking in the Spirit** is the relationship between *myself and others*. **Being filled** is the relationship between *myself and God in the Church*. **Living in the Spirit** is the constant *inter-relationship between the three*. To make it easier to see, I have broken it down:

- Led of the Spirit (contends with the desires of the flesh),
- Walking in the Spirit (contends with desires of the eyes),
- Filled with the Spirit (contends with the Pride of Life).

- Being led of the Spirit (relationship between me and the flesh),
- Walking in the Spirit (relationship between myself and others),
- Filled with the Spirit (relationship between myself and God in the Church)
- Living in the Spirit (the constant inter-relationship between the three).

The ministry of the Spirit is designed to counter all the effects of sin in the life of the believer. We have been equipped to do more than just overcome. We have been given the opportunity to reveal God in our bodies to a world that desperately needs to find Him. In fact, that is the whole point:

**New Testament faith is God's effort in His people
to make Himself visible while still remaining Unseen.**

"His divine power has granted to us all things that pertain to life and godliness, through the knowledge of him who called us to his own glory and excellence, by which he has granted to us his precious and very great promises, so that through them you may become partakers of the divine nature, having escaped from the corruption that is in the world because of sinful desire. For this very reason, make every effort to supplement your faith with virtue, and virtue with knowledge, and knowledge with self-control, and self-control with steadfastness, and steadfastness with godliness, and godliness with brotherly affection, and brotherly affection with love. For if these qualities are yours and are increasing, they keep you from being ineffective or unfruitful in the knowledge of our Lord Jesus Christ. For whoever lacks these qualities is so nearsighted that he is blind, having forgotten that he was cleansed from his former sins. Therefore, brothers, be all the more diligent to confirm your calling and election, for if you practice these qualities you will never fall. For in this way there will be richly provided for you an entrance into the eternal kingdom of our Lord and Savior Jesus Christ." (2 Peter 1:3-11 ESV)

Needless to say, we have our work cut out for us. There are very dark forces in the world that have no desire other than to see a human fall into corruption and sin. The true and living God is actively working to bring people to the knowledge of Himself through His people. His family is the body of Christ, the Church. The Church is comprised of His sons and daughters. However, this mission is not limited to just reaching out to mankind. There is an interaction within God's creation between Him and all of His creatures, including the ones that we don't see. I am referring to the principalities, powers, rulers of darkness, and spiritual wickedness.

These fallen, wicked, spiritual beings are always at work behind much of the evil in the world. In many ways, they labor to deceive and subjugate the human race through false knowledge and vice. They exploit human weakness and frailty through sin and death. Since their rebellion, they have not only pursued the affections of man in the form of worship, but they have also competed for territory in the earth. This competition has played itself out in the form of wars and conflicts throughout history.

In the past, they impressed mankind with the visual element of idols made of gold, silver, stone, and wood. Today, their images are more deceiving with the advent of modern and postmodern technology. These items are not the beings themselves, but they are the physical representation of their likeness. At some point in past history, they all appeared to the human race, either through visions, dreams, esoteric experiences, and so on. They taught mankind how to emulate their own character in violation of God's perfect nature.

These created beings also know that God is invisible and incorporeal. They know that God is everywhere at all times. They know that among all the so-called gods, the Lord God IS the Most High God. They do, in fact, know that He is the King above all gods (Psalms 95:3). Furthermore, along with humans, they actually share in a mutual handicap. Though we cannot see these spiritual beings, they are nevertheless creatures who are visual beings themselves.

Even though they can operate in dimensions beyond our immediate scope of vision, and even though they can interact with the creation under certain circumstances, they are nonetheless restricted to being able to exist in one place at a time. They do not have the quality of being omnipresent as does the Most High. When moving from one dimension to another, between the spiritual realm and the physical world, they are beings that have no choice but to move from one place to another. That is their nature.

Furthermore, they do not have omnipotence to do all that they want whenever they please, even though many of them have made such claims. They can only operate when the conditions of their environment are favorable to them. There is a reason why such limitations exist for these creatures, the first being that they are not the True Living God. They are merely creatures with special abilities above that of those in the physical world but who are themselves also subject to deception and corruption. Their nature is part of and related to the natural/supernatural created order. Even though they can appear and disappear within our earthly realm, they are limited and finite by virtue of their nature that is itself a creation.

Howbeit then, when ye knew not God, ye did service unto them which by nature are no gods. (Galatians 4:8)

CHAPTER 22
The Divine Conflict

The gods of the ancient world have been attempting to make a comeback in recent times. Names such as Odin, Thor, and Loki from the Norse pantheon portrayed as good guys from the Marvel cinematic universe are a clear example, while TV shows like *Lucifer* or *Constantine* depict overt evil as fun, pleasurable, and entertaining. Cable programming such as *American Gods* have made significant headway in re-introducing pagan deities to the secular world while attempting to dethrone the Judeo-Christian God by means of indifference. The media today caters to the rise of these ancient deities in the form of visual entertainment. Even audiobooks series from "DC Comics" begin their storyline with, "GraficAudio, a movie … in your mind" as its preamble. But that is not their only goal. The so-called "gods" still desire to receive man's worship and attention.

Consequently, with the increased exposure of these fallen creatures, many people have begun seeking out these beings in their cultural roots, and returning to the worship of these pagan deities. They have indeed garnered a renewed following. I recently spoke with a close friend and brother in Christ, a retired Navy Seal who informed me that many of the warriors in that elite community have turned to the worship of the war gods of Norse mythology and other religions in order to better align themselves with their chosen occupation.

These pagan deities are not limited to portrayals in superhero movies or TV sitcoms. Other more nefarious means are becoming popular in mainstream culture. Some are dabbling in occult items, such as the Ouija, or *spirit* board, communicating with the dead through the use of shamans and/or self-proclaimed clairvoyants, and even the outright worship of demons. Our cultures are engaging with the spiritual realm in direct violation of the commandments of God, and it is increasing.

Unfortunately, this infiltration is not limited to the secular and pagan worlds. The influence of these beings has even infiltrated into the church. Not long ago, I had an interesting conversation with a family member who happens to also be a born again believer. She loves to draw and do all sorts of art projects. I had asked her to describe in her own words for me how she perceived God in her own mind. Her answer was somewhat disturbing to say the least, although not unexpected. She retorted with, "Well, I imagine God like … well … like Zeus, with like thunder and lightning around him, sitting on a big chair like on a throne."

It is amazing how it is not uncommon for people in the church to draw from pagan sources when they try to "visualize" what God is like. Our inability to differentiate between the true God and these "other guys" has played a significant role in the bold resurgence of these false gods within pop culture, and the indifference has also contributed to the current state of affairs in the church.

In this spiritual war, human beings are the prize. The gods of the nations depend on humans for their power. Part of the reason for this is the obvious fact that human beings were created in the image and likeness of God. But that is not the only reason behind their endeavor. When the Creator made the human race, He did so by decree. In speaking everything into existence, He also created mankind with a stated purpose, which he did not give to these other beings in the day of their creation. He gave mankind dominion over the entire spectrum of the physical universe. We will explore this in further chapters, but for now it is enough to recognized that when God gave mankind dominion, He did not include other non-human beings in that dominion. The Father limited that dominion to mankind alone.

However, after mankind sinned, the entire creation became vulnerable and subject to the influences of these divine beings. Of course, God knew this could and would happen. He knew that once the creation became estranged from Him that He would have to take the necessary steps to bring His creation back into alignment with Himself. He set into motion a plan of events that ultimately would find their complete fruition in His Son, Jesus the Messiah. God knew there would be challenges to having His image restored in man, but also that He would perfect a master plan to reconcile not only humankind, but to include the rest of all creation itself.

Jesus Christ is the perfect embodiment and representation of the invisible God. The mission and the appearing of Jesus in the flesh centered around one single premise: to destroy the works of the devil (1 John 3:8). Those include everything from the fall of Adam until the time when the Father will have put all things under His feet.

"For he must reign, till he hath put all enemies under his feet. ... For he hath put all things under his feet. But when he saith all things are put under him, it is manifest that he is excepted, which did put all things under him."
(1 Corinthians 15:25, 27)

"Thou hast put all things in subjection under his feet. For in that he put all in subjection under him, he left nothing that is not put under him. But now we see not yet all things put under him." (Hebrews 2:8)

Our consignment as believers to preaching the gospel is God's intended method to reintroduce the world to their Creator. Our conduct and behavior is supposed to make the knowledge of God not only appealing, but also revealing. Take a look at the following passage:

"But now ye also put off all these; anger, wrath, malice, blasphemy, filthy communication out of your mouth. Lie not one to another, seeing that ye have put off the old man with his deeds; And have put on the new man, which is renewed

in knowledge after the image of him that created him: Where there is neither Greek nor Jew, circumcision nor uncircumcision, Barbarian, Scythian, bond nor free: but Christ is all, and in all." (Colossians 3:8-11)

The significance of the image of God being renewed in the Christian cannot be over stated. There is an intended consequence to the renewal of God's image in man. Believe me when I tell you there is so much more to this. When referring to the true God, we must remember that He is Spirit and has no body. Yet, He desires to make Himself known to everyone and everything within His creation, even his enemies. This self-revealing act of God in various theophanic forms throughout history carrying a thematic purpose, especially as it relates to those other beings who usurp their power, and presume to take the worship intended for the Creator, and demanding that same worship for themselves. The following events in biblical history contain certain elements in common that you may not have noticed before:

The Old Testament

- The voice of the Lord walking in the garden (Genesis 3)
  - Judgment against the serpent
- The plagues of Egypt and the Passover (Exodus 5-12)
  - Judgment / Destruction of the gods
- The giving of the Law (Exodus 19)
  - Judgments / Destruction of the mountain
- Elijah and Fire from heaven (I Kings 18 and II Kings 1)
- Appearing to Gideon (Judges 6)
  - Salvation for the Nation / Destruction of Pagan System
- The Fiery Furnace (Daniel 3)
  - Salvation for three / Destruction of Pagan System

What may not be obvious in the examples given is that in every one of those instances, when the Lord would make some kind of visible appearance, it would always set into motion judgments resulting in not only the destruction of the gods of other nations (including their system), but directly resulted in the liberation of the people from some form of oppression. This is significant because it sets the precedent that the appearance of God in some form is destructive to evil and liberating to human beings, especially those whose loyalty is toward Yahweh. This is also the case when we fast forward to the New Testament.

The appearing of Jesus Christ on the scene inaugurated the Kingdom of God. He was manifested to destroy all the works of the devil. Every belief system, every deity, and every other creature that was opposed to God was now forced to reckon with the new government of the Creator that was imposing itself on the forces of darkness. The person of Jesus so perfectly manifested the Father that every time He would open His mouth or stretch out His hand, it resulted in the dismantling of the infrastructure of unbelief. The ministry of Christ was designed to bring attention to the invisible God of Israel, beginning with Israel itself, and afterward to the surrounding nations.

The appearing of Jesus Christ on the world scene revolutionized humanity on many levels. His ministry is not limited to Christ alone, nor even that of the Apostles. Since Christ's resurrection and ascension, He left us, the church, with the task of fulfilling His mission by going to the nations where other so-called gods have exercised their control. The point I am making here is that as His sons and daughters, we are God's proxies, and as such, we have a destructive effect on His enemies.

Today, we are the vessels by which God chooses to manifest Himself. He gave us His Spirit, constantly working in us, both to want and to perform God's desires. The Father's good pleasure is to see the nations return to Him, to end the rule of the oppressors, and to set the captives free from the power of the oppressors. As the church, we are tasked with the commission to teach the nations, to preach to every creature the truth that the Lord alone is the true God, and that in Him is the abundance of life. We are tasked with warning everyone about the coming judgment, to command all men everywhere to repent in the Name of Jesus, and to also free them from their ailments and their sin.

Our mission in this New Covenant as Christians is to walk into every nation where our feet can take us and to proclaim the reality of God's government. In doing this, we make the invisible Creator known through His creative power working in us to set the captives free, to give sight to the blind, forgiveness of sin through the gospel, and the breaking of every yoke. If we are to fulfill this destiny that was begun in Christ, then we must also understand the role we play in God's plan for the world. In the following chapters, we begin to explore what it means to walk by faith, and the essential part it plays in manifesting the God of Israel to all creation.

> *"For you did not receive the spirit of slavery to fall back into fear, but you have received the Spirit of adoption as sons, by whom we cry, "Abba! Father!" The Spirit himself bears witness with our spirit that we are children of God, and if children, then heirs—heirs of God and fellow heirs with Christ, provided we suffer with him in order that we may also be glorified with him. For I consider that the sufferings of this present time are not worth comparing with the glory that is to be revealed to us. For the creation waits with eager longing for the revealing of the sons of God."* (Romans 8:15-19 ESV)

The most intriguing aspect of our role as sons and daughters is not even really about God's invisible nature by itself. Rather, it is more about how He desires to make Himself known. In other words, it is less about how God is unseen, and it is more about revealing Him by and through His proxies. **It is about the church making God visible to the creation through our obedience!** God desires for His creation to know and to recognize Him within the creation. He wants His enemies to see Him because it results in their demise and our freedom! Being created in His image and after His likeness means that being His proxies collectively, He can fulfill every mystery of His being. He can reveal the deep truths of His essence through those who bear His likeness.

As humans, we are lesser than those other beings that operate in the spirit realm only in that we can suffer death. But as redeemed sons and daughters, we are given the right to act as sons through the authority the Father has bestowed, and the ability to act as His children through the power He has given by His Spirit. Our redemption is the catalyst for the fall of all the so-called gods of the nations. The revealing of the sons and daughters of God forces those powers that are opposed to God to not only come out of hiding, but also to become displaced from their positions of prominence in the world.

God gave man the right to rule when He decreed that humankind was to have dominion. God wants to restore what was lost in paradise—our rightful place of dominion—and to replace the usurpers with those of us who have the right to rule by decree. This one fact alone distinguishes us from the rest of the physical creation. It is high time that we forsook our worldly ambitions, and stepped into our role … no … plunged ourselves into our birthright as sons and daughters of the God of heaven and earth and of everything in between!

CHAPTER 23
Faith and The Believer

Permit me to ask you: *What do you expect from your faith?* Have you ever bothered to even ask yourself the question? Let it sink in for a moment. Imagine you stepped into a time machine that took you back to around 30 A.D. in Israel to about the same time and location Jesus walked the earth. Now imagine you stroll along a road in Israel, and suddenly, you see crowds gathered across the street from you. In the middle of the crowds, you see Jesus. They have been following Him though the neighborhood until they ended up just across the way from you. What would you expect to see?

According to the New Testament, we would expect to see Jesus teaching the crowds and preaching the good news to everyone. You might pull out a little pocket Bible and read, expecting to see the same miracles, signs, and wonders on those precious pages. Assuming that you have a direct line of sight to Him from across the street, we can agree that you would have an amazing vantage point. But what if you decided to get closer because you wanted to get a better look? With your heart racing, you cross the street to get a "front row seat" to the action.

The intensity of the moment only increases with every step you take toward him. The experience is even better now more vivid and real to you simply because of your proximity to Christ. You lean over and see Jesus lay his hand on some poor blind man. You're right there witnessing one of the most amazing events. The intimacy of the moment keeps you completely on edge. Suddenly, you see the Man's milky whites fade away, and the iris of His eyes begin to change. For the first time ever, He can see. Just then, Jesus, the Son of God, lifts up His head, looks directly at you in the eye and smiles. Wow! What a moment.

Degrees of intimacy are often gauged by distance, whether physical, emotional, or otherwise. The highest natural form of intimacy in human relationships occurs within the act of marriage where two bodies become one. You cannot really go beyond that, otherwise the two bodies begin to separate. Now consider that God dwells *inside* of us. He lives *within* us.

Therefore, if we use this logic, we can conclude that at least in a figure, the highest form of intimacy undergirding our relationship with God as born again believers already exists! In a sense, a marriage of sorts has taken place. So if getting closer would make the experience greater and more intimate, then we already have what we are truly seeking. We just need to recognize it. So, why do we expect anything less in us today than what we would have expected 2,000 years ago? So, I will ask the question again ... what do you expect from your faith?

FAITH

The word *faith* is used so lightly nowadays. It is practically synonymous with the most generic of meanings. If you were to ask almost anyone to define faith in his/her own words, the general consensus and typical response you would hear is that faith means to believe and trust (in God) without having to see with your own eyes. We all know what faith means, right? Well ... perhaps not as much as we might think. I have already mentioned how so much of what we claim to believe is based more on our "Christianeez" than on the Bible, and faith is no exception.

What comes out of our mouth from moment to moment and day to day shapes so much of our Christian experience, like pliable clay. We are not as careful with our words as we ought to be. If the biblical writers were as loose with their semantics as we are today, there would hardly be any consistency, and we would have no hope of interpreting the scriptures accurately. As we have seen, the words we use to describe things really do matter. They help us make sense of things. The Bible has many things to say, and we should take the time to really pay attention to the details. What we understand about God, His nature, character, etc., ultimately affects how we make our decisions and walk out our convictions.

Faith is listed as the second of the six principles of the doctrine of Christ (Hebrews 6:1-2). After 2000 years, we ought to be the subject matter experts. However, as we will see, there is indeed much confusion about what faith really is and how it ought to be expressed. This confusion directly affects how we think and live, what we say, how we preach, and even how we interpret biblical passages. The language we use in church for describing our "Christian experience" is typically not thoroughly grounded in biblical terminology. On the surface, it sounds biblical, but in many cases they either contradict or replace what the Bible actually says.

Have you ever wondered why there is such a stark contrast between what we read concerning the early church compared with the body of Christ today? Just by contrasting the demographics from then to now, you can easily discover many more people claiming Christianity today than when the New Testament was written. Even if you remove the ones who are considered nominal Christians by today's standards and count only the "true believers," the numbers of Christians alive today dwarf the number of Christians from that era. The early church had nowhere near as many possessions as we have at our disposal today. They did not have the freedoms we do, technologies we do, buildings like we do, money like we do, none of the many advantages that we boast in.

Yet, the early church turned their whole world upside down within their generation. Their influence was enormous enough to be viewed as a significant threat to the ruling establishment at the time: Rome. They were considered a threat to Rome, not because they had a military force, or even political leverage in the Senate. They were feared by the highest echelons of Roman power because, even though Caesar was worshipped as a god, the Christians paid homage to another King … Jesus.

Now, what may not be obvious is that in the eyes of Caesar, the lowest peasant Christians were a threat because they walked in such supernatural power, and they were able to do things that only God could do, which Caesar could not duplicate. This threatened the so-called "divinity" of Caesar, and therefore the legitimacy of his government and throne. Supernatural power was commonplace among all church folk back in the day, not just the Apostles.

Furthermore, their commitment to live holy and to be different from the world rivaled our current watered down commitments and shallow spirituality by a considerable margin. It is no wonder why there is so little of that power being displayed today. Why doesn't the modern church have more impact? For the most part, we are viewed by the world with contempt, but not for the same reasons. We are mostly viewed as suspect by the world because of our own sins, and we are maligned because of a litany of church controversy from the misuse of money to abuse of every kind under the sun. The accusations hurled at the church's feet center more around moral decline and compromise. Since when did the world become the standard bearer for the church?

So where are the results? Shouldn't there be more miracles, signs, and wonders today with the same impact or greater? Shouldn't believers be living in victory, free from sin, and overcoming the world and its appeal? If Jesus said, "Verily, I say unto you, If ye have faith, ye shall say unto this mountain, Be thou removed, and be thou cast into the sea, <u>it shall be done</u>," then why is it that so many believers are disappointed with their "faith" for not getting their needs met?

These are real people with real problems who need real results. We can't be insensitive to their plight when they have beloved family members either caught up in a sinful lifestyle or dying of some unknown disease. Their questions and doubts are not unwarranted. Let's just be blunt here. Far too many Christians have been disappointed with the absence of a favorable outcome.

Many sincere and God fearing Christians have said things like, "I had faith, and I prayed, and prayed, and prayed, but nothing happened." I have met and spoken with many of these precious brethren, so I can say with a certainty that many church folk do think this way, especially when it comes to losing a loved one. I do understand what it's like to lose family. But we still need to respond to the questions they raise. We must take a step back and reassess where we went wrong. Think about it this way. If the Lord Jesus says that by having faith, we ought to see results, then why does it not happen? Read the following passage and then follow the logic:

> "Then the disciples came to Jesus privately and said, 'Why could we not cast it out?' So Jesus said to them, 'Because of your unbelief; for assuredly, I say to you, if you have faith as a mustard seed, you will say to this mountain, "Move from here to there," and it will move; and nothing will be impossible for you.' " (Matthew 17:19-20 NKJV)

To paraphrase, Jesus said that if you have faith, then "a, b, and c" ought to happen. He was not being flippant about it. Nor was He being irresponsible with His words. Whatever it is we choose to do, if it does not result in "a, b, and c" happening, then whatever it was we did, we should not call it faith. Many would protest my last statement saying, "But I did use faith, and it didn't work."

Think about what you are implying by that statement. If Jesus said that faith is what works, and if your faith did not, then would not that be the same as calling Jesus a liar? What I propose is that the criteria we use to define faith is not what we think it is. I am of the opinion that what we call faith is not actually biblical faith at all. It must be something else. Now, I don't know about you, but I would much rather let God be true, and every man a liar. I know it is a bold statement, and I intend to demonstrate what I mean. Continue with me, and I am sure you will understand.

CHAPTER 24
Faith and The Divine Profile

How could we be so wrong? In order to understand what it means to be the image bearing children of God, we must first understand our Creator. That is the ground work layed down in the first part of this book. There is an aspect to God's invisible nature that enlists us because of one simple truth: While God is invisible, we are still made in His image.

Andy Bannister once wrote, "That humans bear God's image, the *imago dei*, explains why you have real value, regardless of your gender, race, intelligence, or earning potential—why all human beings are equal. It tells you why human life has dignity, why you must not treat people as means rather than ends, and it also gives a foundation for morality and ethics." [41]

The power of God is ever present to change people's lives. Whether it is forgiving sin or healing of the body, it is all accomplished by faith. Even the knowledge of God is given and received by faith. True biblical Faith unlocks all the hidden mysteries of God, and He has sovereignly decreed it so. His

---

[41] Andy Bannister, "What Does It Really Mean to Be Human?," *RZIM*, last modified 2015, accessed May 30, 2020, https://www.rzim.org/read/a-slice-of-infinity/what-does-it-really-mean-to-be-human.

true essential nature demands that we live by it, walk in it, and if need be die by it. As we go farther, we will discover why faith is so necessary, and the inherent connection it has to God's invisible nature.

Understanding this provides us with a whole new dimension: *"For we walk by faith, not by sight"* (2 Corinthian 29 5:7). You will find out why this is the case. You will also come to see how important your role is, and why you are so needed in the spiritual conflict we find ourselves in. Victory always comes at a cost, and we need to be expected to pay it in this life. If Jesus paid it, then so do we.

PERSONAL LOSS

In the spring of 2005, my mother received a devastating diagnosis: stomach cancer. It was a major shock to us all. She had been unable to keep down food for some weeks, and lost a considerable amount of weight until her bones began breaking through her thin skin from lying in bed so much. She was so weak that getting up for any length of time was exhausting for her. My father took her to every available doctor, hoping there was some cure somewhere. However, they all gave the same discouraging prognosis.

I recall various people coming to the house to pray for my mother. We welcomed their prayers whenever they offered. I would often find myself praying alongside them for my mother's healing. There were some days where I would be praying next to her, and she would look at me with these eyes and say, "Stanley, why isn't God healing me?" My heart would break. The question did not come from any sort of resentment or anything like that. It was just an honest question. She loved God. She just wanted to understand why it was that she was going through this kind of suffering. I did not have an answer at the time. Honestly, I don't think anyone has an adequate answer in these situations.

Still, her question did make me wonder … why? As people came by the house to pray for her, I would on occasion make it a point to eavesdrop. I would like to mention at this point that I am truly grateful for all the goodness they showed to my mother during that difficult time in our lives. It truly meant a great deal to us, and especially to my mother. Still, I recall asking myself, "What is it that makes me feel like something is off? Why do I feel like I'm not quite settled?" They were sincere and did their best to help her. Yet, I felt like we were missing the mark somehow. She did not get better, and eventually her condition grew progressively worse.

On one occasion, there was a group of pastors who came from a local church to pray for her. I recall being in the next room as I heard their prayers for my mother. As always, I was moved by their sincerity and desire to see her get well. But as I listened intently to their words, something kept nagging at me. The prayers went something like this, "Lord, if it's your will, please heal Maria. Please pour out your compassion on her and restore her. Please take this sickness from her. Please have mercy and make her whole by Your power. In Jesus' name. Amen." They truly meant every word and were there with the hopes that the power of God would heal her. So, what was it that kept nipping at my heels every time someone would come over and pray for my mother's healing in this way?

As the pastors were leaving, one of them walked up to me with genuine concern and said, "Son, you need to say goodbye to your mother. You must let her go." Now, when I heard that, the feeling of something being "off" came over me again. I was grateful for him and everyone else that came. But this time, the feeling was more pronounced than ever. As I closed the door behind them, I asked myself, "Why don't I hear more triumph in everyone's voice when they pray? Where is the victory I read about in the scriptures? How come there was so much power being demonstrated in the days of the early church, yet that same power was not as prevalent today, at least not with the majority?"

By digging deeper into the Bible, I came across those verses that brought attention to the amount of tradition I actually believed in. I became more convinced that if I am to see the results I was promised in the Bible, I would have to let go of those very traditions that contradicted scripture, regardless of how authentic they sounded. I then began to discover that the degree to which I conformed what I believed in the scriptures, the more freedom I was able to experience and process. I was able to let go of past struggles with much greater ease, and I found I had an even greater degree of boldness as well. I am not saying I was tempted with things any less. Rather, I had greater strength in dealing with my trials because of what I understood of biblical truth.

As my thoughts and beliefs became more aligned with the written Word of God, I also began to grow in my faith. It was not necessarily an experientially-based faith. Rather, my faith began experiencing more of the reality of what I read and knew to be true in the Bible. I am not saying I have not had trials, nor am I saying I have not made any mistakes, or even that I have not committed some sin since I came to realize these things. You can ask my wife, and she can certainly vouch for what I say about that. What I am saying is that I became increasingly aware of the reality of God. This was a progression on a steeper margin than I had before. I found victory, not just in my own personal walk, but also when I wanted to help others.

Before my mother passed away, I had felt somewhat helpless despite the fact we consistently prayed for her healing. I literally felt powerless to confront something like the cancer that ate away at my mother, even though I knew the Bible promised victory. However, it was the manner in which I approached what I read in the Bible, through the lens of my traditions, that kept me from seeing and probably even experiencing the victory over my mother's sickness. I felt no condemnation, nor resentment about it.

I likened my situation to Aaron's silence when his sons died for violating the tabernacle protocol. He knew their judgment was just, and God was justified in His judgment of them. To clarify, I am not saying that God judged my mother, as though her death resulted from it. What I am saying is that had I understood certain principles of faith then as I do today, my mother's situation might have turned out differently. Basically, I do not blame God for what happened.

I don't think I am being unreasonable for believing what the Bible says about it. I do believe there needs to be an overhaul of those "precious" traditions that so often have kept us from our victory. Let's press on and see where the scriptures take us. Many of us might very well end up in uncharted territory, or maybe not. You will just have to see it for yourself.

Jesus said everyone who believes in Him would do the same works He did and even greater (John 14:12), so what happened to His promise? I could not bring myself to disbelieve in Jesus or the Bible just because someone I loved was dying. I knew others who chose to turn away from God for similar circumstances, forsaking their faith because of some tragedy in their life. I have always thought that was foolish, and I have no desire to ever give up on God because of something that affects us all. Even though I could not see Him, I knew He was there. Still, I did feel like the questions in my mind merited at least some answers.

Just a few weeks after this incident, I was in the house when I noticed my mother was not her usual self. She seemed like she was somewhere else. Her breathing changed and became erratic. She stared out toward the foot of her bed as though someone was standing there. I knew something was happening.

I immediately called for my father and siblings to come. My father arrived first and stayed by her side. I sat next to her behind my dad. Everyone wanted to ease her discomfort, so we played her favorite worship music. I just looked at her not knowing what else to say other than, "Everything's going to be alright, Mom." As I held her hand, I looked intently at her face when suddenly, she was gone.

Even now, I can feel the awe of that moment when she left her body to be with the Lord. I did not really feel the need to cry at that moment, even though there was a deep sadness lingering in my chest. I was comforted that she was finally at peace in the presence of God. I knew my mother was saved and that I would see her again when my own time came. Still, I had questions that I felt the familiar impulse to find the answers to. So to make sense of everything in light of what I knew, I had to make the pursuit of truth my primary goal while trusting in God to show me what I did not understand.

I also knew not to let my feelings of hurt and loss dictate how I saw the world. No one ever really lives if they surrender to the anguish of soul in those moments. You only become a prisoner of your own circumstances if you do. But the scriptures are clear: *If I know the truth, that truth would make me free.* So I made truth my ultimate objective.

The truth of God has this capacity of literally making us free. It literally compels us toward freedom. Truth has this peculiar effect on those who seek it. So what does this have to do with the nature of God? Actually...

everything! By readjusting what we believe to what the Word of God actually says and conforming our thinking to what is written, we can begin to partake in the same experience of the early church and beyond. To do this, we will have to re-visit certain biblical themes in order to put everything in proper context in light of God's essential nature.

Remember, how we respond to difficulties ultimately reveals the reality of the Father to the world around us. His Presence alone has the ability to alter our circumstances. Our own personal disposition can either reveal or conceal the reality of the true God. Much of that hinges on us coming into agreement with the Lord. Yet, there is so much more to it than just agreeing with Him. It takes the abandonment of ourselves to the cause of Christ. It requires us to truly count the cost because there really is a price to pay. At the same time, there is a whole realm of supernatural reality in store for those who surrender to and believe in all that Jesus revealed about the Father and His will toward us.

CHAPTER 25
The Plan of God

When God created us in His image and after His likeness, He decreed that mankind was to have dominion over the entire realm of the physical creation. His intent was to create a race of kings that bore the image of Himself, and by that image, to rule His creation in His likeness. Unfortunately, that image and likeness became marred when mankind fell from his exalted position. As the first man created on earth, Adam was the only human in the Old Testament who was ever referred to as a son of God (Luke 3:38).

After Adam's fall, however, and the subsequent corruption that followed, mankind became more and more separated from God, and not just in the sense that they could not be in His manifest presence. Sin changed the nature of the relationship between God and man. When sin entered the world, the image instilled in man became severely warped as mankind became more and more violent, until they became nearly unrecognizable. Mankind ceased to be sons, and instead, chose to be slaves. The Old Testament is God's undaunting pursuit to rebuild a fractured relationship with an estranged creation.

As a result of their inclination to violence and corruption, their life span became shortened. God placed a cap on their propensity for self-destruction by limiting their life span. They became increasingly alienated from their Creator with each passing generation. The likes of Abraham, Moses, David, and all of the prophets that followed, all foretold of a future redemption that would eventually restore the relationship that was lost in the Garden of Eden. That redemption is what the New Covenant is all about.

The relationship being introduced by the New Testament is one in which a transition is taking place, wherein a servant is being transformed back into a son. The New Testament faith is God's primary way to bring humanity back to its rightful place in His economy by establishing a new and better covenant, built on better promises for a better kind of relationship, "Wherefore thou art no more a servant, but a son; and if a son, then an heir of God through Christ" (Galatians 4:7).

Our role as God's children carries with it certain responsibilities. If we are to properly carry out those responsibilities, we must learn to set aside, even abandon our merely human affinities. It will take sacrifice, hard work, and especially the renewing of the mind to conform to the terms of this New Covenant in Christ. It is often said that it was easier to get Israel out of Egypt than to get Egypt out of Israel. It is high time that we as believers come to ourselves, and arise from feeding in troughs of swine to return to our Father's embrace.

By first laying the groundwork for understanding God's nature, we can better process the role we play in God's Kingdom. In doing that, we can further explore various aspects of His nature and character that directly relate to us as His "sons and daughters" who willingly seek their Father's face, and bless His holy name. As God's children, we ought to understand how the "family business" works. God is our Father. He makes those who are born again into His house to be His heirs.

Since our Heavenly Father is a King, that makes us more than just citizens of Heaven. That truth makes us heavenly royalty on the earth. It may shock some of you to read that Jesus never intended to bring a religion. That statement may sound crazy to some, but it is true. He came to bring a government, a Kingdom. But His Kingdom is fashioned and molded after

Himself. The Holy Spirit of God is the active influence behind the nature and character of this Kingdom. Through His agents (the sons and daughters), His Spirit shows what this Kingdom is supposed to *look* like.

Lamentably, we tend to fall acutely short of who and what we were born again to be. I believe what we are about to cover will change all of that. Now that we have a more accurate understanding of God's nature, we can begin touching on what we have learned so far to better position ourselves into realizing all that we are destined to be. Above all, we must never forget to always be about our Father's business.

> *"For it is time for judgment to begin at the household of God; and if it begins with us, what will be the outcome for those who do not obey the gospel of God? And "If the righteous is scarcely saved, what will become of the ungodly and the sinner?" Therefore let those who suffer according to God's will entrust their souls to a faithful Creator while doing good."* (1 Peter 4:17-19 ESV)

We must get settled within our own household first. As modern Christians, I think we have a difficult time understanding what it means to be children of God. Most of us are more comfortable with the idea of being servants of God than we are with being sons. We are a people who profess to be children of a Father who cannot be seen in the conventional sense. We carry inside of us a precious gift that enables us to introduce the world to our family, primarily our Father and our Brother, the Messiah, Jesus, the firstborn Son by the Spirit.

> *"For it was fitting that he, for whom and by whom all things exist, in bringing many sons to glory, should make the founder of their salvation perfect through suffering. For he who sanctifies and those who are sanctified all have one source. That is why he is not ashamed to call them brothers, saying, 'I will tell of your name to my brothers; in the midst of the congregation I will sing your praise.' And again, 'I will put my trust in him.' And again, 'Behold, I and the children God has given me.'"* (Hebrews 2:10-13 ESV)

The Lord's invisible qualities are such that He cannot be "contained," and all that exists in either the physical or spiritual realms, whether in this life or in the world to come, are all created things that exist within the Eternal

God as it is written, *"For in Him we live, and move, and have our being ..."* (Acts 17:28a). His invisible quality dictates His eternality, which reinforces His incorruptible and unchanging nature and self-existent reality.

Being unlimited and not tethered to a physical body means He can display His power and reveal His person in any way or form He chooses within the physical realm. God has made Himself known and relatable to His creation, not only through the different forms He has taken, but also by those methods He ordained in the scriptures. These revelations are what distinguish Him from everything else that purports to call itself god.

Through the covenants He made with man, God prescribed those ways that most reflect his invisible qualities. Every commandment, ordinance, statute, teaching or law ever given to man was given with the express intent to reveal something about the true God Who is invisible. God's works and ways reveal the mysteries within His eternal nature. His creation depends on Him to accomplish this.

God had revealed Himself in specific ways by the different covenants He made with Israel. Since God is a completely unknowable, invisible being who desires to reveal Himself to His creation, He uses His unlimited power and knowledge to produce a relatable context for the creation's sake through functional revelation. The nature of the Lord's relationship to His people is dictated by the terms He lays out in those covenants. In the case of the Old Covenant, God was revealed as Husband, Father, and Master (Lord). These titles were functional in relation to God's invisible nature, and the title was in direct response to the manner in which the people of God responded to Him.

In the New Covenant, God is revealed as the Father, the Word (Son), and the Holy Ghost. Each of these titles, again, have a specific function as it relates to His invisible existence in light of a new relationship formed by this New Covenant. The Father, the Word, and the Holy Spirit are titles that all refer to the one and self-same God. The title of *Father* is the revelation of the new relationship that the invisible God has toward mankind as His children. The Word is God Himself as His communication to man. The title of Son refers to the body that is produced by God and inhabited by His Word to communicate and express His intent to fellowship with humankind. Therefore the Son is the Word of God revealed in bodily form; He is called the Christ (Messiah), who is God manifested or revealed in flesh.

The Holy Spirit is God, and *is* the very nature of God Himself. It is that essence of the invisible God that moves within Himself to give evidence of the unseen God by the creation, through the creation, and for the creation. The Spirit of God is aptly titled as "Holy" Spirit because of the nature of this newly established relationship by the New Covenant that presupposes all those in whom the Spirit resides must be made Holy because He is Holy. Once a human being becomes born again, they are given a new nature, a holy nature that corresponds to the Holy Spirit who is God Himself permanently dwelling within the believer.

This union of the Spirit to the believer is what makes the Christian become separate and distinct from the rest of creation, in that the believer now takes part in God's divine nature. Believers are made holy in order to participate in those attributes and character traits that emulate the image and likeness of the invisible God, and to occupy sacred space. The new relationship establishes God as our eternal Father, and the believer as His beloved sons and daughters for all eternity. Always keep in mind that this union never ever makes us gods, but it does make us sons and daughters of God.

We can see how the most important earmark of a child of God is holiness. Before we can step into the complexities of walking by faith, we must first establish the importance of making holiness our number one priority. Being a peculiar people, and set apart, makes us available to readily manifest the invisible God as His children. In the new covenant, we have been declared sons and daughters, and the Holy Spirit is given to the believer so that we might receive a new nature that directly corresponds to our title as sons and daughters. By the Spirit, we can live up to our namesake: *Christians*—those who are just like the unique Son of God.

The Spirit of God *IS* Holy. Every effort made by the Spirit is intended above all else to make us holy in order to confirm our status as sons and daughters of God by molding us more and more into the image and likeness of God, who is Himself holy. Living in the Spirit, being led of the Spirit, walking in the Spirit, and being filled with the Spirit are all terms of consecration designed by the Spirit to forge, sculpt, and fashion us into holy vessels to be used by God and to occupy sacred space. This aspect of holiness is not only a matter of status but even more so a matter of identity. Holiness is that which identifies us *with* our Heavenly Father.

One thing that holiness does is that it causes a separation between us and that which God considers evil. Allow me to elaborate. It is not just a matter of God's people keeping themselves from becoming defiled or contaminated by sin or evil things. To a large degree and on many levels, that is still absolutely true. But there is another side of holiness equally important in that holiness also restrains evil from touching the believer. Holiness is not just about the believer keeping away from sin. Holiness protects the believer from evil itself. Just before Jesus was arrested, He made the interesting comment, *"... the prince of this world cometh, and he hath nothing in me"* (John 14:30). The adversary had absolutely no claim on Jesus whatsoever.

Jesus knew that what was about to happen to Him was a necessary evil he had to endure in order to fulfill prophecy. But during the entire time, it was Jesus who was in total control of the sequence of events that led to His crucifixion, death, burial, and resurrection. When the guards came seeking to arrest Him, demanding where He was, Jesus stood forward and said He was the one they were looking for. They fell backward to the ground, completely bewildered. They even felt the need to ask a second time just to make sure. As Peter strikes the servant of the High Priest, Jesus makes a remarkable observation that in those moments He could pray the Father to send twelve legions of angels to aid him.

In my opinion, this is one of the most fascinating occasions where Jesus' statement implies a certain plausibility. Jesus could have called on the Father and in the process even alter, or at least temporarily thwart, the mission for which he was sent to accomplish. Jesus' statement implied that the Father would indeed have interfered in those pivotal moments, and prevented His arrest. The only reason he went through with it was to ensure the Word of God in the Old Testament prophecies would be fulfilled.

Now this is truly remarkable because it demonstrates how far the Father would go to answer His Son's call, even at the expense of His reputation in fulfilling scriptural prophecy. This meant that the events of prophecy would have to either be delayed, or played out differently than they already had. If the Father had answered His prayer in those moments, history would have turned out very different. Circumstances would have been changed, and you and I may very well not be here reading this book.

The point I am making here is that Jesus exemplified what a Holy Son looks like and how He operates. His example reveals the degree of commitment that binds both the Father and His children. Holiness is the glue that makes that bond stick. Furthermore, Holiness is what kept Jesus in perfect control of the situation at hand. Even His enemies stumbled as they approached Him, and they became confused to the point that Jesus had to force their hand by commanding them to take Him, and to let the disciples go free. For Jesus, holiness was not about rules or restrictions as so many of us today might believe it to be. To Jesus, it was the benchmark of His Sonship.

CHAPTER 26
The Plan for Holiness

Holiness in the life of the believer is what emulates God's divine nature most efficiently to the creation. When I say *creation*, I am also referring to the spiritual forces that oppose God. Paul said:

> *"So that through the church the manifold wisdom of God might now be made known to the rulers and authorities in the heavenly places. This was according to the eternal purpose that he has realized in Christ Jesus our Lord."* (Ephesians 3:10-11 ESV)

The more holy something is, the more the Creator becomes visible while yet remaining unseen. The more we pursue holiness, the more we see Him in all things. The writer of Hebrews says, *"Follow peace with all men, and holiness without which no man shall see the Lord"* (Hebrews 12:14). Again, Jesus said, *"Blessed are the pure in heart for they shall see God"* (Matthew 5:8). In both passages, the invisible God can be seen by the believer only by maintaining this separation from sin.

We should consider more carefully what holiness means to our adversary in the spirit realm. The world might see us as a peculiar people who merely act differently than the rest, and may appear to hold to a different view of reality. That might even seem attractive to some, though not fully understood. But for the dark spiritual forces, what they see are living visual images of the invisible God. This terrifies them. Make no mistake, fallen angels, demons, or any other fallen spiritual creature is indeed afraid of Him. Even if they hate Him, they are also exceedingly fearful of Him.

Since they know that God is invisible, then whenever the Lord God chooses to reveal Himself, they know that His manifestation means judgment and their eventual destruction.

> *"Little children, let no man deceive you: he that doeth righteousness is righteous, even as he is righteous. He that committeth sin is of the devil; for the devil sinneth from the beginning. For this purpose the Son of God was manifested, that he might destroy the works of the devil. Whosoever is born of God doth not commit sin; for his seed remaineth in him: and he cannot sin, because he is born of God."* (1 John 3:7-9)

The holiness of the believer as the primary agent created in God's image makes the invisible God visually present before His enemies. Holiness is what makes the believer untouchable in the presence of evil. The holiness factor is what causes believers to be comfortable enough to sit down at a table and even eat in the presence of their enemies. *"Thou preparest a table before me in the presence of mine enemies …"* (Psalm 23:5a). This is the example Jesus demonstrated for us.

The ministry of the Spirit is purposely designed to mold us into the same image as of that Christ: the holy child of God. The way we deal with carnality and sin, as well as how we manage our relationships, and by regularly and daily devoting ourselves to God is accomplished by and through the Spirit. It is the apparatus by which we are transitioned into the image of the holy. Make no mistake, what we do and how we live really does matter. If you have not noticed, many Christians in today's world are to resemble their Savior in the most fundamental ways, by their words and deeds. If we are to efficiently image the invisible God, then we must address the sin problem in the church first.

We experience what I term as the pendulum effect. We swing from one extreme to another. For example: There are certain ministries that hold to the Cessationism view that God no longer does miracles, signs, and wonders today, primarily because He did it only to confirm the ministry of the apostles and prophets of the Bible. This group tends to be growing in popularity as the more "safe" and intellectual route. It appeals to the intellect more than to the supernatural aspect of reality, citing doctrine above experience. However, this group is also so caught up in the intellectuality of Cessationism that they shut out almost all possibility of supernaturalism, such as miracles, signs, and wonders, the exception being the salvation or born again experience.

The other side of the pendulum is the charismatic camp of miracles, signs, wonders, and healings. While this group encourages the reading of the Bible, it also relies more heavily on experience to either support or confirm a doctrine. The charismatic group has also shown great potential for doctrinal error on a number of fronts. From this camp, you have offshoots, such as the prosperity gospel that emphasize giving money in order to "receive a blessing." This has many falling prey to such traps.

The issue that I have with both of these camps is that I agree with some of what they affirm, and I also disagree with some of what they deny. The Cessationism camp does an amazing job of calling out sin for what it is. However, they also deny the possibility that God is willing to do the same kinds of miracles as portrayed in the Bible for today. Furthermore, they are more willing to excommunicate anyone who is not in alignment with their dogma. They go to great lengths to even attack preachers and ministries in the name of doctrinal orthodoxy.

On the other hand, the charismatic camp does a phenomenal job of believing God for the impossible and regularly step out in faith against incredible odds. However, they also tend to fall prey to many charlatans who promote signs and wonders to the point that they ignore important points of theology because of supernatural elements that follow erroneous Charismatic preachers. While holding to some position of authority and influence, they might teach or say something that contradicts scripture, but there is little in terms of critical thinking applied to doctrine in many cases.

So what does this have to do with the invisible nature of God? Well, when factions and schisms arise in the church, we distort the image of God in the body of Christ. This division is unholy in itself because it is a form of godlessness veiled in piety. God cannot be seen (or rather experienced) properly due to either our inability, or most likely our unwillingness, to live holy with one another. It creates a distortion that prevents us and the rest of the world from seeing God as He truly is. Our misappropriation of what the New Testament instructs is in our enemy's best interest.

As long as we misrepresent God in our behaviors and attitudes, especially toward one another within the body of Christ, the world will continue to wallow in their ignorance of God. We must stop making excuses for our sin. He desires for those who do not know Him to recognize Him when He moves in and through His people. Our obedience and disobedience either facilitates or restricts that process. God has chosen the believer as the vessel that carries His presence to evoke change. How we carry ourselves among unbelievers will either reveal or conceal the truth of who God is. We need to abandon the image of fallen man and embrace the image of the incorruptible God. For us to transition into our destiny, we must identify ourselves with God as our Father, forsaking the ways of the world and embracing God's plan and process.

The process God has chosen for us is the application of faith in the life of the believer. As we break down the different elements of faith, keep in mind that every step we take in faith has, at its core, the manifestation of the invisible God as the primary touch point. The faith we display to the world communicates the reality of the God we serve in ways that can even defy logic by worldly standards. It might even seem foolish to them who perish, but it is salvation to those who believe.

It is time we re-learned to trust in God whom we serve and claim to believe in. He not only loves us and takes care of our needs, but He has every intention to make Himself known to the world around us.

Since the first advent of Christ, God's long-awaited Kingdom has been in effect. For the first time since the fall of man in Eden, God has a proper representative in Christ to emulate His government on the earth without restraint. Through Jesus' administration of the Kingdom, God could proliferate the earth with manifestations of His glory and majesty. The invisible God could now be made manifest to His beloved creation through His Son. I should point out that His kingdom is much more than a mere religious ideology. It is God's Master Plan to restore what was lost in paradise. His Kingdom is in fact a manifestation of Himself in governmental form.

The Kingdom is purposefully structured to manifest His will, and it therefore becomes necessary for us to learn the role we play in this Kingdom. Furthermore, faith is built on the premise of governmental power. As believers, we are tasked with representing the Lord's government on the earth, so that those who do not know God might recognize Him and sense the need to be drawn to Him (Acts 17:27). The Kingdom of God is intended to be a visual manifestation of the invisible God through His agents. His character, nature, and power are the key elements of His government. However, biblical faith is the very means by which all these things take form.

It is important to note here that the Kingdom of God is actually a family-run business. His household is His first and only choice to run His business. Our destiny as believers is to rule with Him for all eternity. That is our stated purpose, and primary role to play in this whole story. However, if we are to rule well, we need to learn and re-learn some basic principles about Kingdom rulership. In order to do that, we need to go further and deeper into Kingdom concepts and systems of government.

First things first. Kingdoms are forms of government in which a monarch exercises rulership and ownership over everything within his domain. In fact, the word *Kingdom* is a composite of two words: *king* and *domain* (or *dominion*). Hence, the word *Kingdom* means "a King over his domain." The late Dr. Myles Munroe defines a kingdom as, "The governing influence of a king over his territory, impacting it with his personal will, purpose, and intent, producing a culture, morals, and lifestyle that reflects the King's desires and nature for his citizens."[42]

The will of the King is the law of the land. The culture of the King is

---

[42] Myles Munroe, *Kingdom Principles: Preparing for Kingdom Experience and Expansion* (Shippensburg, PA, PA: Destiny Image Publishers, 2006), Chapter 1, Pg. 36.

the culture of his people, especially of his own household. Whenever the King speaks, His word becomes the governing power and priority that is to be followed and obeyed, because it is considered official legislation. Kings and all levels of royalty operate and rule by decree. These carry legally binding power within kingdoms.

CHAPTER 27
Government and Divine Profile

While serving overseas, I had run into a young man who was reading a book about different forms of government for a college class he was taking. I asked him which government was the most efficient. Without even hesitating he said, "Oh, that's easy. It's a kingdom." I replied by saying, "You're absolutely correct, but that is only true if the monarch is a good King." He agreed. Isaiah said, *"For the LORD is our judge, the LORD is our lawgiver, the LORD is our king; he will save us"* (Isaiah 33:22).

Most of us in the West do not live under kings and kingdoms. The Bible is a book that uses language derived from a monarchical system from antiquity. The late Myles Munroe would often quip, "The Bible is a kingdom book!" When we read the Bible, we can easily make the mistake of reading into the text the biases of our own cultures. We may not realize just how much of our westernized history affects our reading of the Bible and what we believe about it. Think about it this way. We are taught in schools from an early age that the Unites States of America won the American Revolutionary War and declared our independence from the tyranny of Great Britain. This event is also known as the American War of Independence.

Americans relish their freedoms and will fight tooth and nail to keep them secure. In the far reaches of the American psyche, monarchies are historically perceived as something tyrannical to be avoided and resisted. It is generally considered an ideology imposed upon others who are deprived of our "brand" of freedom. I know this might seem a little overboard, but the quandary does exist. This is due to the fact that we are citizens of a country that embraces a different form of government. In America, we are actually a Constitutional Republic, not a Democracy.[43]

Unfortunately, most Americans do not even understand the structure of their own government, much less know their own nation's history. This brings me to another point. If we have difficulty understanding our own system of government as Americans properly living day by day in the United States, then how do we presume to grasp a foreign concept and system of government like … say … the Kingdom of God? Yes, the Kingdom of God is indeed a government! It is ruled by the King of kings.

We read words like "Kingdom of God" and "Kingdom of Heaven," and there is an automatic disconnect in our minds. Being raised in a country like America that boasts of its way of life has a profound impact on how we choose to accept God's idea of government. For some, the concept of being under a king may stir up feelings of unwanted control or even oppression, even though we are talking about God's Kingdom. I believe this is partly an undergirding factor as to why so many people in church are duped into believing that Christianity is all about rules, rather than a relationship.

You are probably wondering how this has anything to do with God being invisible, or even faith? It has everything to do with it! Jesus said, *"The kingdom of God is not coming in ways that can be observed"* (Luke 17:20). We are in a conflict between different governments. There are certain realities that are always unpleasant in the midst of war. You may not have considered it before, but every work we do by faith is in all practicality an act of war against the usurpers who took up residence illegally on the earth so long ago.

---

[43] Contrary to public opinion, we are not a Democracy. I think it is shameful that our leaders keep perpetuating mixed truths and half lies by calling us a Democracy when, in fact, we are a Constitutional Republic.

We must put things into proper perspective if we are going to experience true victory. We are important to God's plans, and He has decreed it so. No one is expendable, and no one lacks value or usefulness in God's Kingdom. All of us have a part to play in this. Our conduct dictates to the world the nature of His government. Additionally, faith is not an illusion, nor is it a special handout to a select few with some exclusive "special" anointing. Faith is what gives tangible properties to the invisible aspects of God and His Kingdom in this life, and it is the holiness that most resembles His being. As sons and daughters of God, His dominion is our birthright, our inheritance, our household.

We have been made holy by the work of God through His Son Jesus the Messiah. However, we as believers do not always remain focused on keeping ourselves sanctified. Too many people think it is too difficult a path to follow, or even that it is impossible. I believe the reason we have made it seem so difficult is because we have been conditioned to focus on God from a "visual" concept, rather than an invisible one. Early on in this book, I mentioned that our understanding of God affects our beliefs and behavior. By not having adopted an understanding of God's invisible nature, we have conditioned ourselves to a version of God that does not correspond to reality.

When God's true invisible nature is embraced, our spiritual senses and experiences become conditioned to His reality by revealing God as He really is. Our approach to spiritual matters takes on the same dimensions of God's own nature. So why bring up the whole idea of the Kingdom? Primarily because the Bible is a book built on Kingdom principles. God has chosen this paradigm as the approach to understanding every doctrine of scripture, including His nature. Whether we are accustomed to it or not, there needs to be an adjustment to our understanding of what God intends to communicate. It affects how we interpret and define terms, read chapters and verses, as well as how we wrestle with doctrine and theology.

God is King, and He is the One who determines and defines the boundaries of how His government operates. We are subjects of that Kingdom and form of government. We ought to know how to operate within the framework God has provided for us. As sons and daughters of God, we have certain rights and privileges that belong to us, those who are created in His image and likeness. A necessity exists in our having to learn and relearn the protocols of royalty. Yes, we are considered royalty on the earth. We were created by God with the express purpose of exercising dominion within His creation.

THE DUTY OF KINGS

Laying aside the fanciful and often sinful Hollywood-style depictions of kingdoms, let's consider the basic function of how kings really operate. The main difference between the rule of a monarchy and that of a democracy is defined by the body of leadership. In a democracy, the "will of the many" determine the direction of their nation. But in a kingdom, the direction is determined by the "will of one." This can be problematic when any human government is run by corrupt leaders. When the monarch is benevolent, kingdoms are run efficiently, and the people prosper by virtue of the king's benevolence.

Furthermore, all monarchies rule by decree. Anytime a king or queen issues forth a decree, it becomes an official ordinance of the nation. In other words, the will of the monarch becomes the law of the land. When he or she issues forth a decree, that word spoken by them becomes official legislation. When a king issues forth a decree, it then becomes irrevocable because of the role the monarch plays. The immutable nature of royal decree conveys the idea of the king as the final authority.

Unlike a democratic forum, there is no deliberation between congress, judiciaries, parliaments, or anything like what we experience in the US, or the UK for that matter. You can see how being subject to someone who has great potential for corruption can be a discouraging premise to the American mind. But when it comes to the Kingdom of God and of Christ, corruption is not a part of the equation. God, Who is our Father, cannot be corrupted by sin. Jesus Christ, who is our King, never sinned and therefore was never corrupted. The Kingdom of which I speak has a good and benevolent King at its helm.

An observation should be made at this point of a careful reading into the biblical text that gives us some peculiar insight into the aspect of royal decrees. When we look at certain kings mentioned in the Old Testament, there are nuances behind the decrees of various kings, Jewish and Gentile alike. A casual reading might cause us to overlook the fact that, many times, the scriptures refer to King David by his proper name "David" most of the time, except when his rule as King was being emphasized. At times, he is referred to as "king David" or "David the king."

However, whenever David acted in His full capacity as the reigning monarch by making a decree, the scriptures aptly referred to him as "the king" rather than using his proper name with the title as in other cases. This peculiarity seems to apply to both good and evil decrees because the act of decreeing is the legitimate method of rule by kings. We see the same thing even with the pagan king Xerxes in the book of Esther. When he issues a direct decree, Xerxes is referred to as "the king." It's just a quick observation, but I digress.

A kingdom is structured around the monarch. The culture of the monarch is the culture of the citizenry of his kingdom. The state of the people reflects the state of mind of the king or queen. The decrees issued by the monarch are the means by which laws are passed, armies are led, and how people are governed. Everything is done by decree. When citizens request to be seen by the king or queen, it is an appeal to the monarch's benevolence.

To be seen by the king or queen, i.e., to be brought before the presence of the king, is to be heard by the king. This assumes that the monarch is not only able enough to meet the needs of his citizens, but he is also good enough to answer their need. If the king speaks with an answer in favor of the citizen, a law in favor of the citizen is being issued. Therefore, if it comes from the king, it cannot be contested.

Of course, even though this is how kings in general ought to operate, we are actually talking about God and His kingdom. God is good. He is a good King who is not only able, but also willing to answer His people. Consider the language used of God in relation to His people, especially in light of the nature and character of God. He is everywhere, has all power, and is completely and utterly good. To seek His face is to come before Him. To be seen of Him is to be in His presence.

To be in His presence is to be heard by Him. If He hears you, then it means He answers you. If He answers you, then you have whatever you desire of Him. All of this is a play on His goodness. It is a system designed entirely around the nature and character of the eternal God. Though human governments fall exceedingly short of what He considers legitimate, God's kingdom stands forever as a rock that cannot be moved.

CHAPTER 28
Faith and the Kingdom

Faith and God's Kingdom are intricately connected. The nature of God's Kingdom was exemplified through Jesus' life. He preached the Kingdom of God and His righteousness by faith, thereby changing history through His decrees. Everywhere He went, He proclaimed the superiority and supremacy of God's government over everything, whether it was sin and sinner, sickness, or disease.

When the King appeared, His mission was to establish a new order. He set the legal precedent of how His Kingdom would operate. Everything Jesus did during His lifetime was the model and example for us to follow. This is a very rudimentary introduction into Kingdoms, and it is certainly not much to chew on, but it is enough fuel to get us to our destination.

When it comes to faith, this principle of decree is the basis upon which faith operates. I will admit here to my personal departure from the conventional definition people often ascribe to faith. I say this because most people define faith as "believing without having to see." This way of accepting faith is prevalent in the church, and everyone blindly assumes it to be true. In the coming chapters, I intend to make the case that what is generally understood about faith by the laymen and theologian alike is incorrect and misapplied. It is a bold statement, I know, but as I said before, allow me to make my case.

Has it ever occurred to you to ask, "Why Faith? I mean, why does God in His infinite wisdom choose faith as the means by which we are to live?" Think about it. God could have picked anything, but He chose faith. God does nothing by accident. For this reason, we must go back to the beginning at creation to understand what the Bible means by using the word *faith*. The creation account depicted in Genesis can be very enlightening, primarily due to the various precedents the Father sets in those first few chapters. The book of Genesis is the book of beginnings. Every aspect of the creation sets a precedent for what follows.

When God created the universe, how did He do it? He did it by decree! He literally spoke the universe into existence. In fact, the English word *universe* literally means "a single spoken sentence." All creation came about by the Word of God. God spoke, and things just came into being. When God said, *"Let there be light ..."* (Genesis 1:3), it simply became a matter of fact from that moment on. Light was. Think about the kind of power God must have for Him to simply speak His Word, and then His will is accomplished with no strain nor diminishing of energy. The enormity of that power simply cannot be defined or measured.

As King, God exercises His right as Creator by bringing things into existence. As He does this, He also sets a precedent. There are so many tidbits that can be gleaned from the first chapter of Genesis alone. I will select only a few to make an important point. As each day that is created passes, patterns emerge revealing details that communicate what faith is supposed to look like. These patterns are loaded with ramifications for future generations coming into existence. Allow me to elaborate with just a few examples.

CREATION

On the first day, God created light. The Bible gives a peculiar phrase concerning His creation of that light with *"God saw the light, that it was good"* (Genesis 1:3). When we get to the second day, nothing about goodness is stated. But when we get to the third day, God says **twice** that it is good! That is not there by accident! This ought to be an indicator to the reader of something God deems as important. Remember, when the Creator of the Universe speaks, it is not by happenstance, nor is it without relevance. There is a purpose behind every single thing He says and does. By revealing that He calls "the third day" as being good twice, it is His way of telling us there is a special significance He associates with the third day.

This special significance of the third day can be seen in other passages, revealing something of profound importance to God's intentions where the third day is concerned. Here are a handful of examples of things that happened on the third day:

- Genesis 22:4 – Abraham saw the place where he was to sacrifice his son (Akedah).
- Exodus 19:11-20 – God descends on Mount Sinai to give His Holy Law, the Torah.
- Hosea 6:1-2 – Future prophecy of the people of God repenting and returning to God.
- Matthew 27, Mark 10:34, Luke 18 – Resurrection of the Son of God from the dead.

When we get to the fourth day, God creates the sun, moon, and stars. The passage reads, *"And God said, Let there be lights in the firmament of the heaven to divide the day from the night; and let them be for signs, and for seasons, and for days, and years: And let them be for lights in the firmament of the heaven to give light upon the earth: and it was so"* (Genesis 1:14-15). This passage tells us the reason for the creation of the lights was primarily for signs and seasons, for days and years, and to provide illumination on the earth.

The fourth day signaled the last phase of the environmental aspect of creation. After the environment was established, God then created animals, commencing with sea creatures and birds on the fifth day. And then we finally arrive at the sixth day, when God created the land animals. He ended the day with the creation of Mankind.

There is a peculiar method to the creation account that should draw attention to its order. When something (a) is made for something else (b), which one is more important and takes priority? In the order given, which one has the preeminence between a and b? Put it another way, if your clothes (a) were made for your body (b), which of the two have the most value? The clothing or the body? Obviously, it is the body. Likewise, when the Bible says that the sun, moon, and stars were made for the earth, which one has the most importance in order of precedence? The sun, moon, and stars, or the earth?

Again, the obvious answer is that the earth is more important in terms of priority. I am not saying the earth is necessarily the center of the universe. What I am saying is that as far as priority goes, the earth is more important than the sun, moon. and stars because it serves as the immediate environment for the living creatures. One way of visualizing this order of precedence is shown below with the least important on the bottom and the most important on the top tier:

~ LIVING CREATURES ~
~ EARTH ~
~ SUN, MOON, STARS ~

The importance of bringing this up stems from the creation of mankind. The very last thing God made was humankind, and God has a habit of always saving His best wine for last. Here is the account in question:

> *"And God said, Let us make man in our image, after our likeness: and* **let them have dominion** *over the fish of the sea, and over the fowl of the air, and over the cattle, and over all the earth, and over every creeping thing that creepeth upon the earth. So God created man in his own image, in the image of God created he him; male and female created he them"* (Genesis 1:26-27 [emphasis added].

When man is created, he is formed by God with a design that is compatible with the stated purpose given to him. God said that man is to have dominion over everything He created, including the animals, and the earth itself.

Man is positioned at the top of the hierarchy. Why? Because he has DOMINION over all of it. Only kings exercise dominion. By God's sovereign decree, Adam was appointed king over the creation. As a direct creation of God, Adam was called God's son (see Luke 3:38). God intended Adam to be the first in line of the race of kings. All of humanity was to have this title. Every descendant of Adam that was to follow would qualify for the position. Interestingly enough, God's appointment of Adam and his descendants to such a lofty position is such that no other being is given such dominion within the physical creation.

Genesis 2 elaborates with further detail concerning the creation of humankind and what followed immediately afterward. God made Adam from the "dust of the earth," which is the same material that is higher in priority from that of the sun, moon, and stars. This can be construed to mean that mankind's authority reached over the entire physical creation. Even though man was made from the same material as that of the animals, his dominion was established by God's sovereign decree placing humanity above them. Now, for the first time, the physical creation had in humanity a frame of reference for the image and likeness of the invisible God.

This new being called "Adam" was uniquely designed to project onto the creation the very image of the invisible God by way of dominion. With that in mind, where does humankind fair in the grand scheme of things after it's all said and done? See the updated hierarchy below:

~ **GOD** ~
~ **SON(s)** ~
~ **MANKIND** ~
~ **LIVING CREATURES (ANIMALS)** ~
~ **EARTH** ~
~ **SUN, MOON, STARS** ~

It is imperative to note here that the list provided above is in order of precedent. God is above all, with humankind as God's absolute ruling authority over all of creation, by representing God in every possible way through mandated dominion. I would also like to note here that the living animals are in a higher order of precedence than the earth, sun, moon, and stars. I am of the opinion that God's emphasis on placing a higher priority and value to living things, and life itself in particular, above matter is the whole point. God is in the business of creating and giving life. This will play a significant role in what is to come.

Humankind is in a unique position to influence the creation. In the grand scheme of things, humanity was given authority to govern the entire physical creation as it saw fit. Our place in the order of things is above that of the entire universe. The authority invested in man was so complete that when Adam fell, the entire physical creation fell with him and was made subject to his condition. Death and decay became interwoven in the fabric of the universe.

Whether it is the chaos of a star exploding in a galaxy somewhere, or whether it is sickness and even death, these are all results of the fall of man. When the Bible says that death came into the world, it is referring to the laws of entropy that are inherently within the creation as it is now. Entropy is the measure of degradation or disorder over time. As time passes, entropy increases its effect and things break down.

Adam's position was that of a king. To gain proper perspective of this reality, imagine the notion that every governor over every individual state in the United States of America was actually a king. If the king over any state were to die, that state would cede from the union. That is the nature of kings and kingdoms, and that was also the state of creation under Adam. When God gave mankind dominion, He did so in a unique way. We need to look at the creation of man, and see how God set in order the rule of creation.

> "And God said, Let us make man in our image, after our likeness: and let them have dominion over the fish of the sea, and over the fowl of the air, and over the cattle, and over all the earth, and over every creeping thing that creepeth upon the earth. So God created man in his own image, in the image of God created he him; male and female created he them." (Genesis 1:26-27)

The one major aspect of man that is preeminent above all other creatures within the physical realm is that we were made in God's image and after His likeness. The invisible God chose to put together a being that would represent His invisible qualities most efficiently and accurately through a stated purpose: dominion. That image and likeness is the status that qualifies us for rulership over God's creation. However, what makes the creation of man even more impactful was in what God did *not* say. When He created man, He did not say, *"Let us make man ... and let us have dominion with them ..."* Instead, God purposefully omits Himself from the equation!

CHAPTER 29
The New Creation

God chose to give His new creation a dominion that was so complete, so thorough and absolute that when man was approached in the garden, God did not interfere. Think about it. By giving man this dominion, God was in effect instituting the legal boundaries of rulership. Only a being like Adam, of His seed, could be allowed to exercise dominion. That is, only a being created in the manner of Adam could freely operate in the physical realm without restraint. That meant that even if God Himself issued a decree, Adam would still be free to choose contrary to the command. That is what we see being played out in scripture.

MAN'S CREATION

> "And the LORD God formed man of the dust of the ground, and breathed into his nostrils the breath of life; and man became a living soul." (Genesis 2:7)

Having been made from the same material as the earth, and receiving the breath of life from God, man became a living soul especially designed for the task set before him. When God decreed that man should have dominion, He did so knowing in a way that only a being that was made from the dust with His breath of life would have the legal right to govern the physical creation with righteous rule. However, this also created a quandary in that by giving this dominion, God set into motion a series of necessities that did not exist prior to issuing His decree.

Since God is spirit and is Himself not a man, then that meant that in order for God to interact with His new creation in the way He intended, then He would need a man to cooperate with Him. That is why the Lord God did not interfere in the garden. He would not interfere because He could not! If God did interfere, He would have been violating His own blessing of dominion to man. In fact, I would go so far to say that if God had done so, all of creation would have come apart at the seams.

This might seem strange to you and I, but the concepts of kingdom realities are usually foreign to us. Everything about the creation account is based on a kingdom paradigm. When Adam fell (Genesis 3), his dominion was not handed over to the serpent. If the serpent's guile was able to take the dominion from Adam, then the condition of creation itself would have been unaffected. That is not what happened. The creation followed the mandated dominion of man given by its Creator.

Now, that is not to say the creation cannot be influenced by the enemy of mankind. Rather, it was the control that man exercised over circumstances which was relinquished. That control is what governed the creation under the dominion of man. It was the act of Adam's refusal to exercise control over the serpent that resulted in him losing that control. However, even the spiritual enemy of man still has to use mankind in order to subject the creation to his will. The entire creation responds to the disposition of man because of God's decree for man to have dominion.

You might ask, "What about God? Doesn't He have a say in all this? Isn't He in control of everything?" Well, according to the account in Genesis, though God is sovereign, He is not in complete control of every decision made by His creation. They can and do things that are contrary to His will. God's sovereignty and power is revealed in His ability to govern in spite of everything contrary to His will. His greatness is not subject to the whims of a serpent, nor even that of man. He is God overall who is wise enough and strong enough to create a world in which His perfect will can be accomplished regardless of the opposition.

This autonomy he instilled in mankind's volition is an essential component to the dominion He mandated. This freedom is inherent within the design of the mandate. God freely chose to give man this liberty so that he can emulate God's own choice through willful obedience. By giving man this freedom, God's image and likeness can be projected through human beings who willingly submit to righteous rule. That willingness is necessary in order for true peace to be peace. If mankind had not rebelled the entire creation would be like heaven today, where God's perfect will is always accomplished. Again…that is not what happened.

Even though humanity would progressively digress in its condition, God knew from the beginning what it would take to bring about reconciliation. He knew that He would have to have a human to come into alignment with Him in order to fulfill His will on earth. When God wanted to bring a flood, He needed Noah. When He wanted to deliver Israel out of Egypt, He needed Moses. When He wanted to call Israel to repentance, He needed a prophet. When He wanted to deliver the nation of Israel from an oppressor, He needed a deliverer. When God wanted to save the world, He needed Christ. Now He wants to reach the world, and right now He has the Church, the body of Christ.

I understand that you might have some hesitation about saying that God needs anything. I get it. Understand, that it is not a need inherent within His nature. It is a need that arises by virtue of His own decree. Remember, God is Himself King with unlimited power. The moment God says anything, He becomes subjected to His own decree because it defines all boundaries of reality. He cannot contradict Himself, therefore God cannot lie. When God dictates anything from His authority and seat of power, He abides by it because every command He issue in the scripture is a direct reflection of His own nature and character. His own decree for dominion accounted for all the circumstances stemming from his decision. God's wisdom and greatness is beyond what we can comprehend, and His goodness is better than we might give Him credit for.

Since God's invisible things are intended to be seen through the things that are made, we ought to embrace our destiny as the children of God who are called to show forth His greatness. Jesus is our template. He is our model. He perfectly demonstrated what a fully submitted Son looks like. As redeemed sons and daughters, we are given the lofty role of ruling with Christ as those who sit on His throne. That is not something that can be taken lightly.

Some time ago, Psychologist Jordan Peterson interviewed Jonathan Pageau on his Podcast. In it, Dr. Peterson gave an emotional response to the reality of what it means to truly believe in Christ. Dr. Peterson may or may not be a born again Christian, but his tone and comments in this interview carried the profound weight of the realization of everything we have discussed thus far. With tears, Dr. Peterson stated:

> "… We have a narrative sense of the world. For me that's been the world of morality. That's the world that tells us how to act. It's real … we treat it like it's real. It's not the objective world, but the narrative and the objective world touch; and the ultimate example of that in principle is supposed to be Christ. But I don't know … that seems to me oddly plausible. But I still don't know what to make of it. It partly is because it's too terrifying a reality to fully believe. I don't even know what would happen to you if you fully believed it!" [44]

The interviewer then asked him, "Do you mean if you believe in the story of Christ, or if you believe that history and the narrative meet? Jordan's response to him was equally profound, "Both, I think, because when you believe that, you buy both those stories. You believe that the narrative and the objective can actually touch."

The truth concerning God's ultimate plan to make Himself known to the world in the New Covenant has been severely curtailed through our ignorance and unbelief. It has also been stifled by the traditions we elevate above God's own Holy Word. Of course, God knows these as well. Knowing

---

[44] Peterson, Jordan B. *The Perfect Mode of Being | Jonathan Pageau - Jordan B. Peterson Podcast S4 E8 quote time marker 23min 32sec to 24min 08sec* YouTube, 2021. Accessed March 12, 2022. https://youtu.be/2rAqVmZwqZM.

this in advance, God saw fit to mention the following by the mouth of the prophets:

> "I will praise thee with my whole heart: before the gods will I sing praise unto thee. I will worship toward thy holy temple, and praise thy name for thy lovingkindness and for thy truth: for thou hast magnified thy word above all thy name." (Psalm 138:1-2)

If you recall, God's name is His very Presence in identity. He chooses to set His Word that carries His intent above His own Presence. This is because man disobeyed God's Word, thereby becoming alienated from God. Therefore, in order for mankind to be restored to his rightful place, man must respond to God's Word so that he can live again in God's Presence. Just as God's Word spoken at creation produced humanity, it is God's Word that produces a new creation, a new humanity wherein the image and likeness of God is restored. God knew this monumental task could only be accomplished by Himself, through Himself, and for Himself. In these final chapters, we will delve deeper into what it means that God was in Christ reconciling the world to Himself. There is more to this than meets the eye.

CHAPTER 30
The Word of Reconciliation

We need to take a step back for a few moments and meditate on the reality of what it means that God has made Himself visible in any capacity, but infinitely more so in Christ. What we are about to embark on will challenge some of your most fundamental notions of theology. We know *who* this narrative is really about. We also know *what* it entails. We even know how it plays out in history to the present day. Yet, the other more pressing question still remains to be fully explored ... *why*?

Why would God go to such great lengths in manifesting Himself in the capacity of the Son of God? I think at some point, we have all taken for granted the testimony of Christ, how Jesus came into the world, died, was buried, and rose again the third day. But there is so much more to it than that. I believe some retrospect is in order here. For us to see God's ultimate intent, we must look back at Jesus Christ Himself for the answers we seek.

The Lord Jesus Christ is the absolute and most perfect representation of the Father there has ever been. Everything about Him is a perfect reflection of God's nature in the form of character. Everything Jesus both said and did on earth communicated the Father's truth to the world as a whole. Every generation since His first advent has been impacted by His appearing. We even measure our history and time with Christ as the singular reference point.

So what is it exactly that God wanted to reveal about Himself? Well, the answer is found in the mission of Jesus Christ. Every lesson Jesus taught, every miracle He did, every encounter He had, all of it communicated God's heart for His creation. What was the core of Jesus' mission? In a nutshell, the most simple answer is: ***He forgave, and He healed.***

It is simple but exceedingly profound. You see, it was the Father's plan all along to use these two methods to reveal Himself. The works of Christ were no accident, nor were they an afterthought in God's mind. They were the arrows in God's quiver, and through Christ, they would pierce the hearts of God's enemies.

Since the fall of man, the spiritual powers in opposition to God took their places to usurp themselves and to impose their will on mankind. We became enslaved to their will, and as sin increased in the earth, the image of God was distorted. Eventually, we morphed into the image of the corruption propagated by those spiritual forces who wanted to make us forget the Creator. Humanity was now alienated from God, and without hope in the world. Of course, God knew all these things would happen. He would devise a plan that would result in the ultimate dispossession of the entire creation from its usurpers.

The Father's plan would involve Him manifesting His Word in flesh, to extend the hand to heal. He reached out in mercy to forgive every sin committed, reconciling mankind back to Himself. Everything Jesus did and taught was the Father's unrelenting effort to reconcile His image bearers, to undo the alienation. He did this by doing two basic things: He would heal their bodies from sickness and disease brought on the world by sin, and He would also forgive them of their sin that corrupted His image and likeness within them. In this way, God would make it possible for the world to behold Him, to once again walk in a new Eden as it were.

The healing of the bodies has a purpose. The body is a vessel, an instrument of projection. While the Father cannot be seen, the body can make Him visible through godly character. Christ Jesus lived out that character as an example for us to follow. He made it possible. As the Son of

God, Jesus brought together two different and separate worlds—the mostly invisible, spiritual, divine world with its perfection, and the human, natural world with all its messiness and imperfection. He made them both one in Himself. Whenever Christ would touch a sick body, or speak from a distance to heal a dying soul, He made the Father visible. As the writer of Hebrews says:

> *"Who being the brightness of his glory, and the express image of his person, and upholding all things by the word of his power, when he had by himself purged our sins, sat down on the right hand of the Majesty on high …"*
> (Hebrews 1:3)

In a human body, God would intimately share in humanity's weakness, and we were in the audience with front row seats. We could see with our very own eyes what a frail human body was capable of with the living God inside of him. His mouth would speak words carrying the power to restore and make whole. He could compel water molecules to join together without freezing for his feet to walk on. Storms would calm and the dead would rise at the mere sound of His voice calling out.

Every healing, miracle, sign, and wonder was an open display of that which could not be seen. The enemies of God could stop the course of events that would lead to the liberation of humankind. As for these fallen divine beings behind the corruption of the world, the appearing of the Son of God was the mark of their destruction, by building back the bodies they destroyed. The restoration of those vessels, fitted to image God, communicated to them that the Father was revealing Himself. That notion terrifies the powers of darkness. They know that His appearing means their destruction.

Every healed body, the opening of deaf ears, the walking of crippled feet, and dead bodies being given life again was the signal of impending judgment. In fact, every one of the miracles performed was a judgment made by decree of the Son of God that all were being made free from their oppressors.

> *"Bless the LORD, O my soul: and all that is within me, [bless] his holy name. Bless the LORD, O my soul, and forget not all his benefits: Who forgiveth all thine iniquities; who healeth all thy diseases; Who redeemeth thy life from destruction; who crowneth thee with lovingkindness and tender mercies; Who satisfieth thy mouth with good [things; so that] thy youth is renewed like the eagle's. The LORD executeth righteousness and judgment for all that are oppressed."*
> (Psalm 103 1-6)

Notice how the benefits of the Lord are *forgiving* iniquity, and *healing* all diseases. These two elements result in redeeming life from destruction, rewarding lovingkindness and mercy, and satisfaction with goodness that prolongs life. All these things are the execution of God's righteous judgment in order to reconcile us who could not be free from our oppression on our own. This is how God wants to be seen. He wants the world to see Him in this light. It is the default measure God utilized in Christ to reconcile the world back to Himself.

We have a nasty habit of divorcing the spiritual from the physical to the point that in certain circles, there can be no correlation between the spiritual condition and physical ailment. One example is how some people hold to the position that sickness and disease does not fall under the category of Jesus' atoning work and sacrifice. While this is a topic that will be addressed in a future work, it should be noted here that regardless of anyone's position on the subject, both the physical and spiritual conditions of humanity were addressed in Jesus' ministry.

The propensity to adamantly oppose the union of both the physical and spiritual conditions as being covered by the offering of Jesus' body is problematic. By not including the healing of the body with the forgiveness of sin as a part of the divine package of Jesus' ministry for today is to deny the Bible's emphatic assertion that God does both. I suspect that this is due to our combining of physical things with evil. If you really want to be accurate, the Bible does not make a distinction between spiritual and physical. We do that with our modern understanding of these terms. Contrary to popular opinion, the distinction is not between the spiritual and physical. Rather the distinction made is more often than not between the spiritual and the carnal.

In other words, the physical world itself is not considered evil. Instead, it is the fallen carnal (or fleshly) nature that is opposed to God and His ways. The view that the physical world is evil comes from gnostic philosophy. The Hebrews do not consider the physical world evil because when God created everything, He saw that it was all very good. Furthermore, the Hebrew view of creation is that everything is considered spiritual, including the physical world. I know this goes against much of the theology we hear in churches in the West, and it is unfortunate because the scriptures themselves do not make the physical creation out to be evil.

If for no other reason, the main purpose of the physical world IS to manifest the invisible God. Therefore, the work of Christ was not limited to forgiving sin. It had to include the healing of the body. This is especially true of the human body because it is God's chosen vessel by which He can be made known in the physical universe.

The New Testament often makes mention of Jesus healing the sick, opening the eyes of the blind, making the cripple walk, casting out demons, and raising the dead with His word. This act of reconciling the body is a part of the divine mission of Christ. It was the Father's word of reconciliation through Christ that restored broken bodies to function in the most efficient design. The manifestation of God through Jesus Christ in fulfilling His mission through forgiving and healing had a singular purpose,

> *"He that committeth sin is of the devil; for the devil sinneth from the beginning. For this purpose the Son of God was manifested, that he might destroy the works of the devil."* (1 John 3:8)

Whenever Jesus did anything during His earthly life, whether it was reconciling of the body through healing, or the reconciling of the soul through forgiveness, it was with the express purpose of destroying the works of the devil. That is not to say that all sickness or that all sin is attributed to the devil alone. By no means. However, it does mean that since the devil sinned from the beginning, by it he introduced the system by which the entire world became corrupted. This corruption led to both physical and spiritual death. Jesus correlated the sinful state of mankind with the sin of the adversary. Jesus did not pin man's sins on the devil, but he did point to the devil as the source of the corruption.

So what does all this have to do with the nature of the invisible God? Well, everything! The human body was designed by God as the most efficient vessel to image or project His invisible qualities within the physical world. When it functions the way it is supposed to function, it brings God glory because we are "fearfully and wonderfully made." Having been made in God's image and after His likeness means that we are an affront to every spiritual power in opposition to God. We are the proxies by which all that oppose God are subdued. You can bet with relative certainty that there will be push back. This push back comes in the form of sickness and disease, sin and rebellion. God knew in advance what the enemy would use to oppress humanity, thwarting destiny to exercise the dominion given to it. If you think it stops there, just keep reading, and you will see what God has in mind.

CHAPTER 31
The Ministry of Reconciliation
(Part 1)

When it comes to forgiveness of sin, many of us often relegate it to a very small area of application. What I mean is that forgiveness is usually taught in the context of showing mercy to someone who sins against you personally. Without question, this is absolutely necessary. We cannot assume we are in the appropriate mode of operation if our hearts are filled with bitterness and resentment against someone with whom we might have contention. Forgiveness is an essential part of our conduct as believers. We need to show others mercy, even when it is not convenient to us. In fact, I doubt that it is ever convenient for that matter. Nevertheless, we must labor diligently to not allow ourselves to become hard-hearted toward others, especially those of the household of faith.

> *"Then came Peter to him, and said, Lord, how oft shall my brother sin against me, and I forgive him? till seven times? Jesus saith unto him, I say not unto thee, Until seven times: but, Until seventy times seven."* (Matthew 18:22)

That being said, we must now take a look at the doctrine of forgiveness from a different point of view. After we are done, I believe you will see it in a way you have never perceived before. I am referring to the role forgiveness plays in revealing the invisible God. The Old Testament provides us with a number of beautiful examples of mercy, such as Joseph and his brothers, or David and Saul. However, these were recorded acts of forgiveness toward those who sinned against them as individuals, and thereby also against God by default. There are other situations where the sins were only against God Himself, like when two of Aaron's sons brought strange fire into the tabernacle, and died as a result. Another example is when Uzzah touched the Ark of the Testimony, also called the Ark of the Covenant, when it tipped over, assuming it was appropriate to do so to keep it from falling. Yet, his presumption also resulted in his death.

The examples given above lack one major element. While these men were forgiven for sinning against other humans, they were not necessarily forgiven for sinning against God. Their actions prevented them from the possibility of recovery. The judgment they endured served as warning to all who would sin against the Most High. An elaborate system of ritual sacrifice was set up to provide a covering of the sins of the people through a series of appointed times. This was especially significant during the feast of Yom Kippur. But this was a covering, not a taking away of sin. Due to this being only a covering for sin, there was a remembrance of the people's sins every year by the repetitive sacrificial system that had to be offered on an annual basis.

If that produces some trepidation in your heart, it should. Even the New Testament affirms this reality of God's stance on sin,

> *"For if we go on sinning deliberately after receiving the knowledge of the truth, there no longer remains a sacrifice for sins, but a fearful expectation of judgment, and a fury of fire that will consume the adversaries. Anyone who has set aside the law of Moses dies without mercy on the evidence of two or three witnesses. How much worse punishment, do you think, will be deserved by the one who has trampled underfoot the Son of God, and has profaned the blood of the covenant by which he was sanctified, and has outraged the Spirit of grace? For we know him who said, 'Vengeance is mine; I will repay.' And again, 'The Lord will judge his people.' It is a fearful thing to fall into the hands of the living God."*
> (Hebrews 10:26-31 ESV)

> "For the time is come that judgment must begin at the house of God: and if it first begin at us, what shall the end be of them that obey not the gospel of God? And if the righteous scarcely be saved, where shall the ungodly and the sinner appear? Wherefore let them that suffer according to the will of God commit the keeping of their souls to him in well doing, as unto a faithful Creator."
> (1 Peter 4:17-19)

This issue is no light-hearted matter. It cannot be approached in some flippant attempt to disregard God's holiness. You may not realize this, but what may increase the feeling of fear is the knowledge that God is NOT required to show mercy. However, He absolutely is required to exercise judgment. This is primarily due to God's nature of absolute holiness. Judgment is inevitable. You might argue saying, "God is love, and therefore, He will not condemn." Well, that is a foolish position to take. In fact, His Love is the very reason judgment must be administered. If you sin against anyone for any reason, including sinning against God Himself, God in His goodness must punish evil for the sake of the innocent. He gives equity because He exercises judgment FOR all who are oppressed. Therefore, it is because He is good that He must judge sin.

On the other hand, what is mercy? It is that aspect of God's character that overcomes judgment. Notice that I said God's *character*, not His *nature*. It is in His *nature* to judge righteously, and it is in His *character* to want to show mercy. This might be a revelation to all those who think they can get away with sin and presume upon God's mercy by simply appealing to His love without repentance on their part. That is not the way it works! Without repentance, there can be no forgiveness. It is for this very reason that the first word of the beginning of the gospel message is *"REPENT ... for the kingdom of God is at hand."* Even the principals of the doctrine of Christ begin with repentance from dead works. This cannot be overstated!

With this in mind, we should make the observation that the New Covenant is based on a relationship where God says, *"... for I will forgive their iniquity, and I will remember their sin no more"* (Jeremiah 31:34). That implies that God intends to blot out the lawless acts of man as He chooses to no longer remember their sinfulness. In order for this to happen, He must change our nature from a carnal one to a redeemed spiritual one.

> "And I will give them one heart, and a new spirit I will put within them. I will remove the heart of stone from their flesh and give them a heart of flesh, that they may walk in my statutes and keep my rules and obey them. And they shall be my people, and I will be their God." (Ezekiel 11:19-20 ESV)

> "I will sprinkle clean water on you, and you shall be clean from all your uncleannesses, and from all your idols I will cleanse you. And I will give you a new heart, and a new spirit I will put within you. And I will remove the heart of stone from your flesh and give you a heart of flesh. And I will put my Spirit within you, and cause you to walk in my statutes and be careful to obey my rules." (Ezekiel 36:25-27 ESV)

Notice, how the process of repentance involves the giving of a heart of *flesh*.[45] This is a physical attribute being correlated with a solution to a spiritual problem. It is not actually referring to the pump in your chest. It is referring to physical humanity being reconciled, not just in a spiritual context. The reason for this is that the entire physical creation is affected by humanity's condition. For the physical creation to be restored, humanity must be wholly redeemed. The physical universe plays its part in God's plan to reveal Himself to every being within the creation. His plan of redemption is not limited to mankind alone. All of creation is to be reconciled.

For this to occur, God would have to formulate a redemption in which an alienated creature (mankind) is transformed, both in nature and character, into something else entirely. God would see to it that His work would be complete and thorough in its execution. It would account for every variable that can ever exist at any given time, including the disposition of humankind. He would use the inclinations of the fallen creation to be used as part of the catalyst by which He would raise it up again. The ministry of Jesus Christ was that catalyst.

Jesus was set to carry out the mission to reconcile the world back to

---

[45] While some Bibles translate the word *flesh(ly)* to mean "carnal," these passages in the New Testament refer to the restoration of humanity to their original state at creation.

the Father through the sacrifice of His own body, to pay the penalty that was due. Jesus' sacrifice is what made possible the forgiveness God sought and planned for because Christ lived a life of character perfectly emulating the Father's nature. This set the stage for what is the greatest act of mercy ever demonstrated. Yet, so much of what Jesus actually did accomplish during His ministry is obscured by our assumptions about how He went about doing it.

"What do you mean?" you might ask. There were a series of instances recorded where the Lord Jesus forgave people for their offenses. There is a detail that is often overlooked in how He actually forgave sin. Let's take a look at the following verses and see if you can catch it.

> *"And behold, some people brought to him a paralytic, lying on a bed. And when Jesus saw their faith, he said to the paralytic, 'Take heart, my son; your sins are forgiven.' "* (Matthew 9:2 ESV)

> *"And when Jesus saw their faith, he said to the paralytic, 'Son, your sins are forgiven.' "* (Mark 2:5 ESV)

> *"And when he saw their faith, he said, 'Man, your sins are forgiven you.' "* (Luke 5:20 ESV)

> *"And he said to her, 'Your sins are forgiven.' "* (Luke 7:48 ESV)

> *"And one of the malefactors which were hanged railed on him, saying, If thou be Christ, save thyself and us. But the other answering rebuked him, saying, Dost not thou fear God, seeing thou art in the same condemnation? And we indeed justly; for we receive the due reward of our deeds: but this man hath done nothing amiss. And he said unto Jesus, Lord, remember me when thou comest into thy kingdom. And Jesus said unto him, Verily I say unto thee, To day shalt thou be with me in paradise."* (Luke 23:39-43)

Did you catch it? If not, then here it is: When we read these passages, our eyes sometimes deceive us. We interpret these passages to mean Jesus said, "I forgive you, my child." However, with regards to administering forgiveness, Jesus not once ever said, "I forgive you." Surprised? There is not a single instance where Jesus ever mentions anything like "I forgive you" to anyone. In fact, with the thief on the cross, though forgiveness was implied, it was not even mentioned. The words He used in these passages reveal something significant about His method.

When addressing the person's sin, He never treats the offense as though it were His own. In other words, He treated every sin as though it were directed at the Father alone. Even when He received the brunt of punishment at the hands of sinful men, He never once forgave anyone as though the offense was directed toward Himself. He always saw the offense as toward the Father.

What Jesus would actually say was, "Your sins are forgiven ..." Why? Precisely for the same reasons He never admitted to being God with words like "I am God," even though He would allude to His divinity in other ways. Jesus did not say that He Himself would forgave their sins because of one thing:

> "Search the scriptures; for in them ye think ye have eternal life: and they are they which testify of me. And ye will not come to me, that ye might have life. I receive not honour from men. But I know you, that ye have not the love of God in you. **I am come in my Father's name**, and ye receive me not: if another shall come in his own name, him ye will receive." (John 5:39-43) [emphasis added].

Jesus Himself did not forgive the people's sins because He could not do so in His own Name. That's right! While He certainly did administer forgiveness, He did so ***on behalf of the Father***, because **He came in His Father's Name**. You see, Jesus represented the Father as the One through whom the Father performed the works. As a human, Jesus could not lay claim to forgiving sin in His own name, but He could do so in the Father's Name. As a human, Christ exercised the dominion mandate by healing everyone who came to Him, and forgiving others under specific conditions. It was in this way that Jesus validated His ministry as the Redeemer.

> "Then came the Jews round about him, and said unto him, How long dost thou make us to doubt? If thou be the Christ, tell us plainly. Jesus answered them, I told you, and ye believed not: the works that I do in my Father's name, they bear witness of me." (John 10:24-25)

You see, Jesus *administered* forgiveness. He Himself did not forgive because it was not about Him. It was about the Father, and the offenses were against Him, the Father, and the breaking of His Law. What we observe in Jesus' actions was a form of protocol in the administration of forgiveness. Protocol is the code of behavior and procedure for state and diplomatic affairs.[46]

Remember, Jesus did not come to bring a religion. He came to establish a government. He had to follow proper protocols of the Kingdom in order to administer the forgiveness offered by the New Covenant He was instituting. For Jesus to have simply said, "I forgive you," He would have been bypassing all formality, precedence, and etiquette. As the King of kings and Lord of lords, Jesus knew exactly what He was doing in the Kingdom. He understood how the government of the Kingdom is supposed to operate. He did not miss a beat, and neither should we.

So what part do we as Christians play in this ministry of reconciliation? I believe you will be surprised by what you will read from here on out. While Jesus carried out His mission without fail, it did not end with His death, burial, and resurrection. That was just the preamble to what was to come. The Church plays an integral role in carrying out and continuing the mission. Of course, we have our work cut out for us in the guise of the New Testament. You see, Jesus set the example for us to follow, and we have a lot of catching up to do.

---

[46] "Protocol Definition and Meaning." *Dictionary.com*. Dictionary.com, n.d. Accessed March 17, 2022. https://www.dictionary.com/browse/protocol.

CHAPTER 32
The Ministry of Reconciliation
(Part 2)

Forgiveness is precious. It is the one thing that only God can do. If you never considered it, forgiveness is tied to the Person of God in His very nature, primarily because He is the Creator. If God did not exist, there would be no concept of sin, therefore no need for forgiveness. It is unique in that it stems from the very existence of God's Presence. Every sin we commit is an affront to His Presence who beholds all things. We seek forgiveness solely because He is the reason for it. As the Judge of both the living and the dead, He is truly the only One to whom we must answer for our offenses.

This creates a conundrum for us, a tricky problem. Many of us malinger, feigning illnesses to avoid responsibility, and carry around our guilt not knowing how to rid ourselves of its weight. Knowing our plight, God devised a perfect plan to not just forget our sin, but to take it away altogether. None of the so-called "gods of the nations" could ever do this because they are not the Creator, and they do not have the power to erase any offense. God alone reserves this right to Himself. He alone has the power to redeem and to forgive. He alone knows how to make it possible for sinful men to be forgiven.

When Christ came into the world, the penalty of human offense was not just suffering. The cost of committing sin is death itself. Yet, God saw fit that humanity was worth Christ's own life to save it from perishing. Being alienated from God meant that man could no longer fellowship with Him as He intended from the day of creation. His plan would culminate in His Word taking on human flesh, becoming one of us, sharing in our suffering, paying the penalty for humanity's offense, then rising again to bring His redemption to its zenith.

By making forgiveness possible, humankind can be restored to their rightful place in the order of things in creation. However, Jesus did not just suffer and die for humanity. Sure, that was the price of our redemption. Yet, He did so much more than that. He taught us how to forgive and be forgiven. He displayed the kind of life the Father intends for all of His sons and daughters. This can be a handful, so please bear with me.

Jesus left us a template, a model that each believer is destined to follow after. His life demonstrated what a true Son looks like, just like His Father. Jesus is God's final answer to our fallen condition. What He did during His life was the perfect expression of what God desires for humanity. After His death, burial, and resurrection, He came to His disciples and showed Himself to them, encouraging them to touch Him and see that He was truly alive and real.

> "'See my hands and my feet, that it is I myself. Touch me, and see. For a spirit does not have flesh and bones as you see that I have.' And when he had said this, he showed them his hands and his feet." (Luke 24:39-40 ESV)

His disciples must have been terrified seeing Christ standing in their midst. Knowing He had physically died, His bodily appearance in that setting had to have been a message in itself, one to which they were about to get a profound reintroduction.

Jesus did not waste any time getting down to business. Each of the gospels provides us different details and insights into the words of Christ after rising from the dead. In Matthew's gospel, Jesus comforts the women who came to His tomb, telling them that the disciples will see Him, followed by His second appearance to the disciples, encouraging them to touch Him and see. He eats some food to show He is real and then immediately rehashes His mission to the disciples. Then He goes to "the great commission" where He declares all power is given to Him, commanding them to teach all the nations. Mark follows a similar pattern, except it includes a tidbit in which Jesus rebukes the disciples for their disbelief, followed by "the great commission" again. This time, however, He adds that believers who are saved will perform healings, signs, and wonders in His Name.

In Luke's account, another detail is added. While no commission is mentioned, He does reiterate the mission, and then tells them He is sending the promise of the Father (the Spirit), and that they should wait in Jerusalem until they are clothed with power. Finally, we come to John's gospel where the first words of Christ upon His resurrection are recorded in the following manner:

> *"On the evening of that day, the first day of the week, the doors being locked where the disciples were for fear of the Jews, Jesus came and stood among them and said to them, 'Peace be with you.' When he had said this, he showed them his hands and his side. Then the disciples were glad when they saw the Lord. Jesus said to them again, 'Peace be with you. As the Father has sent me, even so I am sending you.' And when he had said this, he breathed on them and said to them, 'Receive the Holy Spirit. If you forgive the sins of any, they are forgiven them; if you withhold forgiveness from any, it is withheld.' "*
> (John 20:19-23 ESV)

This is where things become problematic. According to Jesus, every gospel account affirms that Jesus appears to the disciples, basically conferring to the Church His mission, to carry out the exact same works He Himself did during His earthly ministry. Since Jesus will no longer be physically with them on earth, the Church takes up the responsibilities to continue what Jesus began, in the same manner. What am I saying, exactly? I am saying that you and I have been given a mandate to exercise the dominion of Christ by doing the works of Jesus Christ.

Just as Christ was sent by the Father to do the Father's works in the

Father's Name, we are sent by Christ to do His works in His Name. That means that we are called to heal the sick AND to forgive the sinner in the same manner, precedence, and protocol. We are to proclaim the Kingdom of God on earth, and to demonstrate what that Kingdom looks like to the world at large. We are to remember all His benefits, and to proclaim liberty to the captives by stretching forth our hands to heal by conducting a spiritual war, fighting the good fight of faith through the Spirit of God.

The problematic aspect is in Jesus' approach to forgiving sin as a significant part of our responsibilities as the Church. I say problematic because, typically speaking, we are never taught we have the authority to administer forgiveness the way Jesus did. Forgiveness is usually taught by the Church in the context of being sinned against by another individual, but we are never in the context of forgiving others in Jesus' Name as an aspect of our ministry. If we are to image God the way Christ did, we must learn how to administer the authority of Christ as His body on the earth. But for that to happen, we need to make some adjustments to both our conduct and our theology in this matter.

I have a working theory. Far too many Christians today carry guilt over things of their past. Even though they have been redeemed, they still have moments of sin that follow them in the course of their walk of faith. Whether it is arguing with their spouse, telling a "white" lie, or taking something that was not theirs, regardless of size or value. All these things pile up in our consciences, yet we fail to have this weight of sin removed from it. We carry the burden when we ought to have already surrendered it to Christ. The reason, I think, is because we have forgotten what the ministry of reconciliation entails. It is about the Church standing in the place of Christ as His proxies for one another, so that we can be healed from self-inflicted wounds.

You will see in the following the context in which they are given to us:

> "Then said Jesus to them again, Peace be unto you: as my Father hath sent me, even so send I you. And when he had said this, he breathed on them, and saith unto them, Receive ye the Holy Ghost: Whose soever sins ye remit, they are remitted unto them; and whose soever sins ye retain, they are retained." (John 20:21-23)

"Is any among you afflicted? let him pray. Is any merry? let him sing psalms. Is any sick among you? let him call for the elders of the church; and let them pray over him, anointing him with oil in the name of the Lord*: And the prayer of faith shall save the sick, and the* Lord *shall raise him up; and if he have committed sins, they shall be forgiven him. Confess your faults one to another, and pray one for another, that ye may be healed. The effectual fervent prayer of a righteous man availeth much."* (James 5:13-16)

Roman Catholics are usually given a bad rap for doing things considered pagan due to the imagery and iconography prevalent in the institution. While I agree with that sentiment, they do have something at least partially right, and I believe there is something to be learned here. The Roman Catholic priests have a practice of confessional where a person can go to a booth for anonymity to meet with the priest and make confession of things done, where the priest absolves them of their sin by blessing them and instructing them to do penance as a sacrament made with sorrow, demonstrating their intention to amend their ways in order to receive forgiveness.[47] According to Catholic doctrine, only a priest can carry out this sacrament. While this practice is not common or adhered to in Protestant circles, Catholic doctrine is correct at least in part.

You see, as Christians, we are given the mandate to both heal and forgive as the body of Christ. We are not separate from Him. We are "members of His body, of His flesh, and of His bones," as it were, so that we are in effect His proxies. According to the New Testament, and contrary to popular opinion, priesthood is not restricted to a select few. The Church itself, that is, the entire body of believers, is considered priests!

"To whom coming, as unto a living stone, disallowed indeed of men, but chosen of God, and precious, Ye also, as lively stones, are built up a spiritual house, **an holy priesthood***, to offer up spiritual sacrifices, acceptable to God by Jesus Christ. Wherefore also it is contained in the scripture, Behold, I lay in Sion a chief corner stone, elect, precious: and he that believeth on him shall not be confounded. Unto you therefore which believe he is precious: but unto them which*

---

[47] "Penance Definition & Meaning." Dictionary.com. Dictionary.com, n.d. Accessed March 19, 2022. https://www.dictionary.com/browse/penance.

be disobedient, the stone which the builders disallowed, the same is made the head of the corner, And a stone of stumbling, and a rock of offense, even to them which stumble at the word, being disobedient: whereunto also they were appointed. But ye are a chosen generation, a royal priesthood, an holy nation, a peculiar people; that ye should shew forth the praises of him who hath called you out of darkness into his marvellous light; Which in time past were not a people, but are now the people of God: which had not obtained mercy, but now have obtained mercy." (1 Peter 2:4-10)

Notice how the passage first mentions Christ as a corner stone, then it includes the believer in association as the spiritual house (building); a holy priesthood. It refers to the entire Church, not just certain individuals. Every believer plays the role of priest in the body of Christ, regardless of age, gender, or social status.

"For in Christ Jesus you are all sons of God, through faith. For as many of you as were baptized into Christ have put on Christ. There is neither Jew nor Greek, there is neither slave nor free, there is no male and female, for you are all one in Christ Jesus. And if you are Christ's, then you are Abraham's offspring, heirs according to promise." (Galatians 3:26-29 ESV)

Our identity as sons and daughters positions us in the unique role as administrators in the affairs of God's government. That includes everything that Jesus did. That also means we must understand what the protocols of the Kingdom are if we are to be effective in the ministration of our duties.

So how do we go about forgiving others? Is it only about getting over the wound of a friend, or the injury from an enemy? Is there more to this thing we call forgiveness? The answer to the latter is yes, absolutely! Through the ministry of reconciliation, people can be reconciled back to God so they can know Him as He truly is. Generally speaking, the Church is not known for its kindness or generosity, mercy or righteous judgment. Most of the time, the world perceives the Church in a very different light, mostly because of our own sins. Yet, the world as it is today has yet to see what the people of God are supposed to be like. Take a look at the following New Testament passage about a man who was discovered to be having sexual relations with his stepmother, and see what Paul prescribed to the Corinthian church concerning this man's sin:

> "It is actually reported that there is sexual immorality among you, and of a kind that is not tolerated even among pagans, for a man has his father's wife. And you are arrogant! Ought you not rather to mourn? Let him who has done this be removed from among you. For though absent in body, I am present in spirit; and as if present, I have already pronounced judgment on the one who did such a thing. When you are assembled in the name of the Lord Jesus and my spirit is present, with the power of our Lord Jesus, you are to deliver this man to Satan for the destruction of the flesh, so that his spirit may be saved in the day of the Lord." (1 Corinthians 5:1-5 ESV)

We have a situation where Paul instructs the church to "deliver this man to Satan" as a punishment for actively living in his sin while being a part of the congregation. He was non-repentant about it and therefore disqualified from receiving forgiveness. He was to be removed from the fellowship of the church. In effect, they were withholding forgiveness by doing so. To be forgiven is to be in the family of God. If he does not repent and chooses to be unholy, he cannot be called a son of God. So, the church must send him away while he lives in his sin.

Fast forward now to the future concerning this same situation, when the church receives a different instruction on their approach to this same individual:

> "Now if anyone has caused pain, he has caused it not to me, but in some measure—not to put it too severely—to all of you. For such a one, this punishment by the majority is enough, so you should rather turn to forgive and comfort him, or he may be overwhelmed by excessive sorrow. So I beg you to reaffirm your love for him. For this is why I wrote, that I might test you and know whether you are obedient in everything. Anyone whom you forgive, I also forgive. Indeed, what I have forgiven, if I have forgiven anything, has been for your sake in the presence of Christ, so that we would not be outwitted by Satan; for we are not ignorant of his designs." (2 Corinthians 2:5-11 ESV)

Notice, Paul instructs the Corinthian church to receive and forgive him because of the man's sorrowful demeanor over his sin. This means he became repentant after they had administered their judgment by putting him out of the fellowship. What I want you to consider is that he was not sinning against them *per se*. He was living in immorality among them with his stepmother, but he did not directly sin against them. He was in rebellion to the Lord, not the church *per se,* when in fact the church seemed indifferent, inviting Paul's rebuke.

For them to follow Paul's instruction meant that they would have to forgive this young man on behalf of Christ. To maintain the protocol, they would not say, "We forgive you" because the sin was not directed at them. It was directed at the Lord by disregarding His ways in open rebellion. Therefore, they would have had to administer forgiveness by saying something like, "In the name of the Lord Jesus, your sins are forgiven you." Admittedly, this is not recorded anywhere, but they would have to have followed the same method of forgiveness Jesus used because what they did was in Jesus' Name, not in their own name.

Think about it. They were being instructed by the Apostle Paul to administer forgiveness on behalf of Christ, and that Paul himself would agree with them as in the "presence of Christ" to forgive. Paul echoes the words of Jesus, *"Whose soever sins ye remit, they are remitted unto them ..."* when he said, *"Anyone whom you forgive, I also forgive."* Furthermore, Paul points out that their act of forgiving in this manner meant they were "obedient in everything." This implies that they knew this to be a part of the mission of the church. It is part and parcel of the administration of the government that rests on Messiah's shoulders. If we are to walk this out, we need to do some homework. In the next chapter, we will explore what it will take to walk in forgiveness, both for us and for others, so that they, too, can see our Heavenly Father.

> *"You are the light of the world. A city set on a hill cannot be hidden. Nor do people light a lamp and put it under a basket, but on a stand, and it gives light to all in the house. In the same way, let your light shine before others, so that they may see your good works and give glory to your Father who is in heaven."* (Matthew 5:14-16 ESV)

CHAPTER 33
The Administration of Forgiveness

Understanding forgiveness is an essential component of our repertoire. God wants to be seen in a particular way, manifesting Himself through the Church. Love is the basis for this forgiveness. If we do not forgive, then it is because we are not walking in love. It requires us to love in order to properly forgive:

> *"Whoever confesses that Jesus is the Son of God, God abides in him, and he in God. So we have come to know and to believe the love that God has for us. God is love, and whoever abides in love abides in God, and God abides in him. By this is love perfected with us, so that we may have confidence for the day of judgment, **because as he is so also are we in this world**. There is no fear in love, but perfect love casts out fear. For fear has to do with punishment, and whoever fears has not been perfected in love. We love because he first loved us. If anyone says, 'I love God,' and hates his brother, he is a liar; for he who does not love his brother whom he has seen **cannot love God whom he has not seen**. And this commandment we have from him: whoever loves God must also love his brother."* (1 John 4:15-21 ESV) [Emphasis added].

Notice how John makes the correlation between loving our brother whom we have seen and loving our God Who is invisible. This is not an accident. Love is the ultimate expression of character that most clearly defines God in the eyes of the world. Jesus Himself said as much:

> "A new commandment I give unto you, That ye love one another; as I have loved you, that ye also love one another. By this shall all [men] know that ye are my disciples, if ye have love one to another." (John 13:34-35)

God in His infinite wisdom has seen fit to make forgiveness from sin possible in a multitude of ways under the same protocol. I believe He did so in order to account for the different circumstances surrounding each individual. Let's look at the following verses and see how this plays out:

CONFESSION

> "If we confess our sins, he is faithful and just to forgive us our sins, and to cleanse us from all unrighteousness." (1 John 1:9)

Most people make the mistake of confusing confession of sin with admission. These are not the same thing. Admission is nothing more than a disclosure, a list of the dirty laundry of one's life. This does not mean a person repents by admitting to anything. It just means they admit to having done something, but without evidence of a change of heart. Admission might bring to light what someone has done, but it does not remove our alienation from God.

On the other hand, confession of sin implies repentance. Confession is when a person comes to a place of agreement with what God has to say about a particular thing. In other words, admission would be like saying, "Yeah, I stole this, or I did that," while confession says, "What I did was wrong. It was wrong for me to do this or that." That is the major difference between admission and confession. One denies the Father's influence, while the other embraces it.

While any fool can admit to doing something evil, only those who confess are the ones who find forgiveness. Confession brings us back into alignment with the Father's will and initiates the necessary change in the heart that transforms us back into His image and likeness so that the Father can once again be seen through the Son.

I REPENT!

> "Take heed to yourselves: If thy brother trespass against thee, rebuke him; and if he repent, forgive him. And if he trespass against thee seven times in a day, and seven times in a day turn again to thee, saying, I repent; thou shalt forgive him." (Luke 17:3-4)

This passage might be a little harder to swallow if you have difficulty dealing with repetitive sin. All of us have dealt with individuals who seem to do nothing but drive us crazy. This is that person who can't find it in themselves to keep from doing something that offends you. Even then, you are still expected to forgive. However, there is a caveat. Jesus points out that if the person says, "I repent," you are required to forgive him. We are literally compelled by the command to do so. It's not an option.

What makes this difficult to observe is the apparent lack of "repentance" that ought to have resulted in the ceasing of an endless cycle of repetitive sins. However, the problem is not with what Jesus said, but with what we assume is repentance. That is to say, even though we might say repentance, what we probably mean is penance. This is not what Jesus is saying here. The Lord wants us to forgive in the same way He does with us. He wants us to act in His stead as His body, with His heart. I would like for you to consider that sincerity is not a factor in this, primarily because we don't know the offender's heart. The brother or sister may not even mean it when they say they repent. In fact, it's not about sincerity at all. It's about the obedience of the offended party to the Word of Christ.

Answer these questions, and follow the logic: Was Jesus a hypocrite? So he practiced what he preached? The answer is obviously yes. Now consider how many times you have asked someone for forgiveness when it seemed like you did not really mean it, just so you didn't get into any further trouble. I would say it happened rather often because we are still human when it happens. Yet, when we are taught to go to the Lord to be forgiven, what makes you think you are any different in your demeanor?

The point I am making is that while we seek forgiveness, we rarely ever say, "I repent." You see, you and I may not have the ability to see into a person's heart, or even their intent. What we do have is their words "I repent." Jesus mentions this phrase because it generates something in the person who is committing the sin. It produces the fruits of repentance over time. When was the last time you said, "Lord, I repent," after having sinned? I dare say most likely never. Yet, your freedom from guilt and from the power of your sin to continue to overtake you in the future is determined by what you say in the moment.

By saying, "I repent" you are declaring with your mouth what you really believe with your heart. When Jesus hears you say it, He practices what He preaches. He forgives, regardless of whether or not you know you really mean it. He already knows everything. He already knows whether you will sin again. He already knows there is more going on than just your attempt to say certain words. When you say them, the trajectory of your action will change as a result. So the next time you sin, the first thing that should come out of your mouth is "I REPENT." Try it sometime and see what happens next. And when your brother comes to you and says, "I repent," your response should be, "Brother, your sin is forgiven."

CONFESSING YOUR FAULTS ONE TO ANOTHER

> *"Confess your faults one to another, and pray one for another, that ye may be healed. The effectual fervent prayer of a righteous man availeth much."* (James 5:16)

This one requires some vulnerability and introspection on our part. To be pure in heart, humility must be seen as an indispensable asset. Without it you cannot show who God is to the world, and only the pure in heart can see God for themselves. Confessing to one another means we must be approachable to each other, a safe haven for us to go to without the risk of losing status because of some weakness or moral failure.

This is a huge problem in the Church today. It's almost as if we love to crucify our own. That is not to say that people should not be held accountable. Rather, I'm addressing the inability to be vulnerable with each other, and that in itself eventually leads to a place of no return in the mind of many individuals. Imagine how our life would be if we could confess our faults (sins) to one another where we can pray for one another without fear of judgment from one another. Restoration could become possible before there is any real damage done. It might even keep us from the path of destruction altogether. If only we exercised mercy in advance of the depravity, we could have avoided so much of the controversy that plagues the modern church.

How many pastors have been found to have committed moral failures, even to the extreme, because they could not really approach anyone they felt they could trust. I suspect this stems from the fact that, many times, they feel that if they told anyone what they were thinking or feeling, they would be perceived as either perverse. or unfit for ministry. There is history of Pastors being ostracized for situations that could have been resolved differently. Fear, uncertainty, and lack of trust reign supreme in such environments.

Modern ministry nowadays places so much emphasis on status and titles that if a ministry leader does go to someone, they risk their reputation and the respect of both their peers, and their constituents. I have seen it myself, and it can be discouraging. You keep from sharing your weakness because those who hear you will likely find a reason to dishonor you. That is not the reality, but it is how it is often perceived.

At the same time, the infrastructure of church discipline is also lacking. There are those whose sins are so grievous they should be placed in jail for their crimes. The church should have the discernment to exercise proper protocol for discipline just as well. The thing is, if we had taken steps to bridge the gap beforehand, it may not have had to go that far to begin with. We are more willing to admit our sins to God, than we are to confess to our brethren because, most of the time, we won't get a response that is condemning. The better thing is to confess. But even more so, be ready to receive one another with no pretense so that we can stop sin before it destroys us.

COMMUNION

> "The cup of blessing which we bless, is it not the communion of the blood of Christ? The bread which we break, is it not the communion of the body of Christ? For we being many are one bread, and one body: for we are all partakers of that one bread." (1 Corinthians 10:16-17)

This is another method available to the Church by which forgiveness can be administered. Understanding the elements of communion and how we carry out this practice can have heavy consequences on the body of Christ. Paul the Apostle makes no light matter of this, indicating that partaking of communion in an unworthy manner can result in individual members who partake of it either becoming sick, or even dying. That should compel anyone to take a big step back before the next time they take communion.

Jewish Evangelist Dick Reuben once gave a phenomenal teaching on the Patterns of Revival Fire. In it he broke down the concept of communion from a Hebraic perspective. He mentioned that if a person can get sick by taking the bread incorrectly for not discerning the Lord's body, then what is to say that taking it correctly can't heal you? In that same vein, I would add that if drinking the fruit of the vine incorrectly leads to death, would observing it correctly conversely lead to life? I would certainly say so.

There is far too much on this topic alone to be covered at length here. But, for the purposes of brevity it is enough to make the correlation of the bread to the body, and the wine to the blood. The bread correlates to healing of the body, whereas the wine correlates to forgiveness of the soul. If you take the time to study the elements of communion in their proper context, you will discover a whole new appreciation for it.

WORDS OF CAUTION AND WARNING

I would be remiss if I did not mention that there is also potential for great error here. While I stand by every word I have written thus far, I need to emphasize the gravity of what is being implied by all this. We are all called to minister the most holy things within our realm of responsibility in the Kingdom. Yet, it behooves us to consider that misappropriation of these holy things can and will lead to ruin. For this reason, we must account for the possibility of abuse of the liberty we have in the administration of forgiveness.

What do I mean? There would be those who, in their zeal or ignorance, would presume to forgive everyone and/or anyone for any reason, as if that is what is meant by remitting the sins of others. In truth, if we were to be that irresponsible with this gift of grace, we might very well fall into perdition ourselves. So let us be clear: without repentance, there can be no remission of sin. If a sinner is seeking to be forgiven, this individual must repent and show genuine contrition for their sin. At the very least, the individual ought to say aloud that they repent. THIS IS A PREREQUISITE!

The danger lies in our ignorance of protocol. If we flippantly act without regard to the protocols laid down by the example of our Lord Jesus, we risk heaping condemnation on our own selves. By not seeking evidence of true repentance, we cheapen and make light of the sacrifice of Christ. This serves only to reinforce a sinner's self-deception. The writer of Hebrews gave us a clear warning of those who willfully sin, and the condition they are under:

> *"For if we go on sinning deliberately after receiving the knowledge of the truth, there no longer remains a sacrifice for sins, but a fearful expectation of judgment, and a fury of fire that will consume the adversaries. Anyone who has set aside the law of Moses dies without mercy on the evidence of two or three witnesses. How much worse punishment, do you think, will be deserved by the one who has trampled underfoot the Son of God, and has profaned the blood of the covenant by which he was sanctified, and has outraged the Spirit of grace? For we know him who said, 'Vengeance is mine; I will repay.' And again, 'The Lord will judge his people.' It is a fearful thing to fall into the hands of the living God."* (Hebrews 10:26-31 ESV)

There is real danger for those who go on sinning. But there is also grave danger for those who overlook people's sin, and then seek to simply accept those engrossed in their sin.

> "Whosoever transgresseth, and abideth not in the doctrine of Christ, hath not God. He that abideth in the doctrine of Christ, he hath both the Father and the Son. If there come any unto you, and bring not this doctrine, receive him not into your house, **neither bid**[48] **him God speed**: For he that biddeth him God speed is partaker of his evil deeds." (2 John 1:9-11 KJV) [emphasis added].

This is the sort of error perpetrated in the Catholic doctrine of confession. Repetition of multiple prayers and/or simply doing good works will in themselves never produce forgiveness of sin. As I said before, and I will say it again, *without repentance there can be no forgiveness!*

THE PRIESTS OF THE LORD

I recognize that all of this is controversial, and I expect you, the reader, to be somewhat skeptical. However, I would like to offer some perspective. The Old Testament priesthood was responsible for administering the duties of their office through the sacrificial system to provide atonement (a covering) for the sins of the people of Israel. They were required to offer sacrifices in the exact manner prescribed in the Law of Moses. They were not permitted to deviate from the instructions given them to make the people accepted before the Lord.

With all this responsibility, it was always understood that while the Levitical priests fulfilled their requirements under the Mosaic Law, no one ever assumed or believed that it was the priest who forgave the sins of the people. They just acted in obedience to what God had commanded them. It is God who forgives. Just as it was then, so it is now. We do not do the actual forgiving. We only administer it according to the protocols of our office as New Testament priests. The Apostle Peter said, *"Ye also, as lively stones, are built up a spiritual house, an holy priesthood, to offer up spiritual sacrifices, acceptable to God by Jesus Christ"* (1 Peter 2:5).

It is important to recognize here that the sacrifices we are required to offer must be <u>acceptable to God</u> ... not to us! God is the one who sets the

---

[48] The Greek word for "bid" in this passage is often translated as "greet," but it actually means to accept, affirm over, and maintain.

parameters by which we govern our conduct. The Lord Jesus gave us the perfect example we must follow if we are to operate as those who bear the responsibilities associated with the ministry of reconciliation. It only takes our diligent obedience to what He has taught us, and we fulfill our purpose.

THE CHILDREN OF GOD

> *"For I reckon that the sufferings of this present time are not worthy to be compared with the glory which shall be revealed in us. For the earnest expectation of the creature waiteth for the manifestation of the sons of God."* (Romans 8:18-19)

The entire creation is waiting for something. The earth, the sky, the stars in the cosmos, and even heaven itself are all waiting for this one thing: the manifestation of God's children. The creation cannot see the Father with them ... without us who believe. We hold in our being the Presence and Spirit of the Holy One. Our bodies are efficiently designed for the task. Every act of obedience, every labor of love, and every opportunity we have is a gift to the world from the Father.

When the children of God manifest, the impossible happens by default. The sick are healed, the lame walk, blind eyes are opened, captives are set free, prison doors are opened, the dead are raised, and in His Name all oppression comes to an end. That is exactly what happens when God's people choose to think like Him, act like Him, speak like Him, and consequently look like Him. The world is waiting, so prepare to manifest!

ABOUT THE AUTHOR

Stan T. Albuquerque

STAN ALBUQUERQUE served with distinction for 22 cumulative years in the U.S. Navy. While traveling literally around the world, he used his time in service to evangelize and disciple the sailors under his leadership and influence. During six years of this time, he served as the Virginia Beach Life Team Leader for a large, well-known ministry.

Stan is a prolific Bible teacher and dynamic street preacher. During this time, he was responsible for evangelizing the Virginia Beach area by coordinating various public outreach events, as well as training and equipping his home groups to reach the lost and set people free with the message of the gospel. He continues to host online Bible study groups involving families from around the country with a growing online presence.

It has been said that Stan is a gifted teacher! He has a heart to bring the believer's attention back to the text of scripture and refining their faith by shifting the focus from tradition back to biblical truth.

Stan is currently retired from the military and lives with his wife and their four children.

BIBLIOGRAPHY

Page 27

1 Earls, Aaron. "Americans Hold Complex, Conflicting Religious Beliefs, According to Latest State of Theology Study." *Lifeway Research*. Ligonier Ministries, August 12, 2021. Last modified August 12, 2021. Accessed October 12, 2022. https://research.lifeway.com/2020/09/08/americans-hold-complex-conflicting-religious-beliefs-according-to-latest-state-of-theology-study/

Page 30

2 The term "Old Testament" was first used in the second century by Melito of Sardis (the first known Christian Pilgrim). He was mentioned by Eusebius. Some have even postulated that Constantine may have referred to the old testament so as to make people believe that it had no longer any value.

3 Eusebius of Caesaria, "The Church History of Eusebius," in *Eusebius: Church History, Life of Constantine the Great,* and *Oration in Praise of Constantine*, ed. Philip Schaff and Henry Wace, trans. Arthur Cushman McGiffert, vol. 1, A Select Library of the Nicene and Post-Nicene Fathers of the Christian Church, Second Series (New York: Christian Literature Company, 1890), 206.

Page 46

4 Michael S. Heiser, *Reversing Hermon: Enoch, the Watchers & the Forgotten Mission of Jesus Christ (Crane, MO: Defender Publishing, 2017).*

Page 49

5 "USS Abraham Lincoln - Nimitz Class Aircraft Carrier." Naval Technology. Accessed May 16, 2020. https://www.naval-technology.com/projects/abraham-lincoln-nimitz-class-aircraft-carrier/.

Page 53

6 The use of different translations by the author is intended to reflect a broad consensus of understanding from the translators' perspectives on the text to provide as cohesive a context as possible in spite of any loss in translation from the original languages.

7 Brandon J. O'Brien and E. Randolph. Richards, *Misreading Scripture with Western Eyes* (Downers Grove, IL: IVP Books, 2012), p.72)

Page 55

8 Lera Boroditsky, "How Language Shapes the Way We Think," TED (TED Women, 2017), https://www.ted.com/talks/lera_boroditsky_how_language_shapes_the_way_we_think?utm_campaign=tedspread&utm_medium=referral&utm_source=tedcomshare, Min. 1:35)

Page 57

9 "constructs" – This author recognizes that the implementations of "constructs" are unavoidable and practically impossible to omit if there is to be any understanding due to language and cultural constraints. Constructs must be in place to grasp those concepts

Bibliography

foreign to one's culture. However, to solely rely on these constructs without the overall context is problematic in that it may convey something contradictory or unintended to the original content from those who penned the scriptures.

Page 58

10   White, James R. *The Forgotten Trinity: Recovering the Heart of Christian Belief.* Minneapolis, MN: Bethany House, a division of Baker Publishing Group, 2019. Ch. 1, Pg. 1.

11   Roger E. Olson and Christopher A. Hall, *The Trinity, Guides to Theology* (Grand Rapids, MI: W.B. Eerdmans, 2002), 1.

12   One fascinating detail in the structure of scripture is how the Lord God always has attributed to Himself the initial reference as "God" who has the title of Father and Creator. However, when it comes to the Son and Spirit, their titles tend to come first, recognizing to their divinity by association. However, their order is not the other way around. As an analogy, imagine a hand with a finger pointing in a specific direction where the core of the essence as God points toward the Father (God > Father), while the Son and Holy Spirit point back to the core essence of God (Son/Spirit > God). In other words, God IS the Father, while the Son/Spirit ARE God. This is a consistent pattern in scripture where God the Father is always presented as the Supreme centric being, with the Son and Spirit always pointing back to Him.

Page 60

13   Brandon J. O'Brien and E. Randolph Richards, *Misreading Scripture with Western Eyes* (Downers Grove, IL : IVP Books, 2012)

Page 61

14   "replacements" – This term is intended to convey the idea of human "constructs" infused within the interpretations of scriptural passages that completely change the context and overall message of the text. Not all constructs do this, but it does happen.

15   Replacement theology is one of the many evils infiltrating the church because of the inaccurate use of terms, and misappropriation of theological concepts.

Page 62

16   The term gospel tends to have an anecdotal meaning to most English-speaking people. To the non-believing and unchurched, it often carries an overly religious connotation bearing little resemblance to its true meaning. The Greek term is evangelion which literally means good news, while the Hebrew term is Besorah with the same definition. However, the Hebrew use of Besorah has an additional meaning from Israel's historical as a term used to describe good news that comes from victory in battle. The good news, or gospel of God is the message of God's absolute triumph over every adversary in setting every soul free from oppression and sin.

Bibliography

Page 69

17 Matthew 17:9, Mark 8:38, Luke 12:8, John 3:13

18 John 12:34

Page 72

19 "Shekinah" is a term referring to the manifest glory of God usually in the form of some illumination such as supernatural fire or divine light that was visible to both Israelites and Gentiles alike.

Page 74

20 "One important observation in using terms such as "Apostle" before individual names such as Paul, Peter, etc., may cause believers to forget that Jesus and His disciples were in fact Jews, and that most of the new covenant was written by Jews, and that gospel (besorah) is a Jewish message of redemption.

Page 81

21 "Jewish Concepts." *The Nature of G-d.* Judaism 101, n.d. Accessed January 18, 2022. https://www.jewishvirtuallibrary.org/the-nature-of-g-d.)

Page 82

22 We are taught to emphasize in Trinitarian theology that the Father, the Son, and the Holy Spirit are separate and distinct persons of the Godhead. This is mostly because of the logic we follow in our own common language. If a being thinks and feels, that being is therefore his/her own distinct person. We end up reading that into the text and come up with the Trinitarian model of God in three persons, even though the Bible itself does not use this formula. What we often overlook in our rhetoric is that any time God has to manifest Himself in any form or capacity, that manifestation is not fully in the context of who and what the Father is truly like. Since the manifestation itself is lesser than the Father's essence, that manifestation is addressed in a "third person" context without there actually being three separate and distinct beings that make up the one God. If God wanted, He could manifest in 20 different ways, from a human to a dog to a bird, to a burning bush, but it doesn't mean He is 20 different persons because of those manifestations.

Page 83

23 June Hunt, *Biblical Counseling Keys on New Age Spirituality: A New Mask for an Old Message* (Dallas, TX: Hope For The Heart, 2008), Pg. 1.

Page 84

24 Ibid, Pg.4

Page 85

25 F. L. Cross and Elizabeth A. Livingstone, eds., *The Oxford Dictionary of the Christian Church* (Oxford; New York: Oxford University Press, 2005), 1652.

26 Ibid, 87.

Bibliography

Page 88

27 Dale Tuggy, "Judaic and Islamic Objections," *Stanford Encyclopedia of Philosophy* (Stanford University, 2016), last modified 2016, accessed May 21, 2020, https://plato.stanford.edu/entries/trinity/judaic-islamic-trinity.html.

28 Arnold Fruchtenbaum, "Jewishness and the Trinity," *Jewishness and the Trinity* (Jews for Jesus, April 23, 2018), last modified April 23, 2018, accessed May 21, 2020, https://jewsforjesus.org/publications/issues/issues-v01-n08/jewishness-and-the-trinity.

29 Sigal, G. (2006). *Trinity doctrine error: A Jewish analysis*. Bloomington, IN: Xlibris. Kindle Reader, location 471.

Page 96

30 The main difference between a covenant and a testament is this: A covenant refers to the relationship itself, whereas the testament refers to the document that defines said relationship. To illustrate, we can use marriage for our example: The ceremonial union of the man and woman is representative of the covenant, whereas the testament is represented by the marriage certificate. The Old Covenant is the relationship between God and the Nation of Israel as prescribed in Mosaic Law. The New Covenant is a relationship established between God and the House of Israel under the auspices of Israel's Messiah. The covenants reflect the nature of the different relationships as they are described by those written testaments. In the same manner, the changing of names and titles is a biblical method of communication often used to convey a particular nature of something. In the Bible, God establishes all His relationships by way of covenant. Covenants were confirmed and ratified by the sacrifices offered by the people as prescribed. When covenants were made in ancient Israel, the parties involved would kill an animal and divide the parts. The parties would then walk between those parts reciting the words of the covenant. This process was referred to as cutting a covenant.

Page 98

31 The New Covenant God mentioned in Jeremiah was never made with the church, as some may presume. God made it specifically with the House of Israel and the House of Judah. He made this Covenant with the Nation of Israel as a whole. However, aside from Jeremiah, there is no record of God ever officially making this Covenant with the people of Israel, as in the event of the giving of the Law by the hand of Moses, other than the New Testament. Nevertheless, He does stipulate that even though the Covenant was made with Israel, He confirms it would be accomplished by the Messiah when he says, "… I will give you for a Covenant of the people …" The Messiah is Himself the representative of the entire nation with whom God makes this new Covenant. He is also the embodiment of the Covenant itself. Besides this, He is also the One who carries out the terms of the Covenant; He is the Priest who offers the sacrifice, and also the Sacrifice itself. The entire New Covenant begins and ends with the Messiah! Hence, the catalyst.

Bibliography

Page 127

32 Michael S. Heiser, *"The Name Theology of the Old Testament,"* in *Faithlife Study Bible* (Bellingham, WA: Lexham Press, 2012, 2016).

Page 128

33 Michael S. Heiser, *"The Name Theology of the Old Testament,"* in *Faithlife Study Bible* (Bellingham, WA: Lexham Press, 2012, 2016).

Page 36

34 The idea of God existing as a human, or with human features as the very essence of His being is in agreement with Mormon beliefs about God, and is fundamentally not Christian.

Page 149

35 The following verses show the relationship within the Godhead: Matthew 10:20; Acts 20:28; Galatians 4:6; 1 Corinthians 6:17; 2 Corinthians 3:17-18; Ephesians 4:4-6.

Page 163

36 The only other person that comes close to using this phraseology is Peter, "For this cause was the gospel preached also to them that are dead, that they might be judged according to men in the flesh, but live according to God in the spirit" (1 Peter 4:6).

Page 164

37 Scholars have long debated the meaning behind God's reference to "us" in Genesis. Historically, the Hebrews understood it to imply God was addressing His divine counsel who witnessed the creation take place (Job 38:4-7). While God addresses the divine counsel, He alone takes credit for the act. Reading the Trinity into those passages was never addressed in the New Testament by any of the Apostles. It was not until after Tertullian introduced Trinitarian concepts that these references became topics of debate.

Page 170

38 Matthew 4:2 and Luke 4:2

Page 172

39 NOTE: It has often been said in varying church circles that Jesus received his marching orders everyday whenever He got up to pray. The problem with this view is that it is mere speculation on our part. The Bible never says in any text that Jesus received instructions on what to do when He prayed. We assume that because we are taught to do so, but that is not biblical. If we are to use only the biblical text to interpret Jesus act of prayer, then He did so because Jesus understood that while the Spirit is willing, he also knew that the flesh is weak (Matthew 26:41 and Mark 14:38). Furthermore, Acts 10:38 indicates that Jesus often wandered about with no set destination, and did all the good He did simply because God was with Him.

Bibliography

Page 181

40 It should be noted that Jesus requests the Father to glorify His name. The Father glorifies it His name not by saying "YHWH" or even "Jesus". Instead, He speaks aloud for everyone present to hear. The sound that the people around Jesus heard was that of thunder. Though the sound was indiscernible to the people, it was in direct response to Jesus' prayer. The glory was in the voice that was heard. The glorification of the Name that was glorified was the evidence of the presence of the Father in their midst speaking to the Son.

Page 205

41 Andy Bannister, "What Does It Really Mean to Be Human?," *RZIM*, last modified 2015, accessed May 30, 2020, https://www.rzim.org/read/a-slice-of-infinity/what-does-it-really-mean-to-be-human.

Page 223

42 Myles Munroe, *Kingdom Principles: Preparing for Kingdom Experience and Expansion* (Shippensburg, PA, PA: Destiny Image Publishers, 2006), Chapter 1, Pg. 36.

Page 226

43 Contrary to public opinion, we are not a Democracy. I think it is shameful that our leaders keep perpetuating mixed truths and half lies by calling us a Democracy when, in fact, we are a Constitutional Republic.

Page 242

44 Peterson, Jordan B. *The Perfect Mode of Being | Jonathan Pageau - Jordan B. Peterson Podcast S4 E8 quote time marker 23min 32sec to 24min 08sec* YouTube, 2021. Accessed March 12, 2022. https://youtu.be/2rAqVmZwqZM.

Page 254

45 While some Bibles translate the word *flesh(ly)* to mean "carnal," these passages in the New Testament refer to the restoration of humanity to their original state at creation.

Page 257

46 "Protocol Definition and Meaning." *Dictionary.com*. Dictionary.com, n.d. Accessed March 17, 2022. https://www.dictionary.com/browse/protocol.

Page 263

47 "Penance Definition & Meaning." Dictionary.com. Dictionary.com, n.d. Accessed March 19, 2022. https://www.dictionary.com/browse/penance.

Page 274

48 The Greek word for "bid" in this passage is often translated as "greet," but it actually means to accept, affirm over, and maintain.

www.ingramcontent.com/pod-product-compliance
Lightning Source LLC
Chambersburg PA
CBHW070608170426
43200CB00012B/2622